Legal Implications of Brain-Computer Interfaces in Modern Society

Robert Szuchy
Károli Gáspár University, Hungary

Swarnima Gorani
https://orcid.org/0009-0004-2052-6891
Sharda University, India

Laeeq Razzak Janjua
https://orcid.org/0000-0002-1948-5859
WSB University, Poland

IGI Global
Scientific Publishing
Publishing Tomorrow's Research Today

Vice President of Editorial	Melissa Wagner
Director of Acquisitions	Mikaela Felty
Director of Book Development	Jocelynn Hessler
Production Manager	Mike Brehm
Cover Design	Jose Rosado

Published in the United States of America by
IGI Global Scientific Publishing
701 East Chocolate Avenue
Hershey, PA, 17033, USA
Tel: 717-533-8845 | Fax: 717-533-7115
Website: https://www.igi-global.com E-mail: cust@igi-global.com

Library of Congress Cataloging-in-Publication Data

LCCN: 2026028376 (CIP Data Pending)
ISBN13: 9798337397207
Isbn13Softcover: 9798337397214
EISBN13: 9798337397221
British Cataloguing in Publication Data
A Cataloguing in Publication record for this book is available from the British Library.

Table of Contents

Preface xv

Chapter 1
Application of Brain–Computer Interface and Artificial Intelligence in Prisons With Harmonizing Neural Data Rights: Analysis of Legal Framework in India's Correctional and Evidentiary Protection Mechanism 1
Sunaina Mishra, Christ (Deemed to be) University, Delhi NCR, India
Kriti Parashar, Christ (Deemed to be) University, Delhi NCR, India

Chapter 2
Artificial Intelligence and Digital Inclusion for Women With Disabilities: Legal and Ethical Perspectives of Brain-Computer Interfaces in Modern Society 19
Prangya Parimita Behera, Pingalakhi College of Special Education, Odisha, India
Binita Behera, KIIT School of Law, KIIT (Deemed to be) University, Odisha, India
Sanjay Kumar Singh, Uttar Pradesh Rajarshi Tandon Open University, India
Mousumi Raysingh, Pingalakhi College of Special Education, Odisha, India

Chapter 3
Corporate Transparency in Neural Data Collection and Its Impact on Brand Loyalty 37
Amit Kumar Pandey, Institute of Management Studies (Business School), Ghaziabad, India
Prakhar Duggal, Amity University, Noida, India
Ujjwal Bharadwaj, Amity University, Noida, India
Aastha Sawhney, Independent Researcher, India
Ruchika Jeswal, Amity School of Business, Amity University, Noida, India

Chapter 4
Hacking Brains, Unauthorized Access, and Cloud Storage Risks: Legal Admissibility and Evidentiary Challenges 55
Abhishek Srivastava, Amity University, Jaipur, India
Hemant Singh, Amity University, Gwalior, India
Sanjay Kumar Pandey, MIT ADT University, Pune, India

Chapter 5
Law Enforcement Use Toward International Standards: Neurorights Legislation and Responsible Innovation in the Brain-Data Era 69
Deeksha Jha, Amity University, Gwalior, India
Ravina Parihar, Gujarat National Law University, Silvassa, India
Gopalam Sultania, Amity University, Jaipur, India

Chapter 6
Legal Admissibility and Evidentiary Challenges: Neural-Derived Evidence in Courts and Forensic Contexts 87
Pradip Kumar Kashyap, School of Legal Studies, CGC University, Mohali, India
Saurabh Chandra, Symbiosis Law School Noida, Symbiosis International (Deemed to be) University, Pune, India

Chapter 7
Neural-Derived Evidence in Courts and Forensic Contexts: Case Studies 105
Hemant Singh, Amity University, Gwalior, India
Saurabh Kumar, Chanakya National Law University, Patna, India
Pragya Singh, The Neotia University, West Bengal, India

Chapter 8
Neurorights Legislation and Responsible Innovation in the Brain Data Era 121
Arunima Shastri, Christ University, Bangalore, India
Laeeq R. Janjua, WSB University, Poland
Saurabh Chandra, Symbiosis Law School, Symbiosis International (Deemed to be) University, Pune, India

Chapter 9
Neurorights Legislation in the Brain Data Era: Forging Comprehensive Legal Frameworks to Safeguard Cognitive Liberty and Mental Privacy..................... 137
Sukhwinder Singh, School of Legal Studies, CGC University, Mohali, India
Swarnima Gorani, Sharda University, India

Chapter 10
Neurotechnology, Mental Health, and Gender-Neutral Justice: Brain-Computer Interface as a Tool for Addressing Cruelty Against Men 155
Yash Saxena, Amity University, Gwalior, India
Hemant Singh, Amity University, Gwalior, India
Radha Naruka, High Court of Rajasthan, Jaipur, India

Chapter 11
Public Health, Patents, and Neuroscience: Legal Implications and Opportunities of Brain-Computer Interfaces in Modern Healthcare 171
Swati Mehra, Amity University, Gwalior, India
Abhijay Chakraborty, Amity Law School, Amity University, Jaipur, India
Priyansh Samadhiya, Amity University, Gwalior, India

Chapter 12
The Future of Communication Skills Training in Neuro-Digital Workplaces: Brain-Computer Interface Challenges and Opportunities for Human Resource Development 187
Vartika Chaturvedi, IMS Noida, India
Anjali Khanna, Step by Step School, Noida, India

Chapter 13
The Impact of Neural Data Rights Awareness on Consumer Attitudes Toward Neurotechnology Products 201
Aastha Sawhney, Independent Researcher, India
Ankita Bajpai, Inderprastha Engineering College, Sahibabad, India
Amit Kumar Pandey, Institute of Management Studies (Business School), Ghaziabad, India
Shashank Chaudhary, Independent Researcher, India
Vartika Saxena, Institute of Professional Excellence and Management, Ghaziabad, India

Chapter 14
Toward International Standards, Neurorights Legislation, and Responsible Innovation in the Brain-Data Era 219
Mohd Faiz Khan, School of Legal Studies, CGC University, Mohali, India
Saurabh Chandra, Symbiosis Law School, Symbiosis International (Deemed to be) University, Pune, India

Chapter 15
Understanding Emotional Well-Being in Indian Policing Through a Cognitive and Neuroethical Lens 235
Priyamvada Singh, Jagran Lakecity University, Bhopal, India
Priyanka Nema, Jagran Lakecity University, Bhopal, India

Compilation of References 251

About the Contributors 269

Index 273

Detailed Table of Contents

Preface xv

Chapter 1
Application of Brain–Computer Interface and Artificial Intelligence in Prisons With Harmonizing Neural Data Rights: Analysis of Legal Framework in India's Correctional and Evidentiary Protection Mechanism 1
Sunaina Mishra, Christ (Deemed to be) University, Delhi NCR, India
Kriti Parashar, Christ (Deemed to be) University, Delhi NCR, India

The intersection of Brain-Computer Interfaces (BCIs) and artificial intelligence in Indian prisons holds significant transformation potential and presents formidable challenges to neural data rights and personal autonomy while addressing issues of rehabilitation, mental health monitoring, and security. This chapter examines the current legal landscape established by the Prisons Act, Indian Evidence Act and Digital Personal Data Protection Act, 2023, our efforts to ensure protection for sensitive neuro-data from misuse, and opportunities to bridge the existing gaps. It looks at aspects of ethics like informed consent, coercive surveillance and mental privacy, and suggests the need for harmonised Neuro-rights laws, in keeping with the Constitution, under Articles 21 and 20. It analyses the doctrines and the various elements, and comes to suggest a balanced regulatory model protecting the dignity of the prisoner while allowing the responsible use of technology.

Chapter 2
Artificial Intelligence and Digital Inclusion for Women With Disabilities: Legal and Ethical Perspectives of Brain-Computer Interfaces in Modern Society 19
Prangya Parimita Behera, Pingalakhi College of Special Education, Odisha, India
Binita Behera, KIIT School of Law, KIIT (Deemed to be) University, Odisha, India
Sanjay Kumar Singh, Uttar Pradesh Rajarshi Tandon Open University, India
Mousumi Raysingh, Pingalakhi College of Special Education, Odisha, India

Artificial intelligence enabled Brain-Computer Interfaces (BCI) have tremendous potential to contribute to digital inclusion for women with disabilities by facilitating their communication, mobility and cognition. Their speedy assimilation into mainstream society, however, brings up important legal and ethical issues. Gender and disability rights considerations sit alongside data privacy, informed consent, algorithmic bias and equitable access considerations, and can make factors worse. This chapter looks at international and national laws and ethical issues raised within a field of autonomy and dignity and whether the individual might be exploited. It highlights the importance of gender framework policies that address issues facing women with disabilities in the digital world, and to ensure that they are not targeted or left behind if the policies are designed to empower.

Chapter 3
Corporate Transparency in Neural Data Collection and Its Impact on Brand Loyalty 37
Amit Kumar Pandey, Institute of Management Studies (Business School), Ghaziabad, India
Prakhar Duggal, Amity University, Noida, India
Ujjwal Bharadwaj, Amity University, Noida, India
Aastha Sawhney, Independent Researcher, India
Ruchika Jeswal, Amity School of Business, Amity University, Noida, India

In an era defined by rapid advancements in the field of neurotechnology, transparency in corporate data collection practices has emerged as a key determinant of consumer trust and loyalty, soaring to new heights in this digital world. As the use of neurotechnology continues to grow, and as the field attracts a new generation of companies, the level of transparency in how these businesses collect and use neural data has become an important element in shaping customer trust and loyalty. The BCIs and wearable EEG devices, as well as mental wellness products, capture data that is extremely sensitive and generates speculations and privacy concerns. This chapter examines the impact of transparent provision of transparency regarding data policies, consent protocols, security measures and consumer rights on attitudes.

Chapter 4
Hacking Brains, Unauthorized Access, and Cloud Storage Risks: Legal Admissibility and Evidentiary Challenges.. 55
Abhishek Srivastava, Amity University, Jaipur, India
Hemant Singh, Amity University, Gwalior, India
Sanjay Kumar Pandey, MIT ADT University, Pune, India

Brain computer interfaces (BCIs) and cloud neural data storage have placed more than ever before us the risk of "brain hacking" and unauthorized data access. Neural Data or rich in personal thoughts, feelings and memories is the most vulnerable information. This chapter explores cyber vulnerabilities in neuro-technologies, the threats posed by cloud storage and how that poses legal and evidentiary challenges in court. It examines the admissibility problems of tampered neural evidence, concerns of reliability and privacy implications in the light of the current cyber laws. As data breaches and even the possibility for brain manipulation are increasing, the study calls for more stringent boundaries for admissibility standards, tighter legislation regarding neuro-rights and international coordination in order to safeguard mental privacy to achieve justice.

Chapter 5
Law Enforcement Use Toward International Standards: Neurorights Legislation and Responsible Innovation in the Brain-Data Era 69
Deeksha Jha, Amity University, Gwalior, India
Ravina Parihar, Gujarat National Law University, Silvassa, India
Gopalam Sultania, Amity University, Jaipur, India

The modern times, in which brain technologies develop very much, such as Brain-Computer Interfaces (BCIs), have started the Brain-Data era and thus introduced deep-felted challenges to mental privacy, cognitive freedom, and human agency. This chapter explores how law enforcement might leverage brain data in investigations, predictive policing, and interrogation; it will look at the current state of law surrounding brain data with an in-depth look at some of the first bills on the topic to be introduced to any national legislatures and discuss the pros and cons of these directives. It examines "international guidance," such as that provided in the UNESCO 2025 Recommendation on the Ethics of Neurotechnology and the OECD Guidance for Responsible Innovation.

Chapter 6
Legal Admissibility and Evidentiary Challenges: Neural-Derived Evidence in Courts and Forensic Contexts 87
Pradip Kumar Kashyap, School of Legal Studies, CGC University, Mohali, India
Saurabh Chandra, Symbiosis Law School Noida, Symbiosis International (Deemed to be) University, Pune, India

Neural-derived evidence stems from the continued growth of neural networks and generative AI, which have opened a new category of evidence such as deepfakes, AI-generated documents, synthetic media and algorithmically-produced forensic reconstructions. This evidence, particularly in terms of legal admissibility, authenticity and reliability, poses new and formidable problems for both lawyers and the judiciary. The chapter explores both the technical aspects and the challenges of using the traditional legal criteria including Daubert, Frye and Section 65B of the Indian Evidence Act with materials fobtained from the brain. It reviews concerns regarding manipulation, algorithmic bias, need for explainability and associated concerns over fair trials. The chapter points out pressing requirements for the creation of new regulation, detection requirements; and judicial capacities in order to effectively answer this new frontier of digital forensics and criminal justice.

Chapter 7
Neural-Derived Evidence in Courts and Forensic Contexts: Case Studies 105
Hemant Singh, Amity University, Gwalior, India
Saurabh Kumar, Chanakya National Law University, Patna, India
Pragya Singh, The Neotia University, West Bengal, India

Evidence from some areas of the nervous system be it brain imaging or electrophysiological data has been increasingly used in the courts to substantiate allegations of mental state, deception, criminal responsibility, and injury, among other things. Technologies, such as fMRI, EEG, and PET scans, have advanced to a level that can provide information about brain structure and function, however, these technologies bring several challenges for the field of forensics with regard to reliability, admissibility and interpretability when it comes to psychiatric issues. In this paper, the focus is on critical technologies, here are some famous landmark products from the United States, India, and other parts of the world, and there are unsolved evidentiary issues.

Chapter 8
Neurorights Legislation and Responsible Innovation in the Brain Data Era 121
Arunima Shastri, Christ University, Bangalore, India
Laeeq R. Janjua, WSB University, Poland
Saurabh Chandra, Symbiosis Law School, Symbiosis International (Deemed to be) University, Pune, India

Neurorights law has become an important field to protect human dignity, mental privacy, cognitive freedom, and other fundamental rights and freedoms of every person in the Brain Data Era, where excessive amounts of intimate brain data generated by advanced neurotech including brain-computer interfaces (BCIs), neural implants, wearables EEG, AI-assisted neuroimage systems and is collected through thought decoding, revealing thoughts, emotions, intentions and cognitive state. Led by some neuroscientists are proposed rights that address mental privacy as the right not to be subjected to gathering or decoding of neural data without consent, cognitive liberty as the freedom from the possibility of coercive manipulation of one's mind, personal identity as the right not to have one's sense of self, or the right to one's identity, altered, equal access to neuroenhancement, and protection against algorithmic bias and discrimination.

Chapter 9
Neurorights Legislation in the Brain Data Era: Forging Comprehensive Legal Frameworks to Safeguard Cognitive Liberty and Mental Privacy..................... 137
Sukhwinder Singh, School of Legal Studies, CGC University, Mohali, India
Swarnima Gorani, Sharda University, India

The unprecedented threats to cognitive liberty and mental privacy posed by the rapid development and maturing of neurotechnology in the brain data era. This chapter reviews the development of laws that protect individuals against unauthorized access, manipulation and/or the commodification of brain generated information. Attempts are accelerating to form more far-reaching frameworks, from Chile's constitutional amendment through state constitutional bans in California and Colorado, and from UNESCO's Ethical Recommendations. However, there are clearly shortcomings with respect to the perceived mental data and regulatory convergence and enforcement. Enhancing existing laws is crucial to accommodate innovation and human right principles to protect human beings' personal autonomy, identity and freedom of thought in this world of connectivity and communication.

Chapter 10
Neurotechnology, Mental Health, and Gender-Neutral Justice: Brain-Computer Interface as a Tool for Addressing Cruelty Against Men 155
Yash Saxena, Amity University, Gwalior, India
Hemant Singh, Amity University, Gwalior, India
Radha Naruka, High Court of Rajasthan, Jaipur, India

In the field of mental health, public policy and a gender-neutral justice-for-all are where Brain-Computer Interfaces (BCIs) come into play as emerging neurotechnological means. This chapter discusses the potential of BCIs to mitigate experience of cruelty and abuse by the male population such as psychological trauma, and Domestic violence victimization, but also certain biases in legal approaches. BCIs provide opportunities for evidence in the legal system, personalized rehabilitation of mental health and objective assessment of trauma, as well as real-time monitoring and management of neural signals, states of mind, and therapeutic interventions. Although there has been a push to implement gender neutral approaches, privacy, ethical consent, and access to services are key issues to be resolved. The chapter calls for a legal intersectionality of neurotechnology to achieve greater fairness and inclusion, as is required in mental health approaches in the modern world.

Chapter 11
Public Health, Patents, and Neuroscience: Legal Implications and
Opportunities of Brain-Computer Interfaces in Modern Healthcare 171
Swati Mehra, Amity University, Gwalior, India
Abhijay Chakraborty, Amity Law School, Amity University, Jaipur, India
Priyansh Samadhiya, Amity University, Gwalior, India

Brain-Computer Interfaces (BCIs) are a promising multidisciplinary field that combines interdisciplinary areas of neuroscience and engineering and healthcare that provides unparalleled opportunities to restore motor and sensory functions to patients suffering from neurological disorders. This chapter examines the various legal aspects of patents, informed consent, data privacy and regulation in regards to public health. Although BCIs have their merits, there are several difficulties with them including the security of intellectual property rights, ethical uses of neural data and access for people in health systems. There are opportunities to speed up innovation, such as with patent incentives, as well as opportunities to integrate into precision medicine. Politically strong instruments are essential to securing the rights of the patients, risk minimisation and proper interaction with the patient.

Chapter 12
The Future of Communication Skills Training in Neuro-Digital Workplaces:
Brain-Computer Interface Challenges and Opportunities for Human Resource
Development 187
Vartika Chaturvedi, IMS Noida, India
Anjali Khanna, Step by Step School, Noida, India

In the age of Digital Transformation and 'neuroscience' what digital transformation does to workplaces is a paradigm change that we now call the Neuro-digital Workplace. Not only will these spaces be defined by state-of-the-art technology, but the incorporation of neurotechnology as well, which will enable direct brain-computer interaction, thereby changing the ways by which a job worker can communicate, collaborate and pick up skills. BCIs are now beginning to be used for communication skills training, which is taking its place, as a neuro adaptive system based on techniques that involve workshop classes, role playing and feedback. BCIs can transmit brain signals to human-made machines or feedback, which might rectify physical handicaps, cognitive problems, and more they serve as additional challenges for Human Resource Development (HRD) professionals. The present chapter addresses future landscape with a particular emphasis on training within neuro-digital environment based on BCI.

Chapter 13
The Impact of Neural Data Rights Awareness on Consumer Attitudes Toward Neurotechnology Products 201
Aastha Sawhney, Independent Researcher, India
Ankita Bajpai, Inderprastha Engineering College, Sahibabad, India
Amit Kumar Pandey, Institute of Management Studies (Business School), Ghaziabad, India
Shashank Chaudhary, Independent Researcher, India
Vartika Saxena, Institute of Professional Excellence and Management, Ghaziabad, India

Consumer-associated neurotechnology devices, like EEG systems and brain computer systems (BCIs), are proliferating quickly, touching controversial issues of neuroscientific knowledge, which may uncover deep psychological, emotional and cognitive variations that are shared with the wearer amongst a household's constituents or with strangers. The aims of this chapter are to explore consumer attitudes towards the same products based on their knowledge of the rights of the neural data. Based on the surveys, policy analysis and industry reports it finds the following: low awareness is linked to increased privacy concerns and decreased usage; education about rights translates to increased trust and usage. But there is still a lot of work to be done in terms of transparency and regulations in companies.

Chapter 14
Toward International Standards, Neurorights Legislation, and Responsible Innovation in the Brain-Data Era 219
Mohd Faiz Khan, School of Legal Studies, CGC University, Mohali, India
Saurabh Chandra, Symbiosis Law School, Symbiosis International (Deemed to be) University, Pune, India

The current brain-data era requires strong worldwide frameworks, such as regulations and guidelines for appropriate and responsible innovation that will safeguard human dignity and stimulate potential areas of therapeutic and cognitive research. The unique amendments to the Chilean Constitution inspired constitutional initiatives in the region as well as soft-law instruments by UNESCO, OECD and the Inter-American Juridical Committee. The constitutional amendments in Chile created a benchmark for similar initiatives in other nations and for soft-law instruments by UNESCO, OECD, and the Inter-American Juridical Committee. The piece explores how national-level responses have not been uniform but rather a mix of protective measures at the state level in the United States, and the evolution toward harmonized governance to help address concerns regarding cognitive liberty, and ensuring access to mental data and privacy.

Chapter 15
Understanding Emotional Well-Being in Indian Policing Through a Cognitive and Neuroethical Lens 235
Priyamvada Singh, Jagran Lakecity University, Bhopal, India
Priyanka Nema, Jagran Lakecity University, Bhopal, India

Emotional well-being amongst Indian police personnel has been inadequately studied in the context of significant work related stressors such as long hours of work, exposure to trauma, scarcity of resources, sociocultural stressors and more. In this paper, the challenge is explored from a cognitive and neuroethical point of view, drawing upon the field of neuroscience on emotional regulation processes such as amygdala/prefrontal cortex interactions and cognitive reappraisal as well as some ethical aspects of the moral injury concept, the right to decision making and institutional responsibility. It looks into how cognitive tools and neuroethical perspectives can contribute towards building resilience. Recommendations include culturally-informed training, organizational support and ethical guidelines to improve officers' health, efficiency and effectiveness and build community trust.

Compilation of References 251

About the Contributors 269

Index 273

Preface

"Legal Implications of Brain-Computer Interfaces in Modern Society" is an edited book covering the current legal and ethical issues brought about by the swift development of brain-computer interfaces. The book brings together experts in related fields of neuroscience, law, ethics, data protection, technology policy and human rights to analyze brain-computer interfaces (BCIs) and the impact they have on basic rights in today's society.

Applications of BCI include the direct connection between the human brain and external devices, for use in medicine in communication and cognitive enhancement. But these also entail significant vulnerabilities. The book focuses on the legal and technological gaps, such as lacking regulations on mental privacy, cognitive freedom and the ownership and management of digital data. The nature of neural data, which is often considered the most private type of information, creates privacy concerns about consent, ownership, surveillance and potential misuse by corporations, governments or bad actors.

These themes encompass the safeguarding of "neurorights" the effectiveness of existing data protection legislation, liability for harm caused by BCI usage, intellectual property rights over the data generated by the human brain and possible rising of social inequalities due to unequal access to enhancement technologies.

The policy maker, legal and technological and ethical professionals will find the book to be an important reference source. It calls for positive law which encourages innovation and at the same time provides protection as a law that could shape the future all over the world. It also highlights that, without adequate frameworks, the use of BCIs can pose as a threat to basic human freedom on the one hand, as well as a pathway to enhancing human abilities on the other hand.

CHAPTER OVERVIEW

Chapter 1: Application of Brain –Computer Interface and Artificial Intelligence in Prisons with Harmonizing Neural Data Rights: Analysis of Legal Framework in India's Correctional and Evidentiary Protection Mechanism

The intersection of Brain-Computer Interfaces (BCIs) and artificial intelligence in Indian prisons holds significant transformation potential and presents formidable challenges to neural data rights and personal autonomy while addressing issues of rehabilitation, mental health monitoring, and security. This chapter examines the current legal landscape established by the Prisons Act, Indian Evidence Act and Digital Personal Data Protection Act, 2023, our efforts to ensure protection for sensitive neuro-data from misuse, and opportunities to bridge the existing gaps. It looks at aspects of ethics like informed consent, coercive surveillance and mental privacy, and suggests the need for harmonised Neuro-rights laws, in keeping with the Constitution, under Articles 21 and 20. It analyses the doctrines and the various elements, and comes to suggest a balanced regulatory model protecting the dignity of the prisoner while allowing the responsible use of technology.

Chapter 2: Artificial Intelligence and Digital Inclusion for Women with Disabilities: Legal and Ethical Perspectives of Brain-Computer Interfaces in Modern Society

Artificial intelligence enabled Brain-Computer Interfaces (BCI) have tremendous potential to contribute to digital inclusion for women with disabilities by facilitating their communication, mobility and cognition. Their speedy assimilation into mainstream society, however, brings up important legal and ethical issues. Gender and disability rights considerations sit alongside data privacy, informed consent, algorithmic bias and equitable access considerations, and can make factors worse. This chapter looks at international and national laws and ethical issues raised within a field of autonomy and dignity and whether the individual might be exploited. It highlights the importance of gender framework policies that address issues facing women with disabilities in the digital world, and to ensure that they are not targeted or left behind if the policies are designed to empower.

Chapter 3: Corporate Transparency in Neural Data Collection and Its Impact on Brand Loyalty

In an era defined by rapid advancements in the field of neurotechnology, transparency in corporate data collection practices has emerged as a key determinant of consumer trust and loyalty, soaring to new heights in this digital world. As the use of neurotechnology continues to grow, and as the field attracts a new generation of companies, the level of transparency in how these businesses collect and use neural data has become an important element in shaping customer trust and loyalty. The BCIs and wearable EEG devices, as well as mental wellness products, capture data that is extremely sensitive and generates speculations and privacy concerns. This chapter examines the impact of transparent provision of transparency regarding data policies, consent protocols, security measures and consumer rights on attitudes.

Chapter 4: Hacking Brains, Unauthorized Access and Cloud Storage Risks: Legal Admissibility and Evidentiary Challenges

Brain computer interfaces (BCIs) and cloud neural data storage have placed more than ever before us the risk of "brain hacking" and unauthorized data access. Neural Data or rich in personal thoughts, feelings and memories is the most vulnerable information. This chapter explores cyber vulnerabilities in neuro-technologies, the threats posed by cloud storage and how that poses legal and evidentiary challenges in court. It examines the admissibility problems of tampered neural evidence, concerns of reliability and privacy implications in the light of the current cyber laws. As data breaches and even the possibility for brain manipulation are increasing, the study calls for more stringent boundaries for admissibility standards, tighter legislation regarding neuro-rights and international coordination in order to safeguard mental privacy to achieve justice.

Chapter 5: Law Enforcement Use toward International Standards, Neurorights Legislation and Responsible Innovation in the Brain-Data Era

The modern times, in which brain technologies develop very much, such as Brain-Computer Interfaces (BCIs), have started the Brain-Data era and thus introduced deep-felted challenges to mental privacy, cognitive freedom, and human agency. This chapter explores how law enforcement might leverage brain data in investigations, predictive policing, and interrogation; it will look at the current state of law surrounding brain data with an in-depth look at some of the first bills on the topic to be introduced to any national legislatures and discuss the pros and cons of these directives. It examines "international guidance," such as that provided in the UNESCO 2025 Recommendation on the Ethics of Neurotechnology and the OECD Guidance for Responsible Innovation.

Chapter 6: Legal Admissibility and Evidentiary Challenges: Neural-Derived Evidence in Courts and Forensic Contexts

Neural-derived evidence stems from the continued growth of neural networks and generative AI, which have opened a new category of evidence such as deepfakes, AI-generated documents, synthetic media and algorithmically-produced forensic reconstructions. This evidence, particularly in terms of legal admissibility, authenticity and reliability, poses new and formidable problems for both lawyers and the judiciary. The chapter explores both the technical aspects and the challenges of using the traditional legal criteria including Daubert, Frye and Section 65B of the Indian Evidence Act with materials obtained from the brain. It reviews concerns regarding manipulation, algorithmic bias, need for explainability and associated concerns over fair trials. The chapter points out pressing requirements for the creation of new regulation, detection requirements; and judicial capacities in order to effectively answer this new frontier of digital forensics and criminal justice.

Chapter 7: Neural-Derived Evidence in Courts and Forensic Contexts Case Studies

Evidence from some areas of the nervous system be it brain imaging or electrophysiological data has been increasingly used in the courts to substantiate allegations of mental state, deception, criminal responsibility, and injury, among other things. Technologies, such as fMRI, EEG, and PET scans, have advanced to a level that can provide information about brain structure and function, however, these technologies bring several challenges for the field of forensics with regard to reliability, admissibility and interpretability when it comes to psychiatric issues. In this paper, the focus is on critical technologies, here are some famous landmark products from the United States, India, and other parts of the world, and there are unsolved evidentiary issues.

Chapter 8: Neurorights Legislation and Responsible Innovation in the Brain Data Era

Neurorights law has become an important field to protect human dignity, mental privacy, cognitive freedom, and other fundamental rights and freedoms of every person in the Brain Data Era, where excessive amounts of intimate brain data generated by advanced neurotech including brain-computer interfaces (BCIs), neural implants, wearables EEG, AI-assisted neuroimage systems and is collected through thought decoding, revealing thoughts, emotions, intentions and cognitive state. Led by some neuroscientists are proposed rights that address mental privacy as the right not to be subjected to gathering or decoding of neural data without consent, cognitive liberty as the freedom from the possibility of coercive manipulation of one's mind, personal identity as the right not to have one's sense of self, or the right to one's identity, altered, equal access to neuroenhancement, and protection against algorithmic bias and discrimination.

Chapter 9: Neurorights Legislation in the Brain Data Era: Forging Comprehensive Legal Frameworks to Safeguard Cognitive Liberty and Mental Privacy

The unprecedented threats to cognitive liberty and mental privacy posed by the rapid development and maturing of neurotechnology in the brain data era. This chapter reviews the development of laws that protect individuals against unauthorized access, manipulation and/or the commodification of brain generated information. Attempts are accelerating to form more far-reaching frameworks, from Chile's constitutional amendment through state constitutional bans in California and Colorado, and from UNESCO's Ethical Recommendations. However, there are clearly shortcomings with respect to the perceived mental data and regulatory convergence and enforcement. Enhancing existing laws is crucial to accommodate innovation and human right principles to protect human beings' personal autonomy, identity and freedom of thought in this world of connectivity and communication.

Chapter 10: Neurotechnology, Mental Health and Gender-Neutral Justice: Brain Computer Interface as a Tool for Addressing Cruelty Against Men

In the field of mental health, public policy and a gender-neutral justice-for-all are where Brain-Computer Interfaces (BCIs) come into play as emerging neurotechnological means. This chapter discusses the potential of BCIs to mitigate experience of cruelty and abuse by the male population such as psychological trauma, and Domestic violence victimization, but also certain biases in legal approaches. BCIs provide opportunities for evidence in the legal system, personalized rehabilitation of mental health and objective assessment of trauma, as well as real-time monitoring and management of neural signals, states of mind, and therapeutic interventions. Although there has been a push to implement gender neutral approaches, privacy, ethical consent, and access to services are key issues to be resolved. The chapter calls for a legal intersectionality of neurotechnology to achieve greater fairness and inclusion, as is required in mental health approaches in the modern world.

Chapter 11: Public Health, Patents and Neuroscience: Legal Implications and Opportunities of Brain-Computer Interfaces in Modern Healthcare

Brain-Computer Interfaces (BCIs) are a promising multidisciplinary field that combines interdisciplinary areas of neuroscience and engineering and healthcare that provides unparalleled opportunities to restore motor and sensory functions to patients suffering from neurological disorders. This chapter examines the various legal aspects of patents, informed consent, data privacy and regulation in regards to public health. Although BCIs have their merits, there are several difficulties with them including the security of intellectual property rights, ethical uses of neural data and access for people in health systems. There are opportunities to speed up innovation, such as with patent incentives, as well as opportunities to integrate into precision medicine. Politically strong instruments are essential to securing the rights of the patients, risk minimisation and proper interaction with the patient.

Chapter 12: The Future of Communication Skills Training in Neuro-Digital Workplaces: Brain-Computer Interface Challenges and Opportunities for Human Resource Development

In the age of Digital Transformation and 'neuroscience' what digital transformation does to workplaces is a paradigm change that we now call the Neuro-digital Workplace. Not only will these spaces be defined by state-of-the-art technology, but the incorporation of neurotechnology as well, which will enable direct brain-computer interaction, thereby changing the ways by which a job worker can communicate, collaborate and pick up skills. BCIs are now beginning to be used for communication skills training, which is taking its place, as a neuro adaptive system based on techniques that involve workshop classes, role playing and feedback. BCIs can transmit brain signals to human-made machines or feedback, which might rectify physical handicaps, cognitive problems, and more they serve as additional challenges for Human Resource Development (HRD) professionals. The present chapter addresses future landscape with a particular emphasis on training within neuro-digital environment based on BCI.

Chapter 13: The Impact of Neural Data Rights Awareness on Consumer Attitudes toward Neurotechnology Products

Consumer-associated neurotechnology devices, like EEG systems and brain computer systems (BCIs), are proliferating quickly, touching controversial issues of neuroscientific knowledge, which may uncover deep psychological, emotional and cognitive variations that are shared with the wearer amongst a household's constituents or with strangers. The aims of this chapter are to explore consumer attitudes towards the same products based on their knowledge of the rights of the neural data. Based on the surveys, policy analysis and industry reports it finds the following: low awareness is linked to increased privacy concerns and decreased usage; education about rights translates to increased trust and usage. But there is still a lot of work to be done in terms of transparency and regulations in companies.

Chapter 14: Toward International Standards, Neurorights Legislation and Responsible Innovation in the Brain-Data Era

The current brain-data era requires strong worldwide frameworks, such as regulations and guidelines for appropriate and responsible innovation that will safeguard human dignity and stimulate potential areas of therapeutic and cognitive research. The unique amendments to the Chilean Constitution inspired constitutional initiatives in the region as well as soft-law instruments by UNESCO, OECD and the Inter-American Juridical Committee. The constitutional amendments in Chile created a benchmark for similar initiatives in other nations and for soft-law instruments by UNESCO, OECD, and the Inter-American Juridical Committee. The piece explores how national-level responses have not been uniform but rather a mix of protective measures at the state level in the United States, and the evolution toward harmonized governance to help address concerns regarding cognitive liberty, and ensuring access to mental data and privacy.

Chapter 15: Understanding Emotional Well-Being in Indian Policing Through a Cognitive and Neuroethical Lens

Emotional well-being amongst Indian police personnel has been inadequately studied in the context of significant work related stressors such as long hours of work, exposure to trauma, scarcity of resources, sociocultural stressors and more. In this paper, the challenge is explored from a cognitive and neuroethical point of view, drawing upon the field of neuroscience on emotional regulation processes such as amygdala/prefrontal cortex interactions and cognitive reappraisal as well as some ethical aspects of the moral injury concept, the right to decision making and institutional responsibility. It looks into how cognitive tools and neuroethical perspectives can contribute towards building resilience. Recommendations include culturally-informed training, organizational support and ethical guidelines to improve officers' health, efficiency and effectiveness and build community trust.

Chapter 1
Application of Brain-Computer Interface and Artificial Intelligence in Prisons With Harmonizing Neural Data Rights:
Analysis of Legal Framework in India's Correctional and Evidentiary Protection Mechanism

Sunaina Mishra
http://orcid.org/0000-0001-5468-1962
Christ (Deemed to be) University, Delhi NCR, India

Kriti Parashar
http://orcid.org/0009-0000-6483-0431
Christ (Deemed to be) University, Delhi NCR, India

ABSTRACT

The intersection of Brain-Computer Interfaces (BCIs) and artificial intelligence in Indian prisons holds significant transformation potential and presents formidable challenges to neural data rights and personal autonomy while addressing issues of rehabilitation, mental health monitoring, and security. This chapter examines the current legal landscape established by the Prisons Act, Indian Evidence Act and Digital Personal Data Protection Act, 2023, our efforts to ensure protection for sensitive neuro-data from misuse, and opportunities to bridge the existing gaps. It

DOI: 10.4018/979-8-3373-9720-7.ch001

looks at aspects of ethics like informed consent, coercive surveillance and mental privacy, and suggests the need for harmonised Neuro-rights laws, in keeping with the Constitution, under Articles 21 and 20. It analyses the doctrines and the various elements, and comes to suggest a balanced regulatory model protecting the dignity of the prisoner while allowing the responsible use of technology.

1. INTRODUCTION

The introduction of Brain-Computer Interfaces (BCI) and Artificial Intelligence (AI) systems into Indian prisons is a groundbreaking revolution in the field that presents multiple opportunities for prison reform, mental health supervision, security, and predictive crime analysis, while posing significant challenges for the seamless integration of BCI-AI systems into the nation's expanding prison legal framework outlined in the Prisons Act, 1894, Indian Evidence Act, 1872, and the Digital Personal Data Protection (DPDP) Act, 2023 (Muravieva, 2025). Using direct Brain-Computer Interfacing (BCI) technologies, which allow prisoners with significant neurological disabilities or those in high-security settings to now actively control protheses, to articulate thoughts to support their psychological therapies or even for neurofeedback exercise applications that help them improve their cognitive functions and behavior to lower recidivism rates, enables the active use of these devices. In criminal correctional facilities, AI can be used alongside BCI to analyze extensive neural data for targeted reintegration strategies, including AI-based tools for creating personalized learning plans for training and cultural enrichment, AI-powered chatbots for cognitive behavioral therapy to address mental health needs, and AI-assisted decision-making software for parole eligibility determination to risk-prevent self-harm or violent behaviors. In India, where the colonial-era Prisons Act prioritizes custody over more positive fluidity between the individual and the machine, and traditional prisons suffer from poor human resource management, overcrowding and outdated facilities, these integrations have the potential to reshuffle the focus for these prisons, making them scientific institutions in a spirit of the Model Prison Manual, offering scientific interventions and facilities, biometrics and rehabilitation, beyond mere mundane incarceration. For example, brain fingerprinting (BEOSP), which has been employed in Indian investigations to identify concealed information by measuring P300 wave responses, has been used to identify NRCs of criminal intent or guilt, potentially along with other AI-driven risk assessment tools, which could utilize BCI-derived information to support evidentiary processes in assessing criminal intent or rehabilitation readiness (Mia, 2025).

1.1 Background of Brain-Computer Interface (BCI) and Artificial Intelligence in Prisons

Nevertheless, the applications present serious ethical and human rights issues involving mental privacy, informed consent and potential for the abuse of surveillance, where India's legislation needs to be scrutinized in order to balance neural data rights. Neural data, which span raw brain signals, decoded thoughts, emotions and inferred and assumed cognitive states, may have an intimacy that far exceeds current biometric or personal data and demonstrate potential vulnerabilities such as cognitive biases, hidden memories, and potential for post-release monitoring or interrogation. In prisons, voluntary or compelled BCI use could be a murky intersection between therapy and control, while reports of BCI usage in law enforcement and defense circle raised HIT concerns of officer decision-making improved through the use of BCIs, the same way that wearing a gun pushes the boundaries of our interactions with the world (Mouazen & El Bouyed, 2025). The right to personal liberty, personal dignity and privacy as extended by the Constitution of India in K.S. Puttaswamy v. Union of India (in the context of its right to life) gives implicit protection to mental autonomy and that is protected by the prospect of law, but there are still gaps in the legislation. The personal data defined in the DPDP Act 2023 is quite broad and lacks a complete definition of neural data as a special category of data similar to that of health or biometric, sticks to a consent based approach that is not appropriate for such unconscious neural inputs which are generated without the intention or complete understanding of the data subject. Such vulnerabilities also exist in correctional settings, where the loss of autonomy in inmates' operations is intended to eliminate consent for meaningful interferences, and evidentiary use under the Indian Evidence Act, where admission of information from the BCI or AI-derived insights from neural patterns might infringe Article 20(3)'s protection against self-incrimination in the event of compulsion. The precedents in India of brain fingerprinting reveal the difference of opinions over its admissibility, as in some cases, the brain-fingerprint has been used as corroborative evidence and not as conclusive proof, highlighting the need for a Daubert-like reliability test as part of the Indian jurisprudence.

1.2 Significance of Neural Data Rights in Correctional Systems

Targeted upgrades to the DPDP Act are needed to clarify that neurodata represents a group of very sensitive data that requires more protection, including purpose limitation and a right to "neural privacy" which bans non-consensual decoding (e.g., "reading" thoughts), and mandating that there should be independent judges' oversight on scientific validity and volontariness of BCI/AI use in prisons, with aim of replacing Prison Manual with an ethical oversight board for BCI/AI deployments (Kritika, 2026). Their viewpoints are offered by the constitutional neurorights in Chile, for example, and California and Colorado state laws in the U.S., which give higher protections around neural data, which could help serve as models for what India should do to stop a "neuro-surveillance state" becoming a drag on its acceptance of technology's rehabilitative potential. Challenges to implementation abound, including access and connectivity issues among Indian prisons; the risks of an algorithmic bias reinforcing caste or socioeconomic inequality in assigning risk; high costs for secure BCI infrastructure; and the presence or absence of judicial capacity to review complex neuro-evidence. Yet pilot programs under the provisions of technology in the Model Prison Act may help test a balanced approach. Applications such as non-invasive EEG with voluntary mental health neurofeedback, for instance, would help without compromising dignity, lower recidivism with personalized interventions while simultaneously ensuring no misuse in investigations, using AI anonymization techniques.

It is important to recognize that India is at a pivotal moment for having the foresight to embrace legal harmonization, ensuring their correctional system remains one of the world's leading forefigures in the ethical and humanized integration of neurotechnology into law. Principles of cognitive liberty, transparency and accountability (e.g., a dedicated Neurotechnology Regulation Authority) can help policy makers reduce risks of mental coercion, commodification of data, while promoting the welfare of prisoners, safety of society and justice. The crux of all of this is the realisation that the social framework needs to evolve from a reactive, evidence-based accommodation to a future-focused, rights-oriented governance framework on neural interfaces which has the potential to be transformative, while ensuring the inviolability of human mind (Ilhan, 2025).

2. EVOLUTION AND APPLICATIONS OF BCI AND AI IN CORRECTIONAL FACILITIES

Brain-Computer Interfaces (BCIs) and Artificial Intelligence (AI) in prisons are transitioning from confinement to precision justice, a shift that is significant in India where prisons are overcrowded. Initial experiments in the 1970s with basic EEG-based cursor control have since developed into a high-tech system for decoding cognitive states. Under the Model Prison Manual, these tools have been touted as solutions to issues such as helping prisoners with mental health concerns, reducing recidivism and rehabilitating offenders in prisons. This is complemented by AI, which analyzes neural and behavioral signals for predictions, allowing for proactive measures to be taken.

In the past, BCI has been developed in medical settings to enable communication in cases of locked in syndrome or motor impairments, with the help of invasive devices or non-invasive EEG. In India, investigations based on brain electric oscillation signatures of concealed knowledge (BEOSP) started gaining traction as a neurotechnological tool since early 2000s and this area of research is further developing in the field of corrections. AI applications have been implemented in the world in various fields such as risk assessment, research and prediction of violence, individualistic rehabilitation program development and such like. BCI could be expanded to help hack cognitive behavioural therapy or assess remorse in prisons, or be applied to monitoring what goes on on computers via AI, analysing behavioral patterns, communications or biometrics to flag them.

Given the resource limitations and overcrowding prevalent in Indian prisons, the use of BCI-AI may be applicable to reformative objectives, such as the use of neurofeedback to manage anger or customizing vocational training using AI. This development creates neural data rights issues that need to be harmonized with constitutional privacy concerns and the DPDP Act, however. Applications should focus on voluntary participation, not coercion, never at the expense of technologies that strengthen dignity, but not restrict freedom. The non-invasive EEG technology in conjunction with AI analytics could be used for mental health support in pilot programs, creating evidence-based reform in the process, and working around Section 42 of the Indian Evidence Act on the evidentiary admissibility of these technologies (Bhattacharjee et al., 2025). As they continue to grow, India's laws and bodies have to evolve and better accommodate security concerns, rehabilitation and fundamental rights, while ensuring that there is no misuse in an environment that is vulnerable and contains captured vehicles.

2.1 Technical Overview of BCI Systems

Brain-computer interface (BCI) systems allow for direct brain-to-external-device communication without using the motor pathways. Contents from the point of view of technical classification, BCIs can be divided into three categories: They are either invasive, partially invasive, or they are non-invasive. Invasive BCIs use electrodes, typically surgically implanted, like Utah arrays or electrocorticography ("eCoG") grids that are attached or infused within the cortex; they are capable of acquiring high spatial and temporal resolution of the activity and decode very precise neural intentions as demonstrated, for instance, in speech restoration or even in controlling prothetic appendages in patients with ALS or paraplegia.

The most practical for general correctional use, non-invasive BCIs are based on the electroencephalography (EEG) signal recorded using the scalp electrodes. They record the brain's electrical activity, such as event-related potentials, such as P300, which are engaged in brain fingerprinting, or sensorimotor rhythms, of mu/beta waves, generated in motor imagery tasks. For the translation from intent to commands, signals are amplified to boost energy levels, filtered to remove unwanted noise, features are extracted (common spatial patterns or power spectral density), and machine learning (such as SVM, deep neural networks) is used to classify the features. Users might then use steady-state visual evoked potentials (SSVEP) or motor imagery paradigms to do the spelling, without moving from their seat or switching on the computer.

Hybrid systems combine EEG with eye-tracking and/or fNIRS which improve the accuracy of the recording. There is a challenge in the signal noise caused by artifacts (muscle, eye blinks), etc., low bandwidth (5-30 bits/min) in non-invasive scenarios, etc., and there is a need for calibration sessions. Recent developments have introduces AI-based real-time adaptive decoding, shortened training time, and improved robustness (Perlin et al., 2025). While there are theoretical potential uses for both non-invasive and invasive EEG headsets, at this point it seems that the former have more promise than the latter. In prisons, non-invasive EEG could be used to help manage impulses, or to enable communication for patient inmates with disabilities, but invasive options would be limited in their application, both ethically – because of the risk associated with surgery – and practically, since consent would be an issue.

2.2 AI-Driven Rehabilitation, Monitoring, and Predictive Analytics

BCI is complemented by AI-driven tools that are reshaping correctional environments with their ability to offer personalized rehabilitation, real-time monitoring, and predictive analytics for better results. AI uses behavioral, biometric, and maybe neural data to develop individualized interventions for rehabilitation. Machine learning algorithms are used to recommend specific cognitive behavioral therapy (CBT) modules, educational curriculum, or vocational courses to inmates that align with their profiles (which include mental health, criminal history, and engagement history), taken from existing profiles.These algorithms analyze inmate profiles to recommend tailored cognitive behavioral therapy (CBT) modules, educational curriculum, or vocational courses, based on existing inmate profiles, through existing inmate histories, potentially with the use of adaptive chatbots or VR environments.

CCTV monitoring applications use computer vision on CCTV footage, wearables, audio analysis to identify anomalies in real-time such as showing aggressive behavior, signs of self-harm, or contraband. Using predictive analytics, initiatives proactively allocate resources and early interventions to prevent risks that include violence incidents, recidivism, and emergency medical services with the implementation of models constructed from historical data and then supplied with real-time data. For example, if the activity level drops or the language used changes, indicating stress, AI can alert the mental health team.

Combined with BCI, AI could help analyze neural patterns for greater insight, like determining how well an individual is engaged during rehabilitation or identifying subtle emotions during parole proceedings. This may be implemented in India to embark upon a new era of prison reforms as per the intent of the reformative spirit of the Prisons Act, with optimised management to curb overcrowding. Some of the challenges are algorithmic bias (that adds to caste or socioeconomic inequalities), data privacy (under DPDP Act), evidentiary reliability (evidence is not easy to accept). Consent is paramount because forced collection of data may breach the right to privacy (which was confirmed in Article 21 of the UN Declaration on the Rights of Indigenous Peoples) and self-incrimination protections (which was recognized in Article 20(3) of the UN Declaration on the Rights of Indigenous Peoples).

Successful deployment is possible only if there are human checks and balances, independent audits, and transparency in their application. AI personalized path-forward signs of reduced recidivism and can harmonize with neural data rights through purpose limitation and anonymization through pilot programs. Finally, the incorporation of these AI-BCI can transform punishment into transformation by promoting restorative justice over punitive measures and ensure greater safety and reintegration as long as the underlying rules and regulations enable the ethical integration of such technology in the legal system.

2.3 Global Practices and Indian Pilot Contexts

BCI / AI practices around the world for corrections have some lessons for India. AI in the US and Europe is used to aid in risk assessment, predictive violence through behavioral analysis, and rehabilitation through personalized learning platforms (Fabiano, 2025). Real-time anomaly detection capabilities via CCTV powering AI technology are being used by countries such as Hong Kong to mitigate incidents. In the UK, researchers develop AI tools to predict violent behaviour, and in the USA, health facilities use wearables to prevent self harm.In the UK, AI solutions for predicting violent behaviour are under study and in the USA, health facilities adopted

AI-based wearables to prevent self-harm. BCI applications are still primarily used for experimental or medical reasons, with governments interested in brain-computer interfaces for cognitive monitoring, but with concerns about neuro-rights and the use of BCI during detention.

Chile and other countries have made progress on a neurorights bill; safeguards mental privacy from neurotechnology abuse. Globally, ethical guidelines focus on consent, limiting data collection, and the elimination of compulsion in displaying the brain. It is important to set ethical standard globally which involved two major principles, consent and data minimisation, while brain compulsion should be avoided in the exhibition.

3. ETHICAL AND HUMAN RIGHTS IMPLICATIONS

The adoption of Brain-Computer Interfaces (BCI) and Artificial Intelligence (AI) in correctional settings introduces existential ethical and human rights issues, including mental privacy, autonomy and consent, and the possibility of forced surveillance. The technologies that are being developed with BCI can decipher what the brain is thinking, feeling and intending, or what brain states it's in, fusing the boundaries of mind and machine while simultaneously furthering the encroachments of the prisoner's autonomy that had already taken place. The risk of a loss of cognitive liberty, neural data being leveraged for behavioral manipulation, behavioral predictions, possible forced rehabilitation and the violation of mental integrity and personal identity are major points to consider. In prisons "therapeutic" BCI uses, such as neurofeedback or impulse control, can serve as a cover for punitive surveillance and can increase dehumanization, or inequalities in access, adding to socioeconomic and caste inequalities in India.

The issue of informed consent creates reservations in a carceral environment, in which power is not equally distributed, thus limiting voluntariness. Prisons can be placed in an implicit "exploitation" situation such as might arise in the past for other populations, if prisoners are presented with the choice of being released on parole in exchange for participating in BCI. Algorithmic biases in AI-driven predictive analytics exacerbate risks by perpetuating discriminatory risk assessments or sentencing, if not causing it in the first place. Broad human rights concerns call for international guidelines, such as the Universal Declaration of Human Rights and principles of mental privacy as promoted in Chile by Neurological Rights protection via constitutional amendments.

These technologies have relevance with the constitutional values of dignity and liberty of the individual under Article 21 of Indian Constitution. If these robust safeguards are not in place, BCI-AI could be used to create the "neuro-surveillance state", jeopardizing rehabilitation goals and generating resistance. Principles for ethical deployment include independent supervision, transparency of algorithms, minimization of data and bans on automatic monitoring and decoding of conscience. To ensure the application of neurotechnologies to promote enhancement of prisoners' dignity and societal justice, there must be various multidisciplinary ethical review boards and the incorporation of international standards (Gridin, 2026).

4. INDIA'S LEGAL FRAMEWORK FOR PRISONS AND EVIDENTIARY MECHANISMS

The current legal system for prisons and the evidence collection in India, which is based on colonial law, is undergoing modernization but lacks adequate capability to equip them with Brain-Computer Interfaces (BCI) and Artificial Intelligence (AI) to deal with their complexity in prison environment. The Prisons Act, 1894, lays special stress on custody and discipline in prisons while the Evidence Act, 1872, is directed towards admissibility of scientific evidence in the court including the new category of neuro-data evidence. While the Digital Personal Data Protection (DPDP) Act, 2023, provides for measures to tackle data protection, there are some lack of protection regarding the brain as the most sensitive neural data within this framework.

This programme needs to balance the use of technology with the constitutional rights that protect equality, defeating testimony, personal liberty/privacy, e.g., Article 14, 20, 21. Where courts have interpreted evidence derived from BCI as 'corroborative' evidence not conclusive (in a series of applications where brain fingerprinting--a BCI technique--has been used, for example), there are indications that neuro evidence is undermining traditional evidentiary norms.There are precedents where the BCI-derived neural data was treated as corroborative evidence, not conclusive (such as in brain fingerprinting--BCI technique--cases, for example, where the data from the brain was interpreted as corroborative evidence). Both the Model Prison Manual and the recent Model Prisons Act, 2023, demonstrate a shift towards rehabilitation and the implementation of technologies, providing no clear indication on either its application of neurotechnologies, the necessary ethical governance and oversight, nor a specifically dedicated section on neural data governance.

The problem of reliability, bias, and consent is one that is difficult for the EvD mechanisms to address in the case of AI-BCI outputs. While neural information is protected by a minimum standard, existing data protection regulations do not categorically distinguish it, leaving areas of concern in the correctional and judicial sectors. In order to make the amendments harmonize, a clause should be added to include neuro-rights and explicitly include a purpose limitation, and provide standards for admissibility similar to the Daubert criteria. India could be open to legal loopholes that would facilitate misuse, if there were no proactive changes in the legislation, which will also hinder any positive use in the field of mental health and reformation.

4.1 Prisons Act, 1894 and Model Prison Manual

The Prisons Act 1894 is the basic law of prisons in India, which is very old and mostly based on custody, discipline and maintenance of the prisoners without paying any attention towards their rehabilitation or technological integration. It was framed during colonial days; its focus is security and order, outlines a classification of prisoners, the work that could be done to prisoners, and medical treatment but deals little with tools such as BCI or artificial intelligence (Thamma et al., 2025). The custodial focus presents issues with the deployment of neurotechnologies for mental health or behavioral change.

Some gaps are closed by this shift in emphasis in the Model Prison Manual 2016 and progressive Model Prisons Act, 2023 by focusing on reformation, rehabilitation and the use of technology. The Manual encourages practices that are scientific, rely on biometrics, computerize the process, and provide mental health support, all of which reflect the principles of reformative justice. This is furthered this year by adding provisions on technological intervention, video conferencing, individualized planning of sentences, aftercare services, and special attention to vulnerable inmates, which includes mental wellness units, in the 2023 Model Act.

4.2 Indian Evidence Act, 1872 and Digital Evidence Provisions

The Indian Evidence Act (1872) regulates the admissibility and appreciation of evidence before the courts in India including scientific and digital evidence related to BCI and AI usage in Prisons. Section 45 and 45A acknowledge expert opinion on scientific issues and Section 65A and 65B establish guidelines for electronic records, mandating electronic records be certified for admissibility of electronic evidence.

Brain fingerprinting (BEOSP) cases are of interest as showing the judicial approach: courts have accepted neuro-evidence as corroborative evidence, not primary; have raised concerns about reliability, voluntariness and protections in Article 20(3) against self-incrimination. The accuracy, bias and chain of custody would all be brought up when using BCI for obtaining data from which an AI would analyze neural information. There are no specific standards set in the Act regarding emerging neurotechnologies, which, if used, raise certain questions about how reassessable the evidentiary value is for the rehabilitation assessment, the decision on parole, etc.

4.3 Data Protection under DPDP Act, 2023 and Constitutional Safeguards

The Digital Personal Data Protection (DPDP) Act, 2023 is the primary legislation for personal data processing in India, highlighting key principles such as consent, purpose limitation, and rights of data principals. It can, however, only partially solve the neural data from BCI systems, as it goes beyond personal data determined by its connection with thoughts and the mental state of its user.

Mental autonomy and informational privacy is supported by solid constitutional protections, including because of the right to private life under Article 21, further rights to privacy as guaranteed by K.S. Puttaswamy v. Union of India. This is implicitly extended to neural data, which means that there needs to be a proportionality for any effect on the data being parallel within prisons. Articles 14 and 20 provide additional support to equality and protection against self-incrimination.

In the context of corrections, there is a risk of intrinsic coercion in the consent basis of the DPDP Act, and the neural category of the sensitive data is not clearly separated from other categories. In the absence of adequate management and monitoring of AI inferences, or in real-time, there are a need for updates and corrections when it comes to explicit neurorights like that of neural privacy or the right to delete decoded content. Through tiered scrutiny and interim guidelines until lawmakers make changes, judicial interpretation can fill these.

5. HARMONIZING NEURAL DATA RIGHTS IN THE INDIAN CONTEXT

Ensuring that the rights of neural data are harmonized within India's legal landscape becomes crucial as the government considers introducing the Brain-Computer Interface (BCI) and Artificial Intelligence (AI) technologies in prisons, so as to reflect compliance to constitution values and statutory lacks. Neural data, which includes raw brain signals, decoded thoughts, emotions, intentions and cognitive inferences is the most personal of all the kinds of data and therefore requires a higher level of protection than standard biometric or health data (Echeverría Munoz, 2025). The Digital Personal Data Protection (DPDP) Act, 2023, offers a basic consent-based principles framework for personal data, however it is lacking with regards to explicit definition of neural data as an SPPD. The requirement that the consent has to be uncoarscious by the sender and is to be free, specific, informed, unconditional, and unambiguous is not appropriate for subconscious signals which are automatically sent without consent, in coercive environments such as prisons where the autonomy of the sender is constricted.

A stronger basis for its implicitness is given in the Constitution. The expansive Right to Privacy and dignity in Article 21, under the Kasri K. Puttaswamy v. Union of India case also covers the right to mental autonomy and the informational autonomy. This may prevent questioning the mind unconsciously and can be designed towards the ideas of cognitive liberty. The use of the BCI also is limited in investigations and rehabilitations by Articles 14 (equality) and 20 (3) (protection against self-incrimination). There are however gaps that need to be addressed in the judicial-legislative sphere: The Prisons Act, 1894, and Model Prisons Act, 2023, highlight the need to decentralise for rehabilitation and technology utilisation (including technology such as biometrics and individual sentence planning), but e.g. do not provide for oversight related to neuro-rights, or data minimisation, or purpose limitation, or prohibition on non-therapeutic mind-reading.

Multipronged reforms are necessary to experience the harmonization. First, update the DPDP Act to grant neural data a specific category that deserves enhanced protections – as such, a right for neural privacy, a right to have inferences or de-coded neural data deleted and a strong prohibition of secondary use without the explicit and magistrated consent of all parties. Second, make sure that neuro-rights become part of the Model Prison Manual with the establishment of ethical review boards, transparency in the working of algorithms and anonymization for all rehabilitative uses, such as neurofeedback. Thirdly, set up a dedicated Neurotechnology Regulatory Authority for setting standards on the deployment of BCIs and auditing for biases as well as interoperability with evidence under the Indian Evidence Act. Comparative lessons: the constitutional neurorights amendments in Chile that protect the mental integrity and the information that arises out of the brain give insight in the significance of explicit constitutional or statutory protection.

It is important that implementation is done taking into account some of India's particular issues: overcrowding in prisons, digital divide, and concerns around the potential politically charged and caste/socio-economic bias of AI models. For mental health applications, using non-invasive EEG-based pilots that are voluntary could show advantages and adopt the trust of the public (Li et al., 2025). In conclusion, harmonization is the process that shifts neural technologies away from a surveillance role to a reformation one, and ensures that technologies open up the possibility of humane correction without destroying the sanctity of the human mind in India's processes of correction. This rights-based approach puts India at the forefront of responsible Neuro-governance in democratic governance.

6. ANALYSIS OF IMPLEMENTATION CHALLENGES AND CASE STUDIES

Global and local case studies illustrate the complex and multifaceted technical, ethical, infrastructural and socio-legal hurdles that natural justice, BCI and AI pose in Indian prisons. Sophisticated neurotechnologies are stunted in most facilities in India due to problems of overcrowding, lack of adequate staff and outdated infrastructure. Access to high-speed Internet, secure data centers and well-trained staff are becoming rare resources and not possibilities for real-time analytics of BCI signals or AI analytics. Restrictions in technology, such as the cost of using headsets for non-invasive EEG, and AI platforms for prison management further contribute to inequities that may result in a lack of access to smaller prisons and/or neglect of them, while maintaining better access to urban or higher-security ones.

There is a high risk from algorithmic bias. An AI tool based on a historical dataset of criminal justice records could continue the cycle of a skewed caste, class and gender/binarized risk assessment system or rehabilitation programmes (Aguilar-Herrera, 2026). A criminal justice distance bias information set could be used by an AI tool to perpetuate biases related to caste, class or gender issues related to an individual's risk assessment or rehabilitation programme. Until data quality is improved through cleaning the records - incomplete data and incorrect data entry - predictive accuracy is reduced. The level of privacy and security concerns is high: if data breaches occur in the brain, they may leave open secrets about the brain, which could result in stigma or abuse. However consent is still tricky as it may depend on power differentials that give rise to the possibility of forced consent in the sense of obtaining consent to be identified as a "voluntary" parolee.

We will illustrate these tensions with case studies. Brain Electrical Oscillation Signature Profiling (BEOSP)/brain fingerprinting has been a reality of Indian experience since early 2000s and poses evidentiary and ethical faults. The Selvi v. State of Karnataka (2010) decision by the Supreme Court has struck down involuntary neuro-tests, noting the importance of protecting mental privacy and placating the limits on testimonial compulsion, where they may be held. This case sets a precedent that suggests problems with admitting evidence that originates from BCI without giving proper attention to voluntariness and reliability.

Internationally, there are concerns regarding bias amplification and over-surveillance, issues U.S. prisons that uses AI in recidivism prediction and surveillance face in the country.Similar to potential pitfalls in India, there are concerns of bias amplification and over-surveillance in U.S. prisons with AI in recidivism prediction and surveillance more broadly around the world. The case of Chile provides a positive one, as the country has a policy of neurorights which allow ethical neurotechnology pillots to exist as well as protecting mental integrity. Pilot programmes in India under the Model Prisons Act, 2023, focusing on the use of AI for chatbots for mental health or on biometric monitoring could be implemented to explore solutions such as federated learning to enable greater privacy protection of AI solutions and independent audits.

6.1 Potential Integration Scenarios in Indian Prisons

The possibilities for having BCI and AI technology used in Indian prisons are many and varied, to match the rehabilitation principles of the Model Prisons Act, 2023, including in the areas of rehabilitation, monitoring, security, and evidence-based support for prisoners. BCI systems based on EEG and made anthropomorph would be able to implement training of brain rhythms in the treatment of addiction, impulse control or anger management. During sessions, prisoners are provided with a portable headset that connects to an AI system that can interpret brain wave patterns (alpha/theta brain states for example) and give real-time feedback through an adaptive app to help create cognitive behavioral shifts, and/or a drop in recidivism. This is in line with the mental wellness provisions in the Model Manual (van Kolfschooten, 2025).

AI-powered predictive risk tools might be incorporated into BCI to give a complete profile of risk. Neural correlates of stress or aggression, together with behavioural data, can help to identify children who may be at risk of harming themselves or towards violence in a timely manner. Artificial intelligence could be used to make educational experiences or vocational training programs more personalized using information gathered by a BCI to design an education program segment after decoding an individual's cognitive profile, thereby providing support for individualized sentence planning.

6.2 Comparative Analysis with International Jurisdictions 6.3 Judicial Precedents and Evidentiary Admissibility Issues

Learning from Comparative Analysis it is observed that the lessons and policies that can be learnt for the protection of neural rights and maintaining balance on BCI-AI innovation are helpful for India. Chile was a pioneer in the field of neurorights in 2021 when it changed their constitution to protect mental integrity, brain activity, and activity results. This platform, which has since been incorporated into a bill on the regulation of neurotechnologies as medical devices, calls for consent and forbids unintended decoding and ensures basic access, alongside other obligations.

As in Chile, judicious decisions by courts like data removal from consumer BCI devices exemplify its enforcement nature in India which the courts currently lack.

The United States has various states which have neural data privacy policies that classify it much like biometric data, and impose increased consent and prohibition standards. These cover consumer neurotech, but provide guidance and/or models for prison-based neurotech, specifically regarding the reduction of bias in the tool and transparency (Khanam et al., 2025). The state laws, however, are ambiguous enough to bring to light the possibility of regulatory arbitrage - a risk with India's federality.

7. CONCLUSION AND FUTURE PROSPECTS

The intersection of BCI and AI with Indian prisons feels like a fascinating and multifaceted combination with the potential to revolutionize how we think about rehabilitation, mental health, security, and evidence-based justice, but also with the potentially precarious challenge of rights to neural data, mental privacy, autonomy, and dignity. This examination of the India's legal landscape shows that while the Prisons Act, 1894 (with its progressive model Act, 2023), the Indian Evidence Act, 1872, and the Digital Personal Data Protection (DPDP), Act, 2023, all provide some framework, namely, with an emphasis on the implementation of technology, reformative justice, electronic evidence and consent of the data, they have failed to ensure that they have the framework to cater with the unique intimacy of neural data. There is a need for harmonization highlighted by the gaps in categorizing any neural signal as a truly “sensitive” signal; meaningful consent in the context of a coerced or “persuaded” experiment; reliability standards for the signal-to-behavior connectivity evidence provided by a BCI; and the absence of algorithmic bias or coercive surveillance monitoring. However, in addition to constitutional protection as in Selvi v. State of Karnataka (2010), there is also a need for proactive, constructive statutory evolution to ensure that these constitutional protections are put to good use for prosecuting these technologies and ensuring good governance for their development.

If viewed from a rights-based perspective, the integration of BCI-AI within the Indian correctional system has promising future. Apart from reducing recidivism, decreasing the overcrowding and facilitating voluntary communication assistance, less time is required for rehabilitation than with the current system, which could also be made highly effective through individualization using artificial intelligence deriving from the non-invasive EEG-based neurofeedback method, and could also help support mental well-being as the Model Prisons Act strives to do while preventing self-harm, and avoiding or mitigating the need for invasive EEG systems. Well budgeted facilities with public-private partnerships, ethical review boards, and capacity building, have a role to play in the pathway to responsible deployment through phase piloting. Today's gaps can be filled by legislative changes, like revising the DPDP Act to include clear quantumization and protection of neural data as sensitive personal data that are subject to special protections, such as purpose limitation and data minimization, as well as providing a right of "neural privacy" (including a right to "neural ignorance"); and revising evidentiary rules to put in place a Daubert-like framework.

Internationally, ideas conveyed from Italy, Chile, and other Great Lakes states such as the USA, and from the global debate on cognitive liberty, can help India create new, democratic models for good governance. In 2030, as portable BCIs and AI advances, India might be leading the way in ethical usage of neurotechnology in the Global South, ensuring access while minimising the risk of developing a "neuro-surveillance state." Longitudinal impact studies, bias auditing in various patient populations and interdisciplinary research on interactions among neuroscientists, legal and ethical specialists, and policy makers should all be emphasized in future studies. In the end, balancing the rights attached to neural data will make the difference between the processes understanding human dignity as an opportunity for reformative justice or debating such justice's destruction. If India takes the lead in adopting a pro-active, people-centred approach to the regulation of new technologies, it will help shape our understanding of the inviolability of the mind while these technologies extend possibilities of correction and societal reintegration.

REFERENCES

Aguilar-Herrera, A. J., Hernández-Aguado, C. O., Monarres-Sokolovskaya, J. A., Pacheco-Ramírez, M. A., Khaleghian, B., Grassi, E., . . . Contreras Vidal, J. L. (2026, January). An Artistic BCI–GenAI System Enabling Real-Time Co-creation in Balinese Performance. In *International Workshop on Creative AI for Live Interactive Performances* (pp. 25-41). Cham: Springer Nature Switzerland. DOI: 10.1007/978-3-032-16893-1_2

Bhattacharjee, A., Pilkington, J., & Farahany, N. (2025). Fiduciary AI for the Future of Brain-Technology Interactions. *arXiv preprint arXiv:2507.14339.*

Echeverría Munoz, D. E. (2025). *Legal impact of Artificial Intelligence (AI) hallucinations* (Master's thesis, Quito, EC: Universidad Andina Simón Bolívar, Sede Ecuador).

Fabiano, N. (2025). *Artificial Intelligence, Neural Networks and Privacy: Striking a Balance between Innovation, Knowledge, and Ethics in the Digital Age.* goWare.

Gridin, E. (2026). Digital Jurisprudence by Design: The Digital Warrant, Neuro-Symbolic Compliance Architecture, and Evidentiary Non-Repudiation in Transnational AI-Assisted Legal Practice. *Neuro-Symbolic Compliance Architecture, and Evidentiary Non-Repudiation in Transnational AI-Assisted Legal Practice (March 23, 2026).*

Ilhan, M. A. (2025). *Predictive Artificial Intelligence Tools in the US Criminal Trial: Reflections on Technology and Justice* (Doctoral dissertation, Université Côte d'Azur).

Khanam, T., Siuly, S., Ahmad, K., & Wang, H. (2025). A novel channel reduction concept to enhance the classification of motor imagery tasks in brain-computer interface systems. *PLoS One, 20*(10), e0335511. DOI: 10.1371/journal.pone.0335511 PMID: 41171945

Kritika, M. (2026). Ethical and legal dimensions of integrating neurotechnology with cybersecurity, a critical reflection for information and communication technology (ICT) policy and practice. *International Cybersecurity Law Review, 7*(1), 1–61. DOI: 10.1365/s43439-026-00168-6

Li, W., Gao, C., Li, Z., Diao, Y., Li, J., Zhou, J., Zhou, J., Peng, Y., Chen, G., Wu, X., & Wu, K. (2025). BrainFusion: A Low-Code, Reproducible, and Deployable Software Framework for Multimodal Brain–Computer Interface and Brain–Body Interaction Research. *Advancement of Science, 12*(32), e17408. DOI: 10.1002/advs.202417408 PMID: 40470749

Mia, A. P. (2025). From Brain Evidence to Neurorights: Rethinking Criminal Responsibility in the Age of Neurotechnology. *Available at SSRN* 5588370. DOI: 10.2139/ssrn.5588370

Mouazen, B., & El Bouyed, Z. (2025). Toward Ethical and Transparent Brain-Computer Interfaces: Challenges and Perspectives in EEG-Based AI.

Muravieva, L. (2025). Regulating Neurotechnologies and AI-driven neural implants in the European Union: Legal and ethical challenges.

Perlin, M., Ellis Cucolo, H., & Kulesza, J. (2025). Artificial Intelligence, Algorithmic Bias, and Mental Disability Law: Ethical Challenges and Regulatory Solutions. *Algorithmic Bias, and Mental Disability Law: Ethical Challenges and Regulatory Solutions (December 15, 2025).*

Thamma, S. R., Prajwala, N. B., Pushpa, N. B., & Patra, A. (2025). Neuroimaging: A Computational Lens on the Brain. In *Visualization in Neuroanatomical Sciences* (pp. 53–68). Springer Nature Switzerland.

van Kolfschooten, H. (2025). Towards an EU charter of digital patients' rights in the age of artificial intelligence. *Digital Society : Ethics, Socio-Legal and Governance of Digital Technology*, *4*(1), 6. DOI: 10.1007/s44206-025-00159-w

Chapter 2
Artificial Intelligence and Digital Inclusion for Women With Disabilities:
Legal and Ethical Perspectives of Brain-Computer Interfaces in Modern Society

Prangya Parimita Behera
http://orcid.org/0009-0004-8286-6402
Pingalakhi College of Special Education, Odisha, India

Binita Behera
http://orcid.org/0009-0006-3042-8448
KIIT School of Law, KIIT (Deemed to be) University, Odisha, India

Sanjay Kumar Singh
Uttar Pradesh Rajarshi Tandon Open University, India

Mousumi Raysingh
Pingalakhi College of Special Education, Odisha, India

ABSTRACT

Artificial intelligence enabled Brain-Computer Interfaces (BCI) have tremendous potential to contribute to digital inclusion for women with disabilities by facilitating their communication, mobility and cognition. Their speedy assimilation into mainstream society, however, brings up important legal and ethical issues. Gender and disability rights considerations sit alongside data privacy, informed consent, algorithmic bias and equitable access considerations, and can make factors worse.

DOI: 10.4018/979-8-3373-9720-7.ch002

This chapter looks at international and national laws and ethical issues raised within a field of autonomy and dignity and whether the individual might be exploited. It highlights the importance of gender framework policies that address issues facing women with disabilities in the digital world, and to ensure that they are not targeted or left behind if the policies are designed to empower.

1. INTRODUCTION

Brain-Computer Interfaces (BCI) empowered by AI are one of the most significant technological futures for enhancing the digital inclusion of women with disabilities, but also raise complex legal and ethical questions that need the attention of society. The promise of BCI systems where brain signals are converted into instructions that control computers or prosthetic devices has entered a new level of sophistication in which advanced artificial intelligence techniques learn each person's brain patterns to predict their intentions and communicate in real-time for patients with amyotrophic lateral sclerosis (ALS), spinal cord injuries, cerebral palsy, or locked-in syndrome. The technologies hold particular promise for women with disabilities, who are often confronted with compounding problems of gender discrimination and ableism, including in communication, in control of environments, in education and employment and in digital economy (Omokhabi et al., 2025). But with so many issues of privacy invasion, biased algorithms, unequal access, informed consent and the danger of worsening inequality in modern society to the horizon, the process of inclusive deployment is riddled with hurdles.

BCI's potential in the realm of digital inclusion is to fill in the physical and cognitive gap. Socio-economic, caregiving needs and societal norms often come together with higher prevalence of selected disabilities among women that hinder the use of traditional assistive technologies. By using AI algorithms, BCI can analyze intricate brain signals to create speech, drive wheelchairs with thought, and communicate with smart home devices, it could relieve the burden on care providers and help maintain independence. With AI algorithms, BCI can translate neuro signals into speech, direct wheelchairs with thoughts, or speak to smart home systems, all of which would lower the need for caregivers and thus boost independence. These interfaces, in educational and professional contexts, could help make all spaces virtual and help close the digital divide that disproportionately affects women with disabilities in the virtual world as a whole. Research has shown that women with disabilities face additional challenges such as less access to adaptive technology because it is expensive, a problem with design bias that uses male physiological data as a reference for designing the technology, and a problem with cultural stigmas that discourage using technology. AI-BCIs have the potential to truly empower people who are "passive" recipients, making them active participants as digital citizens and contributing to the better society we seek.

However, an analysis from legal angles shows that existing regulation is not clear enough. According to the UN Convention on the Rights of Persons with Disabilities (2006), among its international focus areas are accessibility, non-discrimination, and access to information and communication technologies, which do not mention anything about technologies like BCI. The General Data Protection Regulation (GDPR) of the European Union (EU) considers neural data to be sensitive biometric information, for which user consent is necessary, but in cases where brain signals are continuously streaming to cloud-based AI systems, it can be difficult with GDPR, to enforce these regulations. Issues come up about who owns the priceless neural data from users? Is this data useful to businesses for AI training and can businesses profit from it? The United States has established laws and regulations, such as the Americans with Disabilities Act (ADA), that prioritize reasonable accommodations, but are less effective at confronting predictions such as algorithmic accountability and neural privacy in the future.

The moral dimensions of the story add on to the complexities, particularly with regard to disability from a gender perspective. An important issue is informed consent; women having communication disabilities may not be able to give fully informed consent, in part because of cognitive disabilities, and in part because of the power imbalance with medical providers. Sentiment sentiment shows that AI algorithms that are largely based on male or able-bodied neural data may contain gender or disability biases, potentially resulting in poorer performance for women and incorrect interpretations of sentiment (Omri et al., 2025). "brain hacking, surveillance or unauthorized access into thoughts" raise deep questions around men and women's psychological confidentiality and autonomy. Furthermore, the enhancement-versus-therapy issue arises – is BCI just to restore functions we've lost, or is it for cognitive augmentation? If one focuses excessively on "fixing" impairments, then ableism and medicalisation of naturally occurring variations might proliferate in the lives of women with disabilities over disability pride and rights campaigns won.Ablerism, medicalisation of naturally occurring variations, may reinforce over the disability pride and rights campaigns gained women with disabilities. The context of equity: there is a huge difference in costs between BCI technology, with wealthy users benefiting while marginalized women have already been at a higher poverty levels. There is the threat of social coercion: the pressure on individuals to get implants to be "competitive" in digital space, which can negatively impact and diminish the real human diversity.

1.1 Background and Rationale

One of the moral aspects is responsibility and liability. Who is to blame for the system misreading the neural signals, such as rendering a false medical diagnosis, or for sending messages to the wrong receiver; the user, the manufacturer, the person who developed the AI system or the provider of the medical system? For women who experience multiple forms of oppression, for instance in the fields of employment, care and service, or law, these are especially relevant when women are denied or unjustly restricted access to support due to discriminatory AI decisions. The acquisition of intimate brain data also raises concerns about its secondary applications, reminiscent of the history of control of women's bodies and minds – for example, "predictive profiling" in insurance, work and even politics. Feminist disability ethics urges the integration of intersectional approaches where lived experience is brought into the fore and diverse voices is integral to the design and governance of BCI, as opposed to a more technologically determined approach (Harrison & Horsfield, 2025).

1.2 Scope and Significance of the Study

Case examples are included to demonstrate potential and pitfalls. Studies such as Neuralink have shown success with helping people see again, and some couples have reported better movement after using an academic BCI, even though it is controversial.But projects like Neuralink and other academic studies aimed at helping people see again and other work aimed at better movement for some participants have resulted in enhanced quality of life for the participants, though some of these look controversial. But initial testing trials have been criticised for not having enough women and transparency. For educational pilots, women with disabilities who had used BCI experienced more independence in digital learning environments, but worries about data security and the potential long-term psychological impacts remain. For this, work must be done that involves disabled women's organizations, ethicists, technologists and policy-makers together.

There should be a push for introducing an all-encompassing neurorights legislation rooted in CRPD principles and AI laws, requiring a gender and disability equity impact assessment. Transparency, continuous consent systems that are flexible to varying cognitive states, and fair access programs (subsidies, training, etc.). The need for a multilateral approach is especially important to avoid creating a multifaceted global world where the rich win at the expense of the poor.

2. BRAIN-COMPUTER INTERFACES INCLUSION FOR WOMEN WITH DISABILITIES: TECHNOLOGICAL FOUNDATIONS

Brain-Computer Interfaces (BCIs) are among the key enabling technologies that directly couple the brain to external devices, and can be used to improve digital inclusion and participation for women with disabilities, bypassing the usual physical constraints. The systems utilize brain signals for communication, mobility, and environmental management, and support women who may be facing multiple barriers because of gender norms, socio-economic inequities and disability specific needs. Utilizing non-invasive, semi-invasive, or invasive techniques, BCI technologies convert various types of electro-, magnetic, and metabolic brain signals into transmitttable signals that can promote greater independence and engagement in digital society. But BCI is a more than assistive technology for women with disabilities, multiple sclerosis, stroke sequelae, or congenital disabilities – it is a mechanism of empowerment for them toward an equal educational, employment, and social life (Olawade et al., 2025). The technological base is built on interdisciplinary research and development within neuroscience and signal processing, and human-computer interaction, marked by increasing user centeredness, which takes into account the physiological differences of female users which may influence the quality of the signal, including hormonal changes and differences in body composition. To move towards an inclusive approach, however, historical dataset skews and a multi-economic context need to be accounted for. BCI's groundwork needs to focus on scalability, affordability, and adaptability in order to accommodate the estimated hundreds of millions of disabled women who are digitally marginalized, and who will form part of BCI's future population. This part will analyze the main technological aspects that support BCI's possibilities and bring the attention to the aspects that are necessary to consider when deploying it in today's society in an equitable way.

2.1 Evolution and Core Mechanisms of BCI

The history of Brain-Computer Interfaces dates back to the early 20th century with the early discoveries in electroencephalography (EEG) during the 1970s, when Jacques Vidal first demonstrated the use of a non-invasive BCI, to the more recent, sophisticated systems based on AI that we are now witnessing today. Though derived to control the cursor in patients with severe motor impairments, BCI technology has come a long way, with a leap in sensitivity of the sensors, computing power, and algorithms (Bruce & Williams, 2025). There are basic mechanisms, such as signal acquisition via invasive (intracortical implants) or semi-invasive (ECoG) or non-invasive (EEG, fNIRS, MEG) techniques, further with removal of artifacts and the extraction of features (search for the relevant brain patterns corresponding to desired device commands such as mu rhythms or P300 waves), and finally classification/translation into device commands. These mechanisms are especially important to women with disabilities, who can benefit from mechanisms that counter the conditions that are specifically disadvantages to women, including chronic pain syndromes or autoimmune disorders. New signal analysis methods such as adaptive filtering and use of deep learning models now allow high levels of accuracy despite fluctuations in the signal of the female brain, which can be caused by changes during menstrual cycles and menopause. Issues of long term stability, biocompatibility of implants, and reducing user fatigue related to calibration sessions, which may be burdensome for women, still exist. New portable and wireless systems have made BCI more user-friendly so it's more feasible for everyday integration. Awareness of this evolutionary course is essential to the understanding of how the refinements of technology can better cater to the needs of women with disabilities, thereby lowering technology set-up complexity, improving reliability, and creating a sustainable digital inclusion framework; as well as the questions raised by having a healthy riskscape and long-term neural effects.

2.2 Integration with Artificial Intelligence

The combination of Artificial Intelligence and Brain-Computer Interfaces has reshaped the power they has, and allowed the creation of intelligent, adaptive systems custom-designed for users with disabilities: an effective mix. Deep neural networks and reinforcement learning algorithms are particularly adept at analyzing brain signals, as they process complex patterns with greater accuracy, allowing for adaptation in real-time depending on the individual's cognitive and physiological conditions. With this synergy, AI can help counteract signal variability that is present with medications, tiredness or hormonal shifts, while also making interfaces more personal to specific needs, like enhanced expression of emotion or context-based communication with others. While machine learning models trained on a variety of datasets have helped to reduce gender-biases that have seen in previous systems, there is still much yet to be done to represent gender-specific disability experiences (Bolarinwa et al., 2025). AI also enables hybrid systems that integrate BCI with other technologies, such as computer vision, natural language processing, and predictive analytics, for example, predicting what the user will want to do to ease cognitive fatigue in extended use. This integration supports advanced applications like thought-to-text generation with high accuracy and multi-modal control of smart environments. It does bring with it issues surrounding data protection, however, as there is always the opportunity for continuous neural streaming to generate massive amounts of data which can be compromised, and algorithmic opacity, where accountability can be difficult. To maximize the benefits while minimizing barriers to inclusion, the design of AI-based decision-making systems must align with principles of fairness, which include fairness and correctness audits of the algorithms and explain the rationale behind the model's actions. In an era of AI-BCI, inclusivity of training data, combined with user's co-design with women with disability, will be taken as a fundamental necessity to achieve equitable technological empowerment in the modern digital environment.

2.3 Current Applications in Assistive Technologies

A closer examination of the present application of BCIs for assistive technologies shows how BCIs are affecting the lives of women with disabilities in the three areas of assistive communication, mobility, and functional activities. Women with severe speech disabilities are empowered to use communication, spellers and speech synthesizers to engage in social media, education and professional interactions, paving the way for them to express their thoughts at better rates without being assisted by caregivers or limited AAC devices. Examples of mobility applications are wheelchairs controlled via BCI, and exoskeletons with BCI that increase women's independence when they have paralysis or a neuromuscular issue. Environmental control systems allow lights, TVs, computers and even smart homes to be controlled by the brain, helping to minimize physical constraints and foster self-determination. In the health care sector, BCI can be implemented in neurorehabilitation using neurofeedback training, which also has potential applications for stroke patients and chronic pain management, areas where women are a prominent group of patients. Developing applications include social aspects being enhanced through VR integration and social, creative expression opportunities for art enthusiasts. These gains, however, have yet to make a significant impact on the rate of adoption among females, as the products are still too costly and, in some cases, due to design, training needs, and awareness that is not necessarily geared towards or for the needs of females (Kopsaj, 2025). Multi-disciplinary teams and customized calibration and support are essential for successful deployments. While the usage of these applications contributes to digital inclusion, the possibilities lead to a greater social engagement but must be combined with measures to increase affordability and accessibility in order to avoid further marginalisation.

3. DIGITAL INCLUSION AND WOMEN WITH DISABILITIES

Digital inclusion is ensuring that a woman with disability is able to have equitable access, use and meaningful participation in digital technologies and online spaces – something that is still not happening for many women with disability even in the face of rapidly changing technologies. Women with disabilities make up a large proportion of a world population that is subject to several aspects of exclusion because of the impact of gender inequality and disability stigma. In Artificial Intelligence and with the introduction of Brain-Computer Interfaces (BCI), digital inclusion opens up to the possibility to benefit from neurotechnologies to improve autonomy, communication, education, employment and social participation. Such technologies have the potential to overcome longstanding barriers and break through them, but many persistent problems—including limited infrastructure, lack of customized training, and discriminatory technology design—still constrain their reach. To achieve digital inclusion, access has to go beyond just being physically available and include learning how to digitally access resources, improve accessibility of the online content, and enable safe online spaces without harassment, especially for women with disabilities. This exclusion can further exacerbate the growing inequality in today's digital era and consequently impact fundamental human rights (Alanazi et al., 2025). This section introduces the diverse facets of digital inclusion problems and opportunities and examines the role that AI-powered BCI can play in driving empowerment, when designed in an inclusive, gender-informed approach that starts from the lived reality of women with disabilities. (Note to student – there is a detailed version of this in subsections which will be used as an aide through the reading of the text that follows.

3.1 Barriers to Digital Access and Participation

Women with disability face hard-to-navigate barriers to digital access and participation, related to economic, technical, physical, cognitive, and societal factors. Primarily, socio-economic barriers apply, with many women, who are already at a higher risk of living in poverty, being unable to afford the devices, implants or subscription services required for access to AsTs, especially AI software updates. Technological barriers consist of incompatible hardware and software that do not support the various disability requirements including visual and motor barriers and barriers related to the processing. Physical challenges include poor or nonexistent Internet connections in poorer neighborhoods and rural regions and absence of accessible public infrastructure, such as computers and other portable technology. Cognitive and sensory barriers are found in complex user interfaces that also expect so-called "normal" user capabilities, and of course calibration processes for BCIs can be rather long or difficult to complete if the barriers are symptoms prevalent in certain diseases like multiple sclerosis or fibromyalgia, which tends to affect women more. Societal barriers include the lack of opportunities for digital literacy education focused on women, ableism and sexism against technology adoption, and caregiver 'gate-keeping.' The risks of digital harassment, breaches, and exclusion are greater for online participation, which also faces a heightened risk. These compounding barriers inhibit access now and often engender cycles of marginalization in schooling, the workplace, and civic engagement. Addressing them requires specific policy measures, more affordable access schemes, as well as universal design in the creation of BCI so that women with disabilities can participate more fully in the digital world (Soldatic et al., 2025).

3.2 Gendered Dimensions of Disability in the Digital Age

Gendered aspects of disability experiences are able to be amplified in the digital age, as women experience intersecting spaces of oppression. There are differences in manifestations of disability according to gender resulting from biological, social and cultural factors, with women more likely to report chronic conditions, mental health issues, and burdens of caregiving occurring in combination with digital exclusion. The intersection of the online realm with a context of gender-based and/or disability-based discrimination reveals algorithmic bias in recommender systems and AI tools that are historically trained on data sets that are dominated by men, performance disparities between male and female, as well as brain structure, hormonal differences, and neural variability. New vulnerabilities in the digital era are also emerging, including gender-based violence through technology, misuses of the deep-fake and surveillance and most notably that specifically harms women with visible or invisible disabilities. Furthermore, the strong demands placed on women's “productivity” and “femininity” mandate that they experiment with new technologies for the enhancement of their bodies, and thereby compel them to “normalize” their bodies, questioning notions of identity and autonomy (Soldatic et al., 2025). There are new communities and platforms for women with disabilities to voice BCI experiences and advocate for inclusive innovation this is a positive development. But the gendered digital divide remains with implications in STEM participation in the development and build of neurotech, for instance, fallustrating the capacity to appreciate how the menstrual cycle affects signal quality and, in instances of implantable devices, how pregnancy and other factors could impact the design. It is important to identify these gendered aspects of creating ethical and equitable BCI frameworks that affirm, rather than marginalise, the wide spectrum of women with disabilities in the current digital society.

3.3 Role of AI in Promoting Inclusive Technologies

Brain-Computer Interfaces adapted for women with disabilities are among the emerging technologies promoted by Artificial Intelligence. BCI is further enhanced by the incorporation of AI, which allows for adaptive signal processing considering individual variability, thus increasing the accuracy and usability of BCI in a wide range of female users. Personalization of calibration, automatic error compensation and predictive support based on machine learning algorithms ease user burden when it comes to dealing with conventional interfaces (Shafik, 2025). Through the power of AI, advanced initiatives like context-aware communication tools with emotional intelligence, intelligent mobility solutions leveraging environmental awareness on the streets, and adaptive tools in education transforming the content delivery approach, bring enhanced possibilities of promoting inclusion. AI can also assist in analysing systemic data on accessibility gaps and making policy decisions. Importantly, AI reduces bias when built and used responsibly, using diverse training data sets and including fairness metrics in the modeling process, to enable better outcomes for women with disabilities. Finally, generative AI helps to develop customized BCI user training materials and simulation environments. But unlocking these benefits means addressing the challenges AI poses, which are related to "black box" decision-making opacity, energy efficiency worries, and, if not managed well, the ability to reinforce stereotypes. This means involving women with disabilities in a collaborative way throughout the design of AI technologies and the need for ethical principles and regulation. Thoughtfully integrating AI with BCI has the potential to greatly improve digital inclusion by developing technology that is responsive, empowering, but grounded in respect and enhanced consideration of the voice and needs of women with disabilities in the modern world (Kchaou et al., 2025).

4. LEGAL PERSPECTIVES ON BCI DEPLOYMENT: INTERNATIONAL AND NATIONAL REGULATORY FRAMEWORKS

The legal aspects within this usage of the Brain-Computer Interface (BCI) emphasize the necessity of robust legal frameworks that would ensure a careful use of machines for humans' benefit, not infringing on their rights, especially for the women with disabilities to achieve a more inclusive digital world. With its rapid development, the use of AI integrated BCI technologies challenges the current legislation focused on traditional medical devices and data systems. Internationally, the UN Convention on the Rights of Persons with Disabilities (CRPD) outlines a broad human rights based approach with the fundamental principles of providing support equipment namely AT (Assistive Technologies) and ICT (Information and Communication Technologies) included in Article 9 and 20. It however does not directly cover any neurotechnologies, areas where loose edges arise such as mental privacy, mental freedom, etc. The and other emerging neurorights concepts, for example in Chile and Spain, call for a special form of protection in relation to the unauthorized use of brain data. On the national level, the European Union's Medical Device Regulation (MDR) and Artificial Intelligence Act have strict safety, transparency and bias reduction requirements on high risk BCI systems. In the USA, the FDA considers BCI as a medical device and the ADA and Section 508 have accessibility issues, but they don't keep up with technological advances as effectively. Global South countries often do not have a complete regulatory framework, which leads to regulatory arbitrage by introducing technologies into the system to be tested on the lower end of the scale by companies, with limited and no oversight. Recommend that legal frameworks holistically consider gender specific issues concerning reproductive health consequences of female implants, and greater vulnerabilities to coercion among women with disabilities. Good governance involves possession of regulations that are adaptive, future-proof, and that encourage innovation in keeping with the basic rights to dignity and inclusion (Foley & Melese, 2025). This section will explore some of the legal aspects influencing the deployment of responsible BCIs in the modern society.

4.1 Data Privacy, Consent, and Disability Rights

Data privacy, consent, and disability rights are important pillars of the legal landscape of BCIs for women with disabilities, particularly in terms of data privacy and consent. The brain data obtained from BCI systems may provide specific information, including thoughts, predictions, feelings and even medical information, which can be classified as 'highly sensitive' data both under the GDPR (General Data Protection Regulation—EU) and California Consumer Privacy Act due to its medical implications. There is a serious concern that the information has several risks of being monitored by third parties for mental purposes, for insurance or employment purposes for the disqualification of anonym, for identity theft. Establishing an informed consent is challenging for women with disabilities, especially those who often need to be cared for by others or placed in institutions, as fluctuating cognitive abilities, communication difficulties and power imbalance can reduce the voluntariness of consent. Dynamic consent models, enabling people to withdraw and control data flows on an ongoing basis, supported by AI tools to simplify explanations, are encouraged as a measure to protect consent in data-driven society.To safeguard consent in a data-driven society, legal experts promote dynamic consent models with flexible and continuous withdrawal, and granular consent to data flows made simpler with AI tools for explanation. Non-discrimination and reasonable adjustment are core to disability rights policies grounded in the CRPD which prioritize the access of BCI technologies and the fact that they do not further disadvantage individuals with disabilities. The cases of forced medical interventions have similarities with threatened BCI involvement. There are country differences: some countries require independent ethics review committees to supervise neural implants, whereas others are behind the times. Neurolaw is fast evolving with a new legislation that wants to see "freedom of thought" as a fundamental right vis-à-vis the influence of algorithms on thought. In addition, intersectional issues arise because the biases of data processing could result in poorer performance or discriminatory outcomes experienced by female users. Charging regimes and procedures, and robust legal tools such as strict purpose limitation, data minimisation, impact assessment, and penalties for violation, are needed to support the stance on privacy and disability rights (Malviya & Rajput, 2025). If it were not for these, BCI could be used to control rather than empower, which negatively affects the efforts on digital inclusion of women with disabilities. Policymakers need to focus on processes for the making of inclusive laws that involve affected communities, and then develop equitable policies.

4.2 Intellectual Property and Accessibility Legislation

Intellectual Property (IP) and accessibility laws are having a very real impact on the use, price and flexibility of Brain-Computer Interfaces (BCIs) for disabled women. The most significant rights holders are the IP regime, mainly in the form of patents held by research institutions and technology companies, which can spur innovation and also enable monopolies resulting in high costs and low ability to customize it. There is a clear link between this tension and digital inclusion, because patented BCI components and AI algorithms add costs, making use of them by the less affluent segment of the global population, even in the wealthier countries, challenging. The TRIPS agreements and national patent laws also include compulsory licensing provisions that may facilitate greater diffusion/decentration in public health settings, but are seldom used in the case of neurotechnologies. There are laws in place that require "accessibility" of digital products and services, including EU Web Accessibility Directive, the Americans with Disabilities Act (or its translation in any country) and national equivalents. Standards for neural interface interoperability, open APIs and open design requirements are needed to extend these to BCI (Sanni, 2025). But existing legislation tends to be generic in its approach to complex and implantable systems or systems with intelligence. IP barriers become additional when traditional software is not modified by the community or localised for languages and different settings for women with disabilities. These solutions include open-source BCI initiatives, patent pools belonging to ATs and "human rights impact assessments" while applying for patents. Tax, or other streamlining benefits, should be encouraged for "inclusive innovation" – gender and disability responsive designs ought to come first. While it is important to safeguard IP rights, it is equally critical to consider accessibility requirements, as this balance is what will underpin the possibility of technological gatekeeping and prevent digital exclusion if balancing it is not achieved, but actually advancement in technological AI-BCI will benefit the goal of digital inclusion. Legislation harmonization in these areas would make it easier to carry these areas to the world in an appropriate manner in order to defend the rights of inventors.

5. CONCLUSION AND FUTURE DIRECTIONS

The bringing together of AI and Brain–Computer Interfaces (BCI) and women's access to digital space introduces both new opportunities and complex legal and ethical issues in a modern society, for women with disabilities. It is clear from this analysis that BCI technologies can have a significant impact on autonomy, communication and participation, and can be of great benefit when deployed thoughtfully. If left unchecked, however, they can exacerbate the inequalities that already permeate gender and disability systems – through algorithms that place women and people with disabilities at a disadvantage, privacy concerns, over-pricing and poor regulations. The legal aspects emphasize the current deficiencies of international and national systems, and the ethical aspects stress people autonomy, equity and dignity. There are various ways of transforming individuals into co-creators of these transformative tools and women with disabilities must not be one of those ways. As the world increasingly becomes more technologically advanced and adopts new technologies that affect the brain, it is important that these technologies are used for inclusion and not for exclusion, and that a human-rights-centred approach is taken to development and integration of new technologies over the next twenty years. Looking forward, the areas needing improvement include the need to advance the technology to enhance access through equitable programming and to engage technologists more effectively with legal, ethical, disabled women's and policy professionals. Whether or not BCI can be considered as a catalyst for empowerment or the latest form of marginalization will be decided from this holistic perspective. Efforts to build inclusive neuro-digital futures require ongoing effort, attention, and flexibility to new realities.

5.1 Policy Recommendations

While policy input for BCIs needs to be integrated and grounded in a gender lens to promote digital inclusion for women with disabilities, it is essential that this objective is fully addressed. States must adopt specific legislation in the spirit of the CRPD and existing data protection legislation such as the GDPR to safeguard mental privacy, cognitive liberty and immunity from any unauthorized action of neuro-intervention on a person's mental constituents. All BCI development and deployment work should be subject to mandatory gender and disability impact assessments and have effective community involvement in design and governance. Subsidized access to both affordable BCI devices and training should be encouraged by the policy-makers through public financing of such access. Proposals for amending regulatory guidelines for medical devices and AI systems need to establish clear standards for long-term safety and provide algorithms and algorithms' performance as checklist translations for gender equivalence. The government can facilitate international co-operation through the WHO and UNESCO, which can help establish standards, and therefore can eliminate regulatory arbitrage. Neurotechnologies should be included under accessibility laws and regulations with specific provisions for open interfaces and interoperability. Ethical review boards conducting BCI trials need to be diverse and need to develop well-informed consent procedures for different degrees of cognitive ability. Responsible development will be supported through incentives for open source and inclusive innovation and robust mechanisms in place to prevent data misuse. Last, but not least, it is essential that adoptions are supported through education campaigns and capacity-building programmes that focus on women with disabilities, women providing support for people with disabilities and health workers. These policy measures are ways to ensure that technology promise turns into actual equity and inclusion, if done decisively.

5.2 Emerging Trends and Research Agenda

New challenges and opportunities are associated with the new research areas of Brain-Computer Interfaces in the context of digital inclusion. Hybrid BCI merges eye-tracking, muscle deployment, and environmental sensing with neural data for greater reliability, and non-invasive, high-resolution systems continue to get more mobile and easy-to-use. As consumer level technologies in neuroscience and brain-cloud interfaces are emerging, they hold promise of greater integration of society, combined with heightened ethical and legal worries over data privacy and cognition enhancement. Personalized medicine and affective computing are pivotal forces providing a new and personalized approach to helping communication and emotional support to women with disabilities. Large-scale, diverse, longitudinal studies of women users should be a priority for the research agenda to account for the gender-specific signal differences and long-term effects. The algorithmic fairness, algorithmic biases, and Explainable AI in BCI environments are in dire need of interdisciplinary research. Clarifications on the socio-cultural implications on the lives of women with disabilities in terms of identity, agency and community in relation to these technologies must be explored. It is important to note that comparative legal studies between jurisdictions can guide best practice and principles in governance about neurorights. Further studies are needed on economic viability of sustainable, affordable access and on co-design methods with disabled women, to inform the research and practice of broader economic change towards sustainable access. Much more philosophical and empirical research on a distinction between enhancing and therapeutic uses of neurobiology is needed. Finally, new hazards like "neural hacking", social coercion and environmental effects of large-scale BCI deployment will play an important role. The proactive and inclusive research agenda will see to it that technological evolution is in keeping with the principles of justice and human flourishing.

REFERENCES

Alanazi, A. S., Salah Alanazi, A., & Benlaria, H. (2025, July). Enhancing healthcare for people with disabilities through artificial intelligence: Evidence from Saudi Arabia. [). MDPI.]. *Health Care, 13*(13), 1616. PMID: 40648640

Bolarinwa, O., Mohammed, A., Igharo, V., & Shongwe, S. (2025). Leveraging artificial intelligence for inclusive maternity care: Enhancing access for mothers with disabilities in Africa. *Women's Health (London, England), 21*, 17455057251326675. DOI: 10.1177/17455057251326675 PMID: 40089873

Bruce, A., & Williams, L. A. (2025). Access and citizenship for those with disabilities: digitally enabled education and AI as a bridge to innovative inclusion. In *Digital Citizenship and the Future of AI Engagement, Ethics, and Privacy* (pp. 31-78). IGI Global Scientific Publishing. DOI: 10.4018/979-8-3693-9015-3.ch002

Foley, A., & Melese, F. (2025). Disabling AI: Power, exclusion, and disability. *British Journal of Sociology of Education*, •••, 1–22. DOI: 10.1080/01425692.2025.2519482

Harrison, A., & Horsfield, N. (2025). The Role and Use of Artificial Intelligence (AI) in Disability Inclusion.

Kchaou, M., Munusamy, Y., Alharthi, K. A., & Al-Mahmodi, A. F. (2025). Industry 5.0 adaptation for disability-inclusive healthcare: A review of emergent and AI technologies for assistive digital health. *Digital Health, 11*, 20552076251395558. DOI: 10.1177/20552076251395558 PMID: 41229932

Kopsaj, V. (2025). The future of social inclusion in the digital age: Challenges and opportunities of AI and digitisation. *Sociology and Social Work Review, 9*(1), 170–181. DOI: 10.58179/SSWR9112

Malviya, R., & Rajput, S. (2025). *Advances and insights into AI-created disability supports*. Springer Nature. DOI: 10.1007/978-981-96-6069-8

Olawade, D. B., Bolarinwa, O. A., Adebisi, Y. A., & Shongwe, S. (2025). The role of artificial intelligence in enhancing healthcare for people with disabilities. *Social Science & Medicine, 364*, 117560. DOI: 10.1016/j.socscimed.2024.117560 PMID: 39612748

Omokhabi, U. S., Erumi, B. S. U., Omilani, M. A., & Omokhabi, A. A. (2025). Empowering women with disabilities: Ai-driven reproductive health solutions. *ShodhAI: Journal of Artificial Intelligence, 2*(1), 40–48. DOI: 10.29121/shodhai.v2.i1.2025.30

Omri, A., Slimani, S., & Afi, H. (2025). The Role of Artificial Intelligence and Digital Solutions in Transforming Educational and Employment Access for Individuals With Disabilities. *The British Journal of Sociology*, *76*(4), 873–897. DOI: 10.1111/1468-4446.13225 PMID: 40344422

Sanni, B. (2025, January). *Leveraging artificial intelligence in women's leadership training: Personalized learning paths for skill enhancement.*

Shafik, W. (2025). The intersection of technology and inclusion for people with disabilities and marginalized communities. In *Global Sustainable Transition with Inclusion: A Focus on the People with Disabilities and the Marginalized* (pp. 185–212). Springer Nature Singapore. DOI: 10.1007/978-981-96-6557-0_7

Soldatic, K., Lee, M., Tunggal, E., Liao, A., & Magee, L. (2025). Rethinking digital and AI inclusion: Participatory and intersectionality-informed methods for disability and migrant justice. *Frontiers in Sociology*, *10*, 1593330. DOI: 10.3389/fsoc.2025.1593330 PMID: 40799256

Chapter 3
Corporate Transparency in Neural Data Collection and Its Impact on Brand Loyalty

Amit Kumar Pandey
http://orcid.org/0000-0001-5767-6333
Institute of Management Studies (Business School), Ghaziabad, India

Prakhar Duggal
http://orcid.org/0000-0002-9273-9712
Amity University, Noida, India

Ujjwal Bharadwaj
http://orcid.org/0000-0002-3159-6332
Amity University, Noida, India

Aastha Sawhney
Independent Researcher, India

Ruchika Jeswal
Amity School of Business, Amity University, Noida, India

ABSTRACT

In an era defined by rapid advancements in the field of neurotechnology, transparency in corporate data collection practices has emerged as a key determinant of consumer trust and loyalty, soaring to new heights in this digital world. As the use of neurotechnology continues to grow, and as the field attracts a new generation of companies, the level of transparency in how these businesses collect and use neural

DOI: 10.4018/979-8-3373-9720-7.ch003

data has become an important element in shaping customer trust and loyalty. The BCIs and wearable EEG devices, as well as mental wellness products, capture data that is extremely sensitive and generates speculations and privacy concerns. This chapter examines the impact of transparent provision of transparency regarding data policies, consent protocols, security measures and consumer rights on attitudes.

1. INTRODUCTION

As companies strive to create compelling new uses for neural data, the need for transparency in the way brands are gathering and exploiting neural data has become a critical enabler of sales and customer loyalty. The data from the neural technology (EEG headsets, sleep trackers, focus-enhancing wearables and brain-computer interfaces) provides previously unobtainable insights into cognitive activity, emotions, attention and mental health. Its nature however, is very personal and it therefore demands a heightened focus on privacy, not only for compliance reasons, but also as part of the brand reputation and consumer relationship. It provides insights from industry audits, regulatory evolution, and behavioural studies as validation that the benefits of increased transparency can be significant in terms of greater trust, lower perceived risk, and higher brand loyalty because of increased retention, positive word of mouth and willingness to pay premiums. But there is insufficient progress due to the persistent problems in practices and unfriendly regulations that are patchy. In this sensitive arena to establish sustainable growth, ethics, and to safeguard consumers' mental privacy and to create long-lasting consumer relationships, transparency is essential (Nguyen et al., 2025).

Transparency means providing clarification about what data is collected, how it is used and processed, stored and shared and how it is protected by the website, as well as allowing the user to easily assert rights to consent, access, correction and deletion. Last year's audit by the Neurorights Foundation on 30 prominent consumer neurotech companies found disturbing deficiencies that left the vast majority of these companies lacking specific information about how their neural data is used, and incubated broad access to neural data within their company with low levels of restriction, along with large rights to share their data with third parties. This can be a direct threat to trust, which causes reservation, reduced involvement, and a decrease in loyalty.

In 2026, consumers are realizing that being open becomes a trait of the brands that they look for. Businesses demonstrating mental privacy by publishing detailed privacy policies, giving granular consent options, having features such as on-device processing and regular transparency reports will help signal their respect for mental privacy. This will help to develop the emotional trust necessary for increasing brand loyalty, and as it turns out, behavioral studies have shown that behavioral trust is equivalent to increasing brand loyalty. These loyal customers tend to ignore minor problems, to solicit suggestions, to stay loyal to the brand in turmoil, etc., making them more likely to look past the issues. Brands, which do not have clear or ethical practices, on the other hand, are likely to face a backlash, negative review and customer churn as awareness of neurorights increases in the media and regulatory milestones.

The need for transparency is further impacted on by regulatory developments. California (SB 1223), Colorado, Montana and other states have laws that treat neural data as sensitive personal information, which require explicit disclosure and opt in consent. The UNESCO Ethics of Neurotechnology Recommendation (2025) urges an active approach to transparency as a standard worldwide (Darmawan, 2025). Organizations with this and more, such as using simple language, visualisations of the flows of data, and independent audits, have a competitive advantage. Brands, for example, that are certain to butch onboarding flows and apps with rights information say higher consumer satisfaction and repeat use rates.

1.1 Background on Neural Data in Consumer Neurotech

There can be a number of pathways that connect transparency and loyalty. First, it helps to diminish consumers' perceived risk; consumers feel safer entrusting data when they know the system includes security measures to deter consumers from having their information stolen, re-identified, or misused. Secondly, it increases perceived control, satisfying psychological needs such as autonomy and cognitive freedom. Third, transparency establishes authenticity and ethical alignment, attracting privacy-focused and younger consumers, where there is a growing influence on values-based purchasing. Fourth, transparency promotes authenticity and ethical alignment, which aligns with and reaches the values-based purchasing segment of younger and privacy conscious consumers. Related research in other areas such as biometrics, health tech demonstrates 20-30% improvements in loyalty ratios such as Net Promoter Scores, retention rates and more.

Examples of these dynamics are highlighted through real-life experience. In cases where companies have taken proactive measures to clean up their policy management following audits and/or regulations, these businesses can gain not only reputation development but also an increase in their user base (Shukla et al., 2025). On the other hand, using this general language around health and wellness and data use that is indistinct is leading to boycotts and investigation. Issues of transparency can prove to become a differentiator in a forecasted significant market - allowing a premium price and an ecosystem expansion to clinical / enterprise applications.

1.2 Importance of Corporate Transparency

Challenges remain substantial. Because of competitive factors, publishing little is an attractive option due to the ability to keep the proprietary algorithms confidential, and because of technofiness, they are hard to explain accurately. However, there are ever fewer companies that still consider electronic devices to be entertainment devices, thereby continuing the inconsistencies. Despite its growth, consumer awareness of these transparency initiatives might have different shapes depending on sectors and on the demographic profile, where the level of education can be an important factor. While awareness has been growing, it may differ in meaning by demographic groups, and digital literacy is an important component of understanding them.

1.3 Link between Transparency and Brand Loyalty

For most of the companies and brands leveraging neurotech, the best approach is to leverage a holistic strategy through; the use of privacy-enhancing technology, periodic third-party audits, stakeholder engagement, and the creation of consumer education campaigns. Policy makers can help in this effort through coordinated federal policies such as a harmonized federal standard (e.g., Moving to a federal MIND Act) and best practice awards.

Neural data gathering in corporations cannot be seen as a cost center, but as a strong loyalty motor. Open acknowledgement of the distinctive sensitivities of brain information can make what may seem like weaknesses into strengths, shaping long-term, loyal relationships with customers. The ones who are open about it will rule the market as more and more neurotechnology becomes mainstream in our life, and those who realize innovation must begin with respecting human dignity that generate sustainable commercial success (Trinh et al., 2026). This leap into radical transparency is ethical first and foremost, and strategic in the neuros era as well.

2. CONCEPTUAL FOUNDATIONS OF NEURAL DATA AND TRANSPARENCY

Neural data and corporate transparency are grounded in the concept of a neural platform, drawing on the insights of neuroscience, data ethics, privacy law, and theories of consumer behavior. Neural data are measures of one's CNS and/or PNS activity. This can be signals generated by EEG, fNIRS or invasive/non-invasive brain-computer interfaces that are able to record brain waves, neural patterns, emotional states, attention levels, cognitive workload and even subconscious processes. The data of the nervous system is more sensitive than the current data of other systems, because it provides entry into the processes carrying out thought, identity, mental life and biological processes.

As concerns transparency, in this instance, it is an intentional and transparent revealing of datasets and activities being collected, processed, security measures in place, sharing policies and the rights of the users. It goes beyond just complying with the law to proactive communications that give consumers quality knowledge and control over their neural information (Reji et al., 2025). The foundation understands that transparency is not only an action but a relationship: It's a key part of the process of gaining consumers' trust and willingness to provide us with detailed brain data.

The foundations of these are interwoven with the human rights discussion, in particular the programmes on neurorights, which focus on the protection of mental privacy (against unauthorized access to mental functions), mental liberty (freedom from interference on mental state, particularly thought control) and mental integrity (freedom from harmful interference). The audit carried out by the Neurorights Foundation in 2024 pointed to the need for speeding up most consumer neural data tech companies had no specific neural data policy, had broad access within organisation and also had extensive rights of third parties on their data. This results in information imbalance in which a company knows more than the consumer and the consumer risks it taking advantage of that imbalance.

In a sense, transparency can be seen as a linkage between technological innovation and ethical obligation. It talks about the dual use of these technologies, such as their applications within the scope of the wellness and focus, sleep and human augmentation, as well as the potential risks of surveillance, discrimination, profiling and subtle manipulation. Legal frameworks, such as Chile's 2021 constitution amendment, UNESCO's 2025 Ethics of Neurotechnology Recommendation and U.S. states laws (California SB 1223, Colorado HB 24-1058) underlie the idea and embed it within a legal system that treats neural data as sensitive information and establishes more robust disclosures.

2.1 Defining Neural Data and Associated Privacy Risks

Neural Data consists of data that can be measured or analysed relating to the activity of the central or peripheral nervous system of the individual. These include the electroencephalography (EEG) signals captured by consumer use of headbands, functional near-infrared spectroscopy (fNIRS) readings, electromyography (EMG) readings, and signals using other new brain-computer interfaces (BCIs). It comprises both the raw brainwave patterns and their derived metrics: attention, relaxation, emotional valence, cognitive load, stress and sleep stages. Using advanced AI can also extrapolate some higher order information, such as the intention, preference, mental health, or even unconscious bias.

Neural data poses a much greater potential threat of privacy loss than most personal data. Since neural data directly reflect mental processes, it can show aspects that people do not want to voluntarily express, like their mind and thoughts and feelings. Unauthorized access can cause mental surveillance and the reluctance to share somebody's neural information that is presented as anonymous - some brain patterns are unique and informative enough to be re-identified - there may be secondary uses like targeted neuromarketing, testing employees, insurance discrimination or/and political profiling (Alzoubi et al., 2025).

Other hazards include the possibility of data breaches compromising individuals' deeply personal psychological states, or having their brains actually modified via closed-loop setups that alter brain activity in response to information gathered. Vulnerable users, such as children, elderly individuals and users who are mentally ill, are especially at risk because they may not be able to give informed consent, and/or they have heightened risk of being exploited.

2.2 Principles and Dimensions of Corporate Transparency

There are a number of key principles that underlie the requirement for corporate transparency in the collection of neural data: openness, accessibility, accountability and responsiveness. Openness obliges businesses to be proactive about sharing information about what data is being captured on these neural networks, why, how, the processing of this data, how it is stored, how it is protected, and how it is sharing. Accessibility should involve making this information easily understood in simple language with the use of visualizations and without using legal jargon that may make the information difficult to understand. Accountability puts in place verifiable commitments: independent audits, breach notification etc. Responsiveness includes effective user controls over consent, access to data, correction of data, data deletion and opt-out.

These include informational transparency (information about data practices), procedural transparency (information on decisions made about data) and interactive transparency (processes for consumers to participate in decisions about data). Privacy by design is another key aspect, which involves transparency features, such as on-device processing, granular consent toggle options and real-time data flow dashboards.

The audit conducted by the Neurorights Foundation uncovered significant gaps in neurosciences and “neuro-tech” around all these aspects in 2024. Few companies met elementary information transparency in neural data details and there was almost none in terms of procedural transparency. On the other hand, top companies apply best practices by sharing transparency reports, providing in-depth privacy centers, and embedding the rights of users into the app experience; and year after year.

The rules are increasingly written down defining these principles. These regulations highlight the need for transparency and ethical use of neural data, particularly sensitive information like that in California's SB 1223 and Colorado's privacy amendments, which call for explicit disclosures of such data, and in UNESCO's 2025 Recommendation, which advocates for international practices by governments and companies that demand thoughtful protection measures (Goncalves & Dangelo, 2025). Transparency means that the information is also timely: provided to the users at the time of collection and whenever it changes; and that it is also complete: includes all possible uses/content and risks.

The power of data dimensions goes beyond two-party relationships to third parties as well: Companies should clearly communicate data-sharing agreements with downstream partners and also make sure they adhere to the same standards. With increasing data, it is of paramount importance to interpret information derived using algorithms from neural signals, such as making them transparent.

2.3 Theoretical Frameworks Linking Transparency to Loyalty

There are multiple theories that can describe the connection between the level of transparency of neural data collection by a company and how it impacts brand loyalty.There are several theories that can explain the connection between the level of transparency of a company's neural data collection and how it affects brand loyalty. According to Signaling Theory, in today's consciousness, transparency is a legitimate signal of quality, ethics and caring-orientedness of a company. However, in situations of information asymmetry such as processing data in the brain, full disclosure helps to build positive brand associations and trigger loyalty actions in consumers because it conveys trustworthiness.

The Commitment-Trust Theory of Relationship Marketing has focused on that trust can be gained from transparency, which in turn is followed by commitment and loyalty (Tkachova, 2025). Emotional attachment, repeat purchase and advocacy happened due to low risk and high benevolence that is perceived by consumers, when a neurotech brand is transparent about the data they gather and the rights of the people using their services.

Another way that this can be understood is through consideration of the Social Exchange Theory: customers maintain their loyalty when they feel they're being treated impartially. When proper measures are taken to store sensitive neural information at least in a non-disclose way; users feel that same fairness and gain that makes them work with brands and recommend them in word of mouth.

3. CURRENT STATE OF TRANSPARENCY IN THE NEUROTECH INDUSTRY

In the midst of an industry that sought greater transparency, overall transparency in the neurotech industry as of mid-2026 is still patchy and insufficient. Many have stepped-up their efforts as a result of audits, but most still fail to have a systematic approach to data disclosure, communication of user rights, or accountability systems. Consumer EEG wearables, sleep trackers, focus devices and the new generation of BCIs still exists in a broken and disorganized marketplace where many companies attempt to sell their products in the wellness or entertainment marketplace, thereby cutting out the red tape.

This leads to inconsistent privacy practices which do not sufficiently consider neural data's unique sensitivities. Technical complexity, competitive pressures and the differential maturity of a company are creating an issue of lack of transparency across the industry. Leading brands have started to reveal much more detailed policies and put in place easy-to-use permission interfaces, but most continue to use legalistic, abstract language to obscure a brand's true data practices. The rapid growth in the market serves as a risk to consumers' confidence and its sustainability in the industry, as between the technological capability and transparent governance, there is a gap. In jurisdictions where regulations are in place improvements are seen, however there is no broad global harmonisation, such that consumers in other parts of the world do not have clarity on how their brain data is being handled. In general, the industry is at a crossroads with a growing need for increased transparency as key to sustainable industry growth (Song et al., 2025).

3.1 Audit Findings and Prevailing Industry Practices

The 2024 Neurorights Foundation report "Safeguarding Brain Data" is still the most detailed industry work that examines privacy policies and user consent notices of 30 consumer oriented neurotechnology firms. Its resulting conclusions found 'extreme transparency deficiencies' which still impact attitudes in 2026. Notably, 96.7% of the 30 companies (29) seemed to have either give themselves "full access" to neural data, or not restrict their access to it at all. More than 60% gave little or no specific detail of an accompanying neural element; almost three-quarters (96.7%) gave rights to transfer accompanying neural data to third parties, in many cases using general wording on the 'sales' or 'brokerage' of such data.

Less than 20% said they used encryption, less than one-fifth said they would notify users if there was a breach and only 10% did implement some of the crucial safety measures. Pre-purchase, only 73% had proffers of relevant privacy policies, and many did not make it clear whether or not their neural data was handled as personal or sensitive information. Low level of responsiveness – only 36.7% responded when asked to by consumers; few provided timely policy change notifications.

The current trends correspond to a tendency towards minimalism. Numerous companies employ vague consent terms, innocuously word the risks while employing wellness frames, and offer weak controls for getting access to information, deleting and opting out. Few companies have endeared themselves to the industry by adopting new features, such as data flow charts, granular consent toggles and an annual transparency report, but these are rare exceptions. The review highlighted the lack of "sufficient information to make meaningful choices" for consumers, which continued to foster information asymmetry and vulnerability of the consumers (Zhang & Liu, 2025). The result of this research is continuing to spur on reform, given that current practices are not meeting the global level of data protection and are causing a loss in trust in the sector.

3.2 Regulatory Influences on Corporate Disclosure

Changes in the regulations are purposeful declinations of corporate disclosure in the neurotech sector but their effect is highly inconsistent at best. U.S. state laws have been the leaders with the introduction of California's SB 1223 (which will take effect in 2025) designating neural data as a sensitive personal information class, calling for clearer disclosures, opt-in consent and improved consumers rights. In 2024, Colorado was the third state to introduce expanded sensitive data protections followed by Montana (2025) and Connecticut (2026). These laws require that users be notified of their rights to access and delete the data and to withdraw their consent and that users be informed about data processing in more visible ways.

Transparency while being proactive, reduction of data volume, and a human rights approach to managing data in a government body are key principles that are encouraged by the constitutional protections existing on Chile and by the UNESCO's 2025 Ethics of Neurotechnology Recommendation internationally. The proposed U.S. federal MIND Act (2025) aims to guide FTC research and potential rulemaking to address the utilization of neural data, focusing on frameworks for transparency and consent for consumers, but has not yet been enacted.

These mandates force businesses to make its disclosures more clear, including clarifying the categories of neural data, why it is being utilized, who it will be shared with and how it will be secured. The highly fractured nature of this landscape, however, poses regulatory difficulties for national operators, and gaps on the part of those states that don't have explicit legislation. A lot of firms still count them as non-medical to keep their obligations to a minimum, which means that they have either partial or boilerplate disclosures. In sum, although regulatory influences are tending to raise overall transparency requirements, this is moving at a gradual pace and is pushing laggard regulators to strengthen policies, while also giving positive incentives to regulators who take a proactive stance, in the form of lower legal exposure and greater confidence with related stakeholders (Shen et al., 2025). There will be ongoing legislative activity that will help to streamline and further advance disclosure standards throughout industry.

3.3 Consumer Perceptions of Transparency Levels

Overall, certain consumers are skeptical of the neurotech industry's levels of transparency and believe that regulators haven't done enough to ensure transparency. According to public surveys and studies, the awareness of neural data risks is increasing and most consumers think that they are not well informed concerning the collection practices, uses and protections. Brain information is often viewed more sensitively (if not more so) than other sorts of data like financial or genetic information, making demands for openness even greater.

The Neurorights Foundation audit has garnered attention so far and caused further inquiries from consumers, who are dubious about the quality of privacy policies that allow companies lots of rights with minimal controls for the customers. Most find it hard to understand if it applies to neural signals, to complicated language, and to find tools to use, such as data visualization or an easy opt-out. This level of opacity can further result in the 'privacy paradox', where users are more willing to use the system for various beneficial purposes, but cut back on actual usage or show negativity towards the system because of a perceived degree of privacy.

Differences in demographics are also significant tech-savvy and younger users basing their purchase decision on a careful analysis of policies, whereas older or less technologically literate users are led by the sensibilities they are more vulnerable and overwhelmed. The perception becomes positive when companies communicate clearly and accessibly, and are responsive to their needs, as well as when consumers are more satisfied and more trusting of the company. But, when there are many reports of ambiguous wellness algorithms and irregular practices, there tends to be a lot of suspicion.

With regulatory shifts and awareness campaigns coming, transparency expectations are rising among consumers (Owusu-Berko, 2025). Perceptions are steadily affecting purchase judgements; more and more people are willing to pay a premium or to change brands because they think open is that.As attitudes become more influential, many can pay more or brand switch to demonstrate openness. Closing the perception gap requires not only an improved policy, but also the conveyed information must be effective enough to enable the user to understand and to be in control of their nervous data content.

4. CHALLENGES AND STRATEGIES

The neurotech sector has a number of challenges to overcome when establishing acceptable transparency about the neural data being gathered at the corporate level but each of these cautions provides nerve center marketers with strategic levers that can be used to build their brand value, differentiate themselves from competitors and build long-term brand loyalty. The main challenges are technical, competitive, regulatory and consumer side. Many brain data processing companies are sensitive about revealing their proprietary algorithms; they can be quite intricate and involve AI technologies, a disclosing of which could erode their competitive edge or result in the loss of intellectual property to others. Many businesses are more interested in initiating innovation, and capturing the market quickly, with minimal transparency than taking the time and effort required to initiate a thorough disclosure. 2024 Neurorights Foundation audit revealed the default position of most companies was to build policies of minimal compliance to ensure flexibility around the use of data, and to include both consent and broad terms.

This fragmentation of regulation can compound these problems. California's SB 1223, privacy amendments in Colorado and others in Montana and Connecticut establish higher protections, but the lack of federal uniformity (with the MIND Act on the verge) means that there is a patchwork of compliance obligations. National or global firms must face varying requirements and conform to them, resulting in varying disclosure levels and greater legal expenses. Many still consider that devices are non-medical, in the range of wellness or entertainment, and consequently fail to meet the tougher medical device regulations in terms of transparency. Internationally, pressure towards a change in ethics is guided by UNESCO's Recommendation on the Ethics of Information and Communications Technology (ICT) 2025 but is not binding.

There are also obstacles to inclusion due to the lack of consumer awareness and digital literacy. Despite efforts by companies to make policies more user-friendly, many users still don't understand "fine print" privacy notices snor can they fully exercise their rights. This leads to further information asymmetry and low value of transparency initiatives (Jbara et al., 2026). Other challenges include the threat of re-identification from rich neural data sets, cyber security issues and providing understandable explanations of real-time dynamic data flows in the brain. There are regional differences in perceptions of privacy that further make it difficult to devise strategies for global application.

These need to be approached proactively with multi-stakeholder strategies to overcome. To reduce sharing of personal data while preserving functionalities, companies need to implement other privacy-enhancing technologies, like implementing on-device privacy processing, federated learning, and homomorphic encryption.

Proposed transparency standards might be harmonized through industry collaborations, which would minimise the cost for individual companies of conforming to the standards and enable standards to be implemented. This can be achieved through incentives for exemplary transparency, voluntary independent audits and definite federal guidance. Education campaigns for consumers, working with neurorights groups and transparency components written directly into the process of product onboarding and applications are also essential.

4.1 Barriers to Enhanced Corporate Transparency

There are important impediments to increasing transparency of how companies collect data from the brain in the neurotech field. The issues of technical and operational difficulties are very significant. Neural signals are highly dimensional and dynamic, and being able to explain such collection, processing, and inferences, without misunderstanding the information or revealing proprietary algorithms, is not easy without being overly simplistic. Detailing disclosures can expose information that a company would consider trade secrets or potentially give a competitor access to the feature to use against the company, causing companies to be hesitant to be too open.

This is worse because of economic and competitive factors. When businesses seek to benefit from the insights that they derive from transposing their data into something useful, they are looking to monetize, find more users and get to market fast – before the expensive infrastructure to provide transparency becomes worth their while. The creation of user-friendly dashboards, regular audits and transparency reports are very resource-heavy and many startups and mid-sized enterprises are resource-challenged. In the 2024 audit of the Neurorights Foundation, it has been found that most of the 30 companies audited chose to be very lax in their disclosure, thereby granting almost unlimited internal access and rights of third parties to limit disclosure to a very general level.

Fragmentation of regulations is also a significant challenge. There is compliance complexity for national operators when faced with the patchwork of U.S. state laws, such as California's SB 1223 (to take effect in 2025), Colorado's law of 2024, and others that have been recently adopted in Montana, Connecticut and elsewhere. If something isn't regulated comprehensively at the federal level (the proposed MIND Act), what do companies have to work with? They don't have a policy that will be all-encompassing or meaningful because it won't be.If no federal legislation is passed and they are not bound by policy everywhere as they are now bound by boiler-plate, instead they'll have a policy they are not truly bound by. There is added complexity globally when each country has different standards ranging from protections contained in its constitution as seen in Chile to UNESCO's 2025 Recommendation (Gabelaia, 2025).

Other critical factors are risk aversion and organisational culture. For many neurotech executives the idea of complete transparency is to risk more legal liability or scrutiny, especially concerning potential misuse or the occurrence of breaches. Marketing often prefers to emphasize warm and fuzzy messaging around wellness aspects and neglects data risks, resulting in an internal disconnect between marketing, compliance and ethics. Whilst short-term financial motives for data monetization further deter strong controls over and deletion options for data are severely limited.

However, the successes of transparency efforts are hampered by barriers on the consumers' side. Public lack of knowledge of neurorights and different levels of digital literacy can result in even carefully-designed disclosures being overlooked and misunderstood. This delivers a reduced incentive to companies to make improvements and continues the "privacy paradox" of users' expressed privacy concerns but continued adoption because of convenience. Systemic change is needed to overcome these barriers. Cooperation between industry/universities, investment in explainable AI through technology, and advocating for a unified policy on regulations are necessary.

4.2 Best Practices and Actionable Recommendations

Top brands in the field of neurotech are showing best practices and ways to effectively connect transparency to increased brand loyalty. The best companies have detailed write-up privacy policies which explicitly explain their collection styles, a list of all the types of neural data they collect, how it is stored, how long it is retained, who they share it with and how it is secured. They embed within their apps interactive features like real-time access/depletion portals, granular consent toggles and data flow visualizations, enabling rights exercise in a natural and convenient way.

Adopting privacy-by-design principles starts with the recommendations for action. Companies should work to use on-device processing wherever possible, to reduce the amount of raw neural signals sent via the cloud. Frequent, independent 3rd party Audit (Summary to public) ensures accountability and credibility. Annual transparency reports that outline requests for data from the reports, incidents arising (if any) and changes to policies provide further trust.

As with all things, communication is essential. Start with a summary; have detailed technical appendices. Incorporating mandatory, informed consent modules of examples of the inferences made by neural data into onboarding flows.Including mandatory, informed consent modules of examples of inferences that can be made from neural data in onboarding flows. A proactive breach notification policy and quick response teams support responding quickly to a breach.

Planning with all stakeholders positively reinforces practice. Close collaboration with others, such as the Neurorights Foundation, for guidance and validation represents a commitment to change. Engagement via feedback mechanisms and creation of features to go along with data controls helps to build loyalty. Ensuring that the staff members are trained to deal with your data ethically, and you have cross-functional transparency committees makes sure that you are in accord within the company (Atreyapurapu, 2025).

From the perspective of policymakers and industry associations, calls for action include promotion of federal level efforts to harmonize around the MIND Act and spread voluntary neurotech practices that are transparent. Offering incentives like tax breaks or quicker approval of privacy enhancing technology will help speed adoption. It is imperative that measurement and iteration are performed. Organizations should use certain indicators such as user understanding of policy, use of data rights, Net Promoter Score and user retention linked to transparency features. There are various ways of disclosure and A/B testing these formats optimizes effect.

5. CONCLUSION AND FUTURE SCOPE

A key driver to the success of corporate transparency within data collection for neural information is how greatly it influences brand loyalty within the neurotechnology market.The importance of corporate transparency in the collection of neural data has to do with its impact on brand loyalty in the neurotechnology sector. With consumer devices now having a direct connection to the human brain, there is an even greater need for open data practices. The audit revealed that the Neurowaits Foundation suffered from multiple issues, but it also made a clear point about the future: transparency is the key to gaining the consumer's trust, reducing risks to their privacy, and strengthening their bond with the business. Growth and developments at the state level, as well as global ethical principles such as the UNESCO 2025 Recommendation, are setting the minimum level,while leadership is defined as going beyond by making things more user-centric and proactive.

Good business practice and doing the right thing is transparency. It mitigates customer concerns of neuro-sensitive information and increases the sense of control, while also steering business behaviors towards the rising customer demand for mental privacy. Due to greater transparency on their products, user rights as well as privacy enhancing technologies, leading brands distinguish themselves in a competitive market leading to increased user retention, positive word of mouth and user engagement. However, the high level of opacity can have a negative effect and cause backlash, churn and slower uptake.

There are several significant hurdles to achieving increased transparency: technical issues, regulatory issues and cultural resistance. But, the strategies and best practices presented - from in-device processing to stakeholders' partnership - are concrete approaches that seek to reduce these impediments. Transparency will increasingly become an expectation of a market as more and more people become aware of the ATs rights to the brain.

There are some research-practicing possibilities to consider in the future. Longitudinal studies would be useful to establish whether a specific transparency measure positively impacts brand loyalty measures over a longer time period. Cross-regulatory comparisons will identify the best policy solutions. What's new like explainable AI, blockchain-based consent management and advanced privacy-preserving computation should be explored for great potential they offer to improving the transparency without hindering the functionality.

Converging neuroscience, behavioral economics and marketing research can help gain a better understanding of information disclosure (ID) through a cognitive lens in a consumer. Due to different norms of privacy across cultures, cross-cultural investigations will be useful. Progress towards common transparency benchmarks and certification at the industry level could help speed up progress and alleviate compliance burdens.

The standardisation of national legislation and international collaboration are important considerations by the policy makers so that it will be able to establish uniform expectations. Transparency for companies goes far beyond mitigating risks; it's an avenue towards sustainable competitive advantage. Enhancing human dignity in a future landscape that balances innovation and mental privacy will foster sustainable brand loyalty, driven by trust and respect. Wherever neurotechnology is becoming part of life, those focused on real openess will form a future where innovation and mental privacy co-exist, to ensure enduring brand loyalty built on trust and respect for human dignity.

REFERENCES

Alzoubi, H. M., Shameem, B., Mushtaq, S., Al Kurdi, B., Joghee, S., & Hamadneh, S. (2025). Unveiling the role of artificial intelligence: Navigating personalized content marketing, customer engagement, and commitment with data transparency and security. *International Review of Management and Marketing*, *15*(2), 343–355. DOI: 10.32479/irmm.18499

Atreyapurapu, L. D. (2025). AI-Enhanced Customer Loyalty Systems: A Collaborative Framework. *Journal of Computer Science and Technology Studies*, *7*(11), 284–290.

Darmawan, D. (2025). Customer Confidence as a Business Asset: The Role of Transparency and Data Ethics in Loyalty and Reputational Resilience. *International Journal of Service Science, Management, Engineering, and Technology*, *7*(3), 35–44.

Gabelaia, I. (2025). AI and Consumer Engagement: Leveraging the Attention Economy for Enhanced Brand Loyalty.

Goncalves, M., & Dangelo, D. (2025). Regulating the Mind: Neuromarketing, Neural Data and Stakeholder Trust Under California's CCPA. *Administrative Sciences*, *15*(10), 386. DOI: 10.3390/admsci15100386

Jbara, H., El Nemar, S., Bakhit, W., Vrontis, D., & Thrassou, A. (2026). Impacting Brand Awareness and Emotions in Retail Consumer Decision-Making Within a Digital Context. *Analytics*, *5*(2), 16. DOI: 10.3390/analytics5020016

Nguyen, K. H., Trinh, A. T., Tran, M. D., & Duong, T. T. T. (2025). Uncovering the evolution of brand transparency in corporate social responsibility: A holistic perspective. *Corporate Social Responsibility and Environmental Management*, *32*(6), 7671–7696. DOI: 10.1002/csr.70099

Owusu-Berko, L. (2025). Harnessing big data, machine learning, and sentiment analysis to optimize customer engagement, loyalty, and market positioning. *Int. J. Comput. Appl. Technol. Res*, *14*, 1–16.

Reji, S. K., Moulya, B., & Rajeswari, P. S. (2025, April). The Role of Ethical Marketing in Building Consumer Trust and Loyalty: A Review. In *2025 12th International Conference on Computing for Sustainable Global Development (INDIACom)* (pp. 1-5). IEEE. DOI: 10.23919/INDIACom66777.2025.11115671

Shen, Z., Li, H., & Zhang, Y. (2025). The mediating role of brand equity in corporate social responsibility and customer purchase intention based on text-CNN model. *Scientific Reports*, *15*(1), 44391. DOI: 10.1038/s41598-025-28118-y PMID: 41436517

Shukla, A., Soni, M. P., & Rawat, T. (2025). Consumer Loyalty to Digital Brands: The Power of Transparency and Ethical Marketing. *Journal of Marketing & Social Research, 2*, 315–321.

Song, G., Gazi, M. A. I., Waaje, A., Roshid, M. M., Karim, R., Rahaman, M. A., Min, Z., & Senathirajah, A. R. B. S. (2025). The neuromarketing: Bridging neuroscience and marketing for enhanced consumer engagement. *IEEE Access : Practical Innovations, Open Solutions, 13*, 40331–40353. DOI: 10.1109/ACCESS.2025.3545742

Tkachova, Y. (2025). Integrating neuromarketing into brand trust building strategies in the digital environment. *Актуальні питання економічних наук*, (14).

Trinh, A. T., Duong, T. T. T., Nguyen, P. T., & Le, N. H. Q. (2026). Examining brand transparency as a driver of customer referral engagement in fashion context. *Journal of Global Fashion Marketing, 17*(1), 94–112. DOI: 10.1080/20932685.2025.2548545

Zhang, L., & Liu, W. (2025, October). Integrating Algorithmic Precision and Emotive AI Design: Two Pathways to Consumer Behavior and Brand Loyalty in Automotive Marketing. In *Proceedings of the 2025 2nd International Conference on Digital Economy and Computer Science* (pp. 1283-1289). DOI: 10.1145/3785706.3785909

Chapter 4
Hacking Brains, Unauthorized Access, and Cloud Storage Risks:
Legal Admissibility and Evidentiary Challenges

Abhishek Srivastava
Amity University, Jaipur, India

Hemant Singh
http://orcid.org/0000-0002-1258-5187
Amity University, Gwalior, India

Sanjay Kumar Pandey
http://orcid.org/0000-0002-7443-0164
MIT ADT University, Pune, India

ABSTRACT

Brain computer interfaces (BCIs) and cloud neural data storage have placed more than ever before us the risk of "brain hacking" and unauthorized data access. Neural Data or rich in personal thoughts, feelings and memories is the most vulnerable information. This chapter explores cyber vulnerabilities in neuro-technologies, the threats posed by cloud storage and how that poses legal and evidentiary challenges in court. It examines the admissibility problems of tampered neural evidence, concerns of reliability and privacy implications in the light of the current cyber laws. As data breaches and even the possibility for brain manipulation are increasing, the study

DOI: 10.4018/979-8-3373-9720-7.ch004

calls for more stringent boundaries for admissibility standards, tighter legislation regarding neuro-rights and international coordination in order to safeguard mental privacy to achieve justice.

1. INTRODUCTION

As the world of neuroscience meets that of digital technology, there is a new frontier of vulnerability where the human brain itself is an object on which hackers may operate. Any system that aims to communicate directly between the brain and a machine (from medical implants such as Neuralink or Blackrock Neurotech, to non-invasive or wearable EEG headsets) is known as a brain-computer interface (BCI) (Demirezici, 2025). These technologies offer hope for revolutionizing treatments of paralysis, epilepsy and mental health disorders, yet have the potential to put thoughts, intentions, memories and emotions into the most private human domain, subject to cyber-attack. Access to neural data, which can be stored and transmitted via cloud platforms, poses some serious issues regarding mental privacy, data sovereignty, and the acceptability of using this kind of data in legal actions and lawsuits. This position could lead to serious violations of human rights as well as a compromise of the fairness of judicial procedures, provided the challenges are not faced.

Brain hacking techniques involve direct cyberattacks on implantable devices where hackers have the ability to intercept, modify and inject signals into the devices. Researchers have shown the potential to exploit the BCIs to control motor activity, gather information that is more sensitive or even to plant false memories, among other things. Timing-related or electromagnetic energy leaks are used in side channel attacks to get information about neural signals. Sophisticated AI-driven malware can be able to identify the individual neural pattern and produces a targeted manipulation. Added to these risks is cloud storage. Real-time decoding is power intensive and therefore information is normally sent to and stored in a remote server for processing. This means that there are several attack surfaces during transit and storage. However, sophisticated state sponsored attacks, privileged user vulnerabilities and supply chain vulnerabilities are still present for the major cloud providers using encryption. At the point of one occurrence could mean millions of neural profiles being uncovered, making mass surveillance, blackmail or behavioral [profiling] more commonplace than ever before.

Evidence derived from the brain via unlawful entry or intrusion is subject of some challenging issues. It is up to the courts to decide whether such evidence infringes upon constitutional rights against unreasonable search, self-incrimination, and/or the right to mental privacy. The 'fruit of the poisonous tree' doctrine may prevent evidence from being used in many jurisdictions where they have stolen information by illegally breaking into a computer system. But it is tricky to distinguish between state-sponsored hacking and corporate breaches and individual cyberattacks and apply them to the two. Another big challenge is "reliability. Data from the neural levels can be readily hacked. An adversary may take measures to supposedly send false messages to the brain which can result in false confessions, memories, and/or motives. This leaves serious questions of authenticity and integrity which are the two cornerstones of Daubert (US), Frye, or parallel experts of other countries (ALlahRakha, 2024). Unskilled with the science of the brain, judges and juries may be confused about the probative value against the prejudice value of such evidence.

There are further challenges to hold evidentiary value: the lack of a clear chain of custody for Digital Neural Stream information. Make copies of logs and hashes for verification tracks is easy in traditional digital forensics, but not possible with neural data as it is strongly dynamic and highly individual. Data stored along international territories may adhere to various different privacy laws, witness GDPR in Europe, DPDP Act in India and CCPA in USA, etc. which renders cloud storage jurisdiction-specific. Issues of consent, data ownership and People's right over their brain activity are raised. To fill these gaps, new "neuro rights" laws are being introduced in countries such as Chile, Spain and legislation is being proposed in the US and in India, which makes mental privacy a new human right.

1.1 Emergence and Concept of Brain-Computer Interfaces (BCIs)

There are only a handful of precedents from case law that are useful and instructive. The addition of neural evidence has been a contentious issue in early BCI related cases, particularly because of the lack of thorough validation by court bodies. In fact, there have already been precedents for liability exclusion and evidence shielding in connection with medical device hacking, like insulin pumps and pacemakers (Hammer et al., 2023). The number of potential litigation cases will explode as more consumers adopt BCI, particularly in the gaming, productivity and mental health apps businesses. India's Article 20(3) and elsewhere, the Fifth Amendment, also come into play since law enforcement agencies could seek warrants to gain access to neural data in the case of terrorism or serious offense investigations.

The implications of this in the larger community are disturbing. Access to the neural network may allow thought crimes, divisiveness, by predicting future behavior, or political manipulation. Cloud providers that are de facto custodians of neural data have a tremendous power, and will have a conflict of interest when they are required to provide information to the governments. Important technologies (such as homomorphic encryption, the work done locally near the user of data (known as edge computing) or quantum resistant cryptography) provide partial answers, but the law is far behind technological possibilities (Mohammed et al., 2025).

1.2 Scope of Unauthorized Access and Cloud Risks

These problems will only be met by reform on a comprehensive scale. Specific Neuro Rights Laws must be passed in Nations, guaranteeing the freedom of thought, the mental integrity and the cognitive liberty are fundamental rights. Clear rules establishing several factors of neural data provenance should be required; as should be independent audits of the neural data and exclusionary rulings of illegally obtained neural evidence. It is reasonable and necessary to urgently need treaties on neural data protection, just like what is posed in the Budapest Convention on Cybercrime. Training programs focused on the neurolaw aspects of BCI and mandatory disclosure of information about potential hacking in BCI evidence studies will strengthen the courts' readiness.

Brain hacking and cloud neural data threats are a serious challenge for the contemporary legal framework (Said, 2025). The admissibility of this evidence should be weighed against the need for safeguarding of core human dignities in a technologically promising balance. If the law doesn't adapt and evolve proactively, societies could step into a new phase where privacy truly becomes the final frontier of the mind–bending digital age.If the law doesn't adapt over the time and evolve proactively, then justice systems can be left open to clever digital manipulation. The next decade will bring out the future of mental sovereignty in the hands of law – or at the mercy of technology and the cybersphere.

2. TECHNIQUES AND METHODS OF BRAIN HACKING AS CYBER ATTACKS ON IMPLANTABLE AND WEARABLE NEURODEVICES

Brain hacking involves using unauthorized cyber technologies and techniques to access, intercept, or manipulate neural signals or to use them for some purpose other than the one intended in the development of Brain-Computer Interfaces (BCIs) and similar neurotechnologies. Ensure that implants used to treat patients like Neuralink's N1, deep brain stimulators (DBS) for Parkinson's disease, cochlear implants and responsive neurostimulation systems for epilepsy do not come into harm's way because they touch brain tissue directly (Moulin, 2022). Though they are becoming ubiquitous, wearable devices like EEG headsets (Emotiv, Muse) or consumer of a type that are used for gaming or meditation with BCIs, offer a larger attack surface since they are, not only technically adopted, but are also dependent on wireless communication (Partick et al., 2025).

Attack vectors are a main concern; one of the primary ones is wireless exploitation. The majority of neurodevices are based on Bluetooth low energy (BLE) or WiFi or private radio frequencies. Researchers have shown how one could get a “bluejacking” or a “bluesnarfing” attack and capture someone's neural information or send in an attack. Security experts from various universities have managed to spy and then accurately re-create users' private thoughts and images in the commercial EEG headsets employed as alarmingly as ever in 2023.

Passive attacks are when a SIGNAL is intercepted or is eavesdropped. Employing Software-Defined Radio (SDR) tools can allow attackers to intercept electromagnetic signals from devices, and attempt to decode neural information. More advanced forms of side channel attacks exploit the device according to its power consumption, timing or electromagnetic rays generated to guess the sensitive information without being able to physically break through the device.

The alarming arrival of active manipulation attacks is more of a worry. Hackers may program a malware to change the stimulation level in an implantable device, causing seizures, mood swings, physical weakness or hallucinations. At extreme levels, an attacker might be able to manipulate signals to the motor cortex so as to control someone's actions, known as “brainjacking.” Because commands in BCI devices have been shown to be easily spoofed, meaning that the movement of a cursor or other action by a user can lead to a different action than intended, it is possible to spoof the commands from a BCI device (Goswami & Khan, 2025).

This is the future frontier of AI-powered neural attacks. An artificially intelligence algorithm, known as a generative adversarial network (GAN), could be used to build a specific neural attack model that can be fitted to stolen neural data to predict and manipulate signals in an individual's brain. There has also been a rise of ransomware in Neurodevices, where hackers are attacking the critical medical devices and threatening the life of those affected.

System-on-a-chip technology can present more problems because implants have a longer lifespan than their host computers, and cannot receive regular security updates. Traditional security measures are challenging with battery constraints, and the risk of surgical removal. There are devices that are still sold with default or low level authentication protocols. Malware can be also be inserted in the manufacturing process, making the supply chain vulnerable. Update-ability is easier with wearable devices, but there is low conscious usage. They typically are linked to unsecured smartphones and open Wi-Fi, which provides easy access points for consumers. Consumer grade hardware coupled by connectivity to the cloud dramatically increases risks.

From privacy concerns to identity theft, through to physical injury, psychological manipulation and national security risk, should it be the case with high-profile individuals or military personnel. With the rise in the number of neurotechnology devices, the security of these devices requires immediate attention including strong hardware security, end-to-end encryption, regular vulnerability checks and regulatory monitoring. If protected infrastructure is lacking, brain hacking could become a mainstream cybercrime and quite literal an attack on a person and society on a scale never before seen (Mathur & Singh, 2026).

3. CLOUD STORAGE RISKS FOR NEURAL DATA

The highly sensitive and private data originating from the brain brings with it dire risks regarding security, privacy, and sovereignty, as the data is stored in the cloud. Neural data (unprocessed brain waves, deciphered thoughts, feelings, intentions and biometric patterns) is sent from a neurodevice to cloud servers for intensive computation, training of machine learning models and further storing. With this architecture, there are a number of points of vulnerability all along the data lifecycle.

However, there are high levels of vulnerability in transmission. To support neural streams in real-time scenarios, data is typically transmitted via public Internet by conventional encryption mechanisms which might not be able to withstand potential quantum computing attacks or advanced persistent threats (APTs). MOA can be used to reconstruct private mental states in the case of the interception of data packets leaving the sender and the receiver of a signal without encryption or with weak encryption.

After uploading the data into the cloud, there is a possibility of data breaches and unauthorized data entry. Major cloud services that host neural repositories are the best targets for black hat hackers, hackers sponsored by the State and cybercrime groups, and rogue employees posing as insiders. The breach can be used to get millions of profiles of neurons that can be used for a large-scale psychological profiling, blackmail or prediction of behaviour. As opposed to financial data or health data that are able to be "changed", once stolen neural data cannot be "changed" which causes the data loss to be permanent and irreversible.

This is not to mention the complications of access and sovereignty by third parties. Neural data is usually stored in other jurisdictions where there is not as robust privacy protection. Governments can force cloud providers to hand over the data with a national security letter or in secret court order. While this leads to conflicts between data protection regulations like GDPR (Europe), DPDP Act (India), and CCPA (California). The place where the users' most sensitive information is stored is often out of their reach (Faqir, 2023).

Systemic risks of mass neural data harvesting. Neural data can be combined by tech firms and/or researchers and used for AI training without revealing the anonymous data's human identity. Attacks that can be re-identified with small quantities of auxiliary information, however, have been shown to be very successful. This may be used for discriminatory practices in insurance, job contracts or credit rating predictions, based on taking their predicted mental state or anticipated thinking.

Heathcare and neurotech cloud repositories have joined the ransomware groups' list of targets and are now identifiable as potentially the next group to be attacked for having threat to leak or ruin their valuable neural medical records (Varsha et al., 2025). APTs can remain present for extended periods of time, without any indication that information is being stolen, for months or years. Other risks involved include data integrity breach. In medical and forensic or legal settings, neural data could be skewed in some subtle way that uses the network to misdiagnose or mislead in a judgment or similar outcome. Yes, the multi-dimensionality and dynamism of neural data make the effective implementation of traditional integrity checks (hashing) more difficult.

The lack of consistency of the encryption, access controls, and audits on various Cloud platforms cases the issue even further. Lots of neurotech start-ups tend to favour speed-to-market approach and consequently, unsecured architecture. Mistakes often made by neurotech start-ups are speed-to-market approach which leads to a weak architecture. These risks demand everything from multiple layers of approach edge computing (for local processing to reduce reliance on the cloud), homomorphic encryption (to compute with encrypted data to a mandatory break notification law for neural data, and regular penetration testing. Ownership rights should be clearly communicated to users, both regarding their data and neural records, specifically the "right to be forgotten." If lawmakers and industry do not step in and make advancements, the cloud will be sure to erode consumer confidence in brain technologies and open the door to the exploitation of humanity's most private place (Tiwari et al., 2026).

4. LEGAL FRAMEWORKS GOVERNING NEURAL DATA PROTECTION

The laws and regulations regulating neural data protection are in their early stages and lag behind the quickly evolving development of neurotechnology and neural data through brain computer interfaces (BCI). At the international stage, the basis is on the instruments related to human rights including the Universal Declaration of Human Rights and the International Covenant on Civil and Political Rights, which indirectly guarantees freedom of thought and mental integrity (Atlam et al.,

2024). But these are less than adequate to meet the special requirements of neural data. As of 2021, Chile is the first country in the world to have implemented specific laws under the umbrella of "Neuro Rights", which ensurestructure the rights to "mental privacy", "personal identity", "free will" and "fair access" to the use of neurotechnologies. This has been emulated by other countries in Latin America such as Spain and Argentina. Responsible innovation in neurotechnology has been recommended to the OECD and UNESCO, focusing on ethical principles along with ensuring protection of human rights.

The General Data Protection Regulation (GDPR), in the European Union, introduces specific rules pertaining to the processing of data concerning neural health and sensitive biometric information, placing stringent constraints on the processing of said data and mandating certain marketing requirements with regards to the data subject's consent and imposing heavy fines for violations. The suggested EU AI Act also classifies high-risk neurotechnologies, bringing new and higher levels of transparency requirements and risk analysis obligations. Protection is piecemeal in the U.S. Consumer-grade BCI data often end up in 'grey areas' of regulatory compliance because it's not fundamentally classified as medical neural data.Although HIPAA applies to some medical neural data, consumer-grade BCI-style data is often in 'grey areas' as far as regulatory compliance goes. Numerous states have enacted bills on "neuro rights" and there are proposals on the federal level to extend privacy rights. The Digital Personal Data Protection (DPDP) Act, 2023, in India classifies neural data as sensitive personal data but does not have any provisions for brain generated data (Krishnapriya, 2025).

Indirect protection is possible by breach notification and critical infrastructure protection laws, like EU's NIS2 Directive, India's Information Technology Act and the U.S. Cybersecurity Information Sharing Act. There are however big gaps as there are significant gaps. Most of the frameworks do not take into account neural streaming in real time, freedom of consciousness and the difference between neuro data used for medical reasons versus non-medical neuro data. To date, in most jurisdictions, the ownership of neural data (whether it the person, the device manufacturer, or the cloud provider) is not clearly understood.

The three emerging principles of the neuro "rights" are: Right to Mental Privacy, Right to Personal Identity and Right to Free Will and Right to Equal Access. Enforcement mechanisms, on the other hand, are weak. Neural data hosted in the clouds of other countries causes cross-border data conflict. The risks of state sponsored neural surveillance of both law enforcement access through warrant and national security exception.

5. EVIDENTIARY CHALLENGES IN COURT: AUTHENTICITY AND CHAIN OF CUSTODY OF HACKED NEURAL DATA; RELIABILITY AND MANIPULATION RISKS; ADMISSIBILITY STANDARDS AND JUDICIAL PRECEDENTS

The most intimidating forms of evidence in court in relation to hacked neural data is authenticity and chain of custody. Unlike the commonly encountered digital evidence emails, CCTV footage, etc. neural data is a highly complex and dynamic set of electrical and hemodynamic signals, and is extremely challenging to verify. The challenge is proving authenticity, or establishing that the information is a true reflection of the person's brain activity at a certain moment and has not been "implanted" in the collector in another way. This is even heavier considering that hacked neural data is just as compromised and suffers from the assumption of compromise.

Perfectly managing chain of custody is difficult. The neural signals are wirelessly transmitted from the device to edge processors, and finally to cloud servers. For each hop there is the possibility of interception points (Kazaure et al., 2023). Once breached, hackers can change what signals are sent at any time, or manipulate the data they store, adding spikes, playing within a range of frequency bands, or simply altering the actual intended meaning, all without creating easily recognizable changes. These traditional forensic methods, such as hashing, are inadequate for time-series, high dimensional neural data, even though a small change in the data's morphology can produce completely different hash.However, a traditional forensic technique like hashing is inadequate for the time-series and high dimensional nature of neural data, where small changes in the morphology may yield entirely different hash value.

Manipulation hazards especially serious. AI can create synthetic neural patterns that mimic a real one providing a false and deceptive appearance to the victim of a sophisticated attack. For instance, generative models can generate "intent" signals to indicate criminal planning or distract or reinforce memory-related patterns to incriminate or clear someone. These manipulations are very hard to be discovered when they are presented in the form of neural data since it is not as explicit in meaning as a textual or available video footage. The timed or frequential modifications of spikes may be within the biologically feasible range and lead to completely different meanings being deciphered.

The second and important one would be the ecological validity problem. How data is collected on the neural level when people engage in normal tasks or when they are stressed is quite different from settings set up in a laboratory for studying the decoding of a learned rule. This gap diminishes the amount of evidential value (Kapoor, 2022). The encoding and decoding of humans' own intentions by their brain with a BCI could be used by prosecutors in criminal cases, but it will be easy for defence experts to show that there are reasonable alternative causes or potential tampering.

Many commercial decoding algorithms are also a black-box making the reliability even worse. They can frequently be used in a proprietary manner by manufacturers, which may restrict independent testing. This opacity goes against fundamental scientific and legal principles of the need for reproducible evidence. Even images of brain data, being seductive and impressive in their colourful illustrations, can also lead to a disproportionate belief by jurors, who, without knowledge of the nature, degree and extent of manipulation, will vouch for such imagery.

The Courts will carefully balance prejudicial value vs. probative value. When there's a potential that neural data is being manipulated, the risks of including it will far outweigh the benefits in most cases and it's just a better judicial decision to exclude it. Frye is still in use in some states, requiring that the scientific community generally accepts the work; and many neurotechnologies aren't yet accepted on the same terms as the Frye in the forensics arena.

There are nascent judicial precedents regarding 'hacked neural' data which are mostly negative. Strategic exploit rulings, with limitations based on the chain of custody, have been issued for early cases involving a medical device hack (like pacemaker data breach). Where neural data is used as evidence in civil litigation in BCI, courts have accepted neural data evidence only when it is gathered under protocols strictly defined, and has traceable provenance. It has been even more circumspect in criminal cases.

Exclusion is often enforced by the "fruit of the poisonous tree" doctrine (or similar rules) in the United States and in other countries, when neural evidence is the result of an illegal hacking. If data becomes vulnerable within the cloud, even legitimate data is in trouble. Motions to suppress could be filed for violation of privacy, particularly in regards to mental privacy rights (Kumar & Sanjaya, 2025). Brain stimulation experiments are often thought to be sophisticated enough to bias the jury. Many decisions only review neural evidence at the sentencing/mitigation phase, but not the guilt phase.

6. LEGAL ADMISSIBILITY OF NEURAL EVIDENCE

A wide range of lines are being drawn by courts across the globe due to its unique position where high-tech science, public privacy and traditional rules of evidence converge. In USA, the main gate keeper is Daubert (1993). Judges should decide if neural evidence is testable, peer-reviewed, has established acceptable error rates, is generally accepted by the scientific community and adheres to reliable standards. These are features that are often lacking when the neural data is hacked, as there are high rates of manipulation, an unknown rate of error in real-world decoding and no standard of practice for brain-computer interface (BCI) evidence. A large number of courts have barred particular fMRI, EEG, or even deciphered neural streams when the authenticity can't be certainly established.

The Frye standard is still commonly used in some States, requiring "general acceptance" in the field—an all-too-uncurrent and unattainable threshold for most current state-of-the-art neural decoding technology that could be used in the forensic field. In the Indian Evidence Act, 1872, there are similar reliability tests in India in other common law nations. There is a big problem in here called the "fruit of the poisonous tree" doctrine. The exploitation of brainhacks and unauthorized access of brain data in cloud storage systems obtained without permission is generally considered as illegal and, therefore, rumor that their data has been copied is rendered invalid.Brainhacks or unauthorized access to brain data in Cloud storage generally comes from outside and amounts to an illegal breach of the brain, and therefore rumours regarding data copying are unreliable (Musa et al., 2025). A right to clarity is solid in India under Article 20(3) (right against self-incrimination) and Article 21 (right to privacy) which was cited in Selvi v. State of Karnataka (2010). The Fifth Amendment in the US allows suppression of compelled neural data extraction and of evidence resulting from breaches for similar reasons.

Flash more intensifies the problems of admissibility due to privacy violations. Privacy violations add to the problems of admissibility. "Cognitive liberty" and "mental privacy" are developing rights that are increasingly being recognized by courts. The use of any neural data ever generated through any unimjustified over-reaching intrusion into mental integrity still poses a problem for the legality, as long as this is not provided by a self-aware entity.Even for lawfully acquired neural evidence there is an issue when its collection or storage involves disproportionate intrusion into mental integrity, unless it is associated to some self-aware entity. Interestingly, rule 403 (US Federal Rules of Evidence) is also an issue because many judges feel there are significant problems of bias when accepting brain pictures for the purpose of determining guilt, opting instead for their use at sentencing and/or when determining civil damages.

Case law is emerging which embodies judicial caution. So far, there are only a few examples of apps fueling BCI that have only been used to verify other types of evidence. Where there is a failure to the patient's neurology or the release of patient data, courts have limited the availability of neural data in civil cases only when it could be documented to have been collected, maintained and validated by an independent expert, and documented with a strong chain of custody. Traditional corroborative evidence is even more strictly required in criminal courtrooms, where neural means of evidence are seldomed considered.

However, taken as a whole, current admissibility criteria are very pro-exclusion or severely restricted in the neural evidence they allow in from vulnerable systems (Agarwal, 2022). This guarantees the sanctity of the court, but it also opens an opportunity to potentially relevant evidence being ignored. Technological advances in the capabilities of encryption and neural stream tracking (such as blockchains), law regarding standard forensics, and the general understanding that these laws will have to be more clear in specifying when these streams can be pulled and used legally, together with other factors are going to influence the future admissibility of such evidence. Even with these advances, the neuroscience evidence will still have great problems of admissibility given its newness and sophistication.

7. CONCLUSION AND POLICY RECOMMENDATIONS

New possibilities of storing brain data in the cloud and brain-computer interfaces have been raising novel dangers of brain hacking and unauthorized access to brain data and put mental privacy, data security and judicial processes at a clear risk. The paper has shed light on advanced cyberattacks targeting neuro-devices, major security challenges with cloud storage, evidence challenges related to authenticity and reliability, evidence threats around evidence manipulations, and the complex legal admissibility issues. The compromise of neural data aims at altering what a person thinks, feels and intends, and the calls into question the integrity of that person's thoughts and feelings and, therefore, his or her human dignity; it is not just an information attack.

Although neurotechnologies offer significant medical and cognitive benefits, the current vulnerabilities in their cybersecurities, and the poor laws currently in place, make for a dangerous environment that allows justice systems to be undermined using manipulated evidence and evidence obtained in illegal ways. Technological innovation and basic rights are still subject of confrontation in most jurisdictions.

There is a desperate need for coordinated, immediate action, both legal and technical, as well as ethical, in the protection of neural data, and in the fair admissibility of neural evidence. In a future where mental privacy will be marketed and justice systems will be subject to a high level of manipulation using this technology, it is important to consider a pro-active approach for policymakers instead two steps behind. If societies make today proactive safeguards, they can take advantage of the opportunities that neurotechnology presents, while upholding the sanctity of the human mind and the integrity of judicial institutions. Whether the law will be able to control this new power frontier or it will undermine the profound human rights it has won are big questions despite its growing sophistication in coming years.

REFERENCES

Agarwal, A. (2022). Information technology vis-a-vis human rights: An analytical and legal approach. *Issue 2 Int'l JL Mgmt. &. Human.*, *5*, 106.

AllahRakha, N. (2024). Demystifying the Network and Cloud Forensics' Legal, Ethical, and Practical Considerations. *Pakistan Journal of Criminology*, *16*(2).

Atlam, H. F., Ekuri, N., Azad, M. A., & Lallie, H. S. (2024). Blockchain forensics: A systematic literature review of techniques, applications, challenges, and future directions. *Electronics (Basel)*, *13*(17), 3568. DOI: 10.3390/electronics13173568

Demirezici, A. S. (2025). The cybercriminal risks and threats of body-hacking crimes under the legal framework of Budapest Convention. *Bioethica*, *11*(2), 8–26. DOI: 10.12681/bioeth.42841

Faqir, R. S. (2023). Digital criminal investigations in the era of artificial intelligence: A comprehensive overview. *International Journal of Cyber Criminology*, *17*(2), 77–94.

Goswami, D., & Khan, M. N. I. (2025). Cybercrime and Contractual Liability: A Systematic Review of Legal Precedents and Risk Mitigation Frameworks. *Journal of Sustainable Development and Policy*, *1*(01), 10–63125.

Hammer, A., Ohlig, M., Geus, J., & Freiling, F. (2023). A Functional Classification of Forensic Access to Storage and its Legal Implications. *Digital Threats : Research and Practice*, *4*(3), 1–14. DOI: 10.1145/3609231

Kapoor, A. (2022). Assessment Of Intrusion Monitoring Methods Using Digital Forensics In A Cloud Infrastructure. *Available at SSRN* 4267941. DOI: 10.2139/ssrn.4267941

Kazaure, A. A., Yusoff, M. N., & Jantan, A. (2023). Digital Forensics Investigation Approaches in Mitigating Cybercrimes: A Review. [JIStaP]. *Journal of Information Science Theory and Practice*, *11*(4), 14.

Krishnapriya, P. (2025). Contemporary Judicial Perspectives on E-Contracts. *Alliance Journal of Corporate and Commercial Law*, 49-58.

Kumar, A. B., & Sanjaya, K. (2025). Ethics, algorithms, and the rules of evidence: new era of ai-driven forensics. In *Forensic Intelligence and Deep Learning Solutions in Crime Investigation* (pp. 103–124). IGI Global Scientific Publishing. DOI: 10.4018/979-8-3693-9405-2.ch006

Mathur, S., & Singh, A. (2026). Cybersecurity and Forensics for Multimedia Investigation. In *Cyber Security, Forensics and National Security* (pp. 244-281). CRC Press.

Mohammed, U. M., Omolara, A. E., Abiodun, O. I., Rasheed, J., Osman, O., Lar, P. M., Adeyinka, P. O., & Olugbenga, A. G. (2025). Cyber threat in drone systems: Bridging real-time security, legal admissibility, and digital forensic solution readiness. *Frontiers in Communications and Networks*, *6*, 1661928. DOI: 10.3389/frcmn.2025.1661928

Moulin, T. (2022). 'I Will Control Your Mind': The International Regulation of Brain-Hacking. *San Diego Int'l LJ*, *24*, 65.

Musa, B. B., Jamal, F., & Yakasai, H. S. (2025). The role of cyber forensics in enhancing police investigation. *Матеріали IV Міжнародної конференції молодих учених та здобувачів вищої освіти „Філософські виміри техніки* “, 65-72.

Said, G. (2025). Brain-Computer Interface 5.0: Potential threats, computational law and protection of digital rights. *Legal Issues in the digital. The Age (Melbourne, Vic.)*, (2), 134–160.

Tiwari, V., Dasari, V. S. R., & Wang, J. (2026, May). The Future of Artificial Intelligence in Forensics: Advancements, Challenges. In *Proceedings of IEMTRONICS 2025: International IoT, Electronics and Mechatronics Conference,* Volume 1 (Vol. 1, p. 351). Springer Nature. DOI: 10.1007/978-981-95-0429-9_24

Varsha, A., Kumar, N. A., Bichanga, S. N., & Chakraborty, P. (2025). Future Direction in Digital Forensics and Cyber Security. *Emerging Threats and Countermeasures in Cybersecurity*, 467-493.

Chapter 5
Law Enforcement Use Toward International Standards:
Neurorights Legislation and Responsible Innovation in the Brain-Data Era

Deeksha Jha
http://orcid.org/0009-0009-4479-6796
Amity University, Gwalior, India

Ravina Parihar
http://orcid.org/0009-0003-2203-7410
Gujarat National Law University, Silvassa, India

Gopalam Sultania
http://orcid.org/0000-0002-2115-1962
Amity University, Jaipur, India

ABSTRACT

The modern times, in which brain technologies develop very much, such as Brain-Computer Interfaces (BCIs), have started the Brain-Data era and thus introduced deep-felted challenges to mental privacy, cognitive freedom, and human agency. This chapter explores how law enforcement might leverage brain data in investigations, predictive policing, and interrogation; it will look at the current state of law surrounding brain data with an in-depth look at some of the first bills on the topic to be introduced to any national legislatures and discuss the pros and cons of

DOI: 10.4018/979-8-3373-9720-7.ch005

these directives. It examines "international guidance," such as that provided in the UNESCO 2025 Recommendation on the Ethics of Neurotechnology and the OECD Guidance for Responsible Innovation.

1. INTRODUCTION

This chapter draws attention to the conflict between public security interests and the fundamental rights, calling for a sensible approach to laws that protect the fundamental rights while avoiding its misuse and promoting moral innovation. It gives the call for the worldwide harmonization, strong safeguards, and inclusive governance for mental integrity in the era of 'thought as data'. The chapter shows a variety of examples illustrating how neuromedicine affects the way we think about human rights, such as mental privacy and the regulation of brain-computer interfaces, while also asserting the importance of responsible innovation and adequate safeguards.

1.1 The Rise of Neurotechnologies and Brain-Computer Interfaces

The Brain-data era is a pivotal move to a phase of utilizing neuro-technologies like Brain-Computer Interfacing (BCI), neural implants, and noninvasive brain monitoring devices to change into data what is going on within the brain. The technologies hold the potential to bring revolutionary treatments to neurological disorders, increased human capabilities and new modes of human-machine interaction (Mia, 2025). They also allow access to thoughts, emotions, and intentions of the mind that is unprecedented, however. Police forces around the globe are investigating the possible uses of these technologies for lie detection, recalling forgotten memories, predicting crime and assessing risk. All this raises time-sensitive requirements for policy on "neurorights" and policy for "responsible innovation" to protect cognitive liberty, mental privacy.

The Police embrace new tech medical drugs due to their ability to provide hard data when that is otherwise lacking. Trial implementations of functional MRI (fMRI)-based lie detection and EEG analysis for intent prediction, and neural pattern recognition for suspect identification have been conducted in several jurisdictions. They have the potential to yield more accurate readings in controlled environments, but also introduce various significant concerns regarding reliability, bias, and coercion. The fear of "brain surveillance," with the aim of silencing dissent, is a special cause for concern in authoritarian settings. In democratic societies, one must wonder how to balance the interests of the general public with the rights of individuals to privacy and free choice of music in the brain. If it is to be discussed at all, then one must ask how to reconcile the rights of the individual rights to privacy and freedom to choose music with the interest of the public in brain monitoring?

1.2 Convergence of Neuroscience, AI, and Big Data

The Chile is a world country now leading in legislation regarding the 'neurorights'. In 2021 it was the first nation to include in its Constitution (Article 19) rights to mental integrity, freedom of will and personal identity in the context of brain activity and information based on it. Setting a strong precedent, in 2023, the Supreme Court in the United States ruled in favor of an order to remove the data of a Chilean senator's brain from a neurotech company. Complementary Bills are meant to "go around" consensual, research, and commercial use. Other Latin American nations have come up with similar proposals, such as Brazil, Mexico and Uruguay. The MIND Act (2025) calls for studying neural data governance in the USA, and the derivation of neurorights in EU law and regulations on AI and data protection is underway.

International standards in constant change. In November 2025, the first global Recommendation on the Ethics of Neurotechnology was adopted by UNESCO, highlighting the importance of respecting human dignity, mental privacy, inclusiveness, and protecting against misuse of neurotechnology. The Recommendation on Responsible Innovation in Neurotechnology from the OECD outlines nine principles, such as the assessment of safety, ensuring data protection and societal deliberation. These soft-law tools urge States to ban non-consensual interventions on the brain, particularly by the police, and for transparency and independent checks.

1.3 Opportunities and Risks for Society and Law Enforcement

The Multi-stakeholder is required for responsible innovation. The proper embedding of privacy-by-design and differential privacy technology and a strict purpose limitation will have to be embedded by the developer. Ethical impact assessment should be carried out in companies and there has to be equity in access to neurotechnologies. The Civil society and ethicists call for institution of special rules governing the use of brain data, such as using a clear, voluntary and cancelable consent, and restricting some applications of brain computers to military use.

The Significant challenges persist. The laws surrounding distinguishing between actual vs. inferred states of mind are complicated. The challenges of enforcing cross border flows, and technological difference between the countries can be an opportunity for exploitation of populations in the "South". Neural analytics based on algorithms may negatively impact marginalised communities. Furthermore, the "therapy to security" and "enhancement to security" angle of neurotechnology poses risks that therapeutic development of technologies can easily be used in military and security environments.

2. CONCEPTUAL FOUNDATIONS OF NEURORIGHTS: DEFINING NEURORIGHTS AND COGNITIVE LIBERTY

The Neurorights are next generation human rights that are dedicated to safeguarding the human brain and mental functions from emerging 'neuro techs' – a class of technologies that impact the brain and its functions. The rights are intended to protect mental intactness, freedom of thought, freedom of memory and freedom of mind – both the psychical and the psychological – in a world given over to decoding, hacking and controlling the human mind (the brain) with Brain-Computer Interfaces (BCIs), neural implants, transcranial stimulation and artificial intelligence (AI) mapping on the brain. Neurorights are still in its early stages of development in academic and policy debates since the mid-2010s, but have emerged as a new branch of human rights to address the special vulnerabilities it causes by direct access to neural activity.

The Neurorights is based on a philosophical foundation of "cognitive liberty. It includes the absolute freedom the individual has to think, believe and to be in a mental state without being imposed upon by others; it also includes control and modification of one's cognition (Di Salvo, 2025). This includes freedom from unwanted/indesisirable use of neurotechnologies as well as the freedom for safe use of neurotechnologies for enhancement or therapy. Cognitive liberty is an extension of the classic idea of free thought, guaranteed in Article 18 of the Universal Declaration of Human Rights, fit into the era of neurotechnologies.

It is based on a concept that the greatest focus of personal autonomy is the mind. Neurorights engage in efforts to set an ethical and legal framework as neurotechnologies push the boundaries between the external system and the internal self. The Neurorights respond to attempts by neurotechnologies to create boundaries between the external and the internal as they attempt to establish ethical and legal boundaries. The key support for proposed neurorights are mental privacy, mental integrity, cognitive enhancement, and the protection from algorithmic bias in neural decoding. They go against the spirit of the current lawmakers and call for a deeper understanding of safeguarding human consciousness itself rather than simply some data. Therefore Building Strong Conceptual Foundations is a fundamental step one should take before developing into a concrete legislation and international standard on neurorights.

2.1 Mental Privacy, Identity, and Agency in the Digital Age

In the brain-data era, mental privacy, identity and agency are more and more at risk. Mental privacy is the right to keep one's thoughts, feelings and nerve patterns private and protected from unauthorised access and decoding. Mental privacy is not about what is public behavior or information disclosed, but it's about the private domain of the mind, the intimate area before even conscious thoughts happen. The latest in neuro-technologies like high-resolution EEG, fMRI and implantable BCIs can now determine political party affiliation, sexual orientation, religious beliefs or an individual's hidden memories and with increasing accuracy which poses groundbreaking threats to privacy (Souza, 2025).

The personal identity is brought into question as the constant flow of neural information can be translated into a detailed psychological profile which can affect a person's perception, treatment or manipulation. Memory editing, emotion technology, and "personality hacking" are some of the implications from the neurotechnologies that have brought questions of authenticity and psychological continuity to the fore. If it is possible to manipulate emotions on an external basis, or to use external systems to plant preferences, then what is the "authentic self"?

The Pressure on agency, or the ability to act as an autonomous agent, is direct when the press of neurodevices affects decision making. This means gentle prompts from brain stimulation or anticipating and influencing decisions even before one knows what to select. Today, with the notion of neurotech combined with AI, such powers, whether government, corporate or malicious, can undermine individual autonomy at the very neurological core.

New legal and ethical protection measures should be in place to ensure the preservation of these elements. Without explicit neurorights, the existing privacy laws fall short, it is claimed, since they are drafted for external data, and not internal processes. Human dignity, psychological autonomy and true self are thus intrinsic principles of fundamental protection that must be reset in order to maintain them, given the digital transformation of the brain in a highly neurotechnological society.

2.2 Distinction between Brain Data and Traditional Personal Data

There are different from traditional personal data, brain data should be treated differently under the law and ethics. The Personal data and personal info consist of those things, which relate to external behavior and choices, such as your browsing history, location, money-spending etc. Brain data is in fact info which reveals your mentals prior to it being illustrated in your actions and even choices. This comes with a huge qualitative improvement in sensitivity and potential harm (Singh et al, 2026).

The Traditional personal data is usually collected through actions of some type that are revealed and/or willingly performed by the external world. Brain information, however, can be gathered passively or even without the individual being fully aware of it by attaching instruments to the body, inserting these into the brain or measuring data on a distance. It's much more of a private one, and it's far more predictive (Sosa Navarro, 2026). Neural patterns can show what information somebody would not be able to realize or would not wish to reveal, like early indicators of neurodegenerative condition, concealed powerful recollections or covert prejudices.

It is also permanent and inferential as it is brain data. Neural signatures can be reconstructed, with high fidelity, once they are decoded to aspects of identity. The risk of re-identification is much higher in the case of health or biometric information compared with anonymized health or biometric information. Furthermore, the brain information can be used for mind reading or for mental manipulation, which presents specially sensitive issues with mental integrity and freedom of thought, not covered by GDPR data protection regulations.

Many experts say that brain data should be considered a "special category" rather than genetic or health data, come with special consent requirements, some commercial restraints, and the banning of non-consensual decoding. The difference is important to policy makers. If scientific data from the brain was considered just an extension of one's own data, then much of the protection of human dignity and cognitive liberty in the neurotechnologic era would be missing.

3. LAW ENFORCEMENT APPLICATIONS OF NEUROTECHNOLOGY: SPECIAL REFERENCES TO INDIAN LAWS

Neurotechnology in law enforcement is a double-edged sword that can significantly aid in crime detection and is also alarming for fundamental rights reasons. These technologies overlap with constitutional rights in India afforded under Articles 20(3) (right against self-incrimination) and 21 (right to life and personal liberty, including privacy and mental integrity) of the Indian Constitution as laid down in the historic K.S. Puttaswamy case (). Although no explicit legislation on neurorights exists in India, the country's police services have been significantly experimenting with neurotechnologies such as Brain Electrical Oscillation Signature (BEOS) profiling, polygraph tests and narco-analysis (Lee, 2026).

Selvi vs State of Karnataka, a case heard by the Supreme Court in 2010, is still the precedent, which ruled that using such techniques on a person is a violation of their constitutional rights. However, it is reported that it continues to be used in investigations, filling in a lag in enforcement. It is understood that the Digital Personal Data Protection Act, 2023 (DPDPA) does not explicitly include 'brain data' as a category of data, hence limiting coverage for neurodata. Such a regulatory void poses problems of achieving an effective balance between good policing and respect for cognitive liberty, mental privacy. India needs to establish laws to regulate their use with clarity and caution while at the same time recognizing their potential for the betterment of justice in the world, as neurotechnologies advance.

3.1 Brain Data in Criminal Investigations and Lie Detection

In India, brain data application is used to a great extent in the field of criminal investigations, especially in Lie Detection and Detection Ar Gotu.In India, specific functional uses of brain data are a particular application of lie detection and lie recognition. Indigenous brain technologies like Brain Electrical Oscillation Signature (BEOS) encourage a response from the brain to an object when it matches a remembered one or is familiar to them (Musole, 2026). Police reportedly have been depending on these tools in hundreds of cases including high-profile investigations.

In Selvi v. State of Karnataka (2010) the Supreme Court has held involuntary polygraph, narco-analysis and brain-mapping tests to be testimonial compulsion that fall foul of Article 20(3). Consent needs to be fully informed, voluntary and provided with legal protections and access to a lawyer. Results obtained from the tests are not admissible in court per se, but the results may contain leads to evidence the results of the other tests, if any, which have been corroborated. These restrictions have been reiterated by recent judgments, one of them being the one issued in 2025 as well.

However, there are practical issues remaining to be addressed, and judicial cautions remain. There are subtle reports of coercion in custodial contexts which compromises "consent." There is scientific doubt and potential for stress-induced and/or memory errors that could create data errors. The techniques exist in a grey area – there are no specific neuro-rights laws. To avoid any compromise in mental privacy without harming the efficacy of investigations, it is important that India have explicit guidelines regarding brain data classification, independent oversight of ethical issues, and ethical compliance of privacy laws in accordance with the DPDPA.

3.2 Predictive Policing, Sentencing, and Risk Assessment Tools

Predictive policing and neuro-informed risk assessment tools are starting to become available in India, mostly through AI based platforms that provide insights into crime patterns, but where the neuro dimension is yet in an experimental stage.

Data analytics are applied to proactively combat crime through initiatives such as Maharashtra's MARVEL system. Incorporating assessment of criminal propensity or recidivism risk measures, such as brain imaging or biomarkers, in neuro-criminology approaches are of greater concern.

There is no specific regulation for using predictive tools based on brain activity in Indian law. These applications can impact on the sentences imposed or result in preventive detention under Section 151 of CrPC, which have a potential impact on equality and non-discrimination set out in Article 14. According to the Puttaswamy decision, the requirement for privacy cannot be fulfilled by any action unless there is compliance with 'tests of legality, necessity and proportionality". In the case of predictive systems, this algorithmic bias works in isolation, impacting on marginalised communities and deepening the inequities of the criminal justice system.

There is a lack of judicial oversight and transparency and no mandate to conduct independent audits of these tools. Ethical issues include "pre-crime" profiling and the loss of the presumption of innocence. India needs to create mechanisms like bias audits, human oversight, and prevention measures in ensuring the use of neural risk assessments for sentencing or preventive measures. If the proposed Artificial Intelligence Regulation in the 'Digital India Act' adopts principles of neurorights, it will contribute to the responsible deployment of AI technologies (Guterres, 2026).

3.3 Interrogation Techniques and Memory Manipulation Technologies

The use of Neurotechnology tools for interrogation of memory and possible memory manipulation present some of the most intriguing ethical and legal issues in India. Current approaches are geared towards recognition-based techniques, such as BEOS, and further techniques based on emerging technologies may allow memory editing or modulation via transcranial stimulation or pharmaceuticals.

The Supreme Court has protected mental integrity by diminishing the use of coerced interrogation techniques. In Selvi and later, the maximum of involuntary narco-analysis and the like was found unconstitutional as it infringes on the right to privacy, both of the mind and body, of the accused under Article 21. If produced for law enforcement, memory manipulation technologies would be subjected to even more serious overscrubble since they would directly intrude upon cognitive liberty and personal identity.

As it stands, India does not have any laws that regulate the process of changing a person's memory without their consent, or extreme neural interrogation. There are some protections, like under the DPDPA and with information technology, but not substantial protections for invasive neuro-interventions (Johnson, 2026). There is a high likelihood of dual use the tools used therapeutically could be adapted for interrogation purposes. Brain data approvals argue for the special status of brain data that includes: explicit consent, judicial warrant and an independent ethics committee approval.

India needs to adopt specific neurorights restrictions and safeguards on non-consensual cognitive manipulations, in addition, to ensure compliance with the international standards, there needs to be strict protocols on neuro-interrogation techniques in place. This would uphold constitutional values, but yet would not glorify a constitutional trend towards mind reading in an authoritarian manner.

4. INTERNATIONAL STANDARDS AND HARMONIZATION EFFORTS: ROLE OF UNESCO, OECD AND UN HUMAN RIGHTS MECHANISMS

Existing international guidance to deal with the specific ethical and social concerns related to the brain data age is in a state of dynamic change.International guidance to address the ethical and social challenges of the brain data age is rapidly evolving. UNESCO and OECD together with human rights mechanisms in the UN family have a mutual and complementary function, and their influence on the formation of global norms is growing. These institutions are striving to harmonise through formulating ethics guidelines, policy suggestions, and mental property rights interpretations that help reconcile technological progress and mental privacy, mental liberty, and human dignity standards. These risks, notably of regulatory arbitrage, cross border data flow and different protections across the globe are dependent on their efforts to ensure that neurotechnologies are not nationalized nor and restricted to trade within its own country.

A normative position has been assumed by UNESCO. The first-ever global Recommendation on the Ethics of Neurotechnology was adopted by UNESCO Member States in November 2025. This historic document provides foundational concepts such as respect for mental privacy and beneficience, autonomy, non-maleficence, justice, and respect for human dignity, as well as proportionality. It explicitly urges, however, the states not to allow regulated non-consensual neurotechnology by especially state agents like the police or military (BUIATTI, 2025). The Recommendation asks for the implementation of the neurorights in national law, encourages the establishment of independent monitoring bodies. UNESCO also encourages the development of capacity-building programmes for developing countries to avoid a "neurotechnology divide". What makes it special is its ethic concern and universal membership, which make it an important forum to achieve consensus across the establishment of various legal systems and cultures.

In OECD, responsible innovation and technology policy is our contribution. The OECD has added new elements to its principles on Responsible Innovation in Neurotechnology, which includes updated recommendations on how to account for possible applications in the context of law enforcement, dual use concerns and commercial brain-datasets market (Kritika, 2026). It highlights nine values including "societal deliberation", "privacy", "accountability", "reversibility", "safety", "inclusiveness", "transparency" and "hopelessness". The OECD guidance supports risk-based governance – which promotes the use of privacy-enhancing technologies and governments to conduct impact assessments with a focus on neuro-specific risks. It is especially relevant to policymakers in the quest for realistic solutions to regulatory frameworks for BCI and neural data classification and for collaborative efforts on standards among different countries.

These efforts are based on a rights-based platform as provided by UN human rights mechanisms. There are influential reports by the UN Human Rights Council, the Special Rapporteur on the Right to Privacy and the Office of the High Commissioner for Human Rights (OHCHR) which have defined neurorights as extensions of the concept of rights as protected in the International Covenant on Civil and Political Rights (ICCPR), particularly in Articles 7 (freedom from torture and cruel treatment), 17 (privacy) and 18 (freedom of thought). The bodies make a point out that freedom of thought should now encompass freedom from unauthorized decoding, alteration or manipulation of mental processes. There have been recent resolutions for the need of a new international instrument on neurorights, and for states to apply stricter scrutiny to any legislation involving neurotechnology and law enforcement.

Even though harmonisation is still difficult because of the discrepancies in priorities among countries. The OECD is more interested in innovation friendly governance, whereas UNESCO is more concerned with human rights and ethics (Yang & Jiang, 2025). They combine in a multi-layered international architecture. But soft-law instruments have no binding force; soft power has been unwilling to link to hard-law treaties; and major powers have been hesitant to join hard law treaties. Going forward, perhaps a hybrid development based on the UNESCO ethics, the OECD technical standards and the UN human rights monitoring system is suitable.

As India continues to strongarm its way into the multibillion dollar AI and biotechnology sector, active participation in these forums will result in positive benefits. Adopting national frameworks in line with such international standards would enhance its constitutional obligations as regards citizens' health, as foreseen in Article 14, 19, 20, and 21, and help place it as a responsible player in global set-ups of regulating neurotechnology. To fill the current gaps in brain data protection, India could participate more in the UNESCO and OECD processes, and support the UN processes.

International harmonization will only be possible if there is a continuing dialogue, mutual recognition of standards and technical interoperability. Unless concerted international action takes place, the brain data revolution may once again result in an unequal and rights-negating environment. All of these institutions together present a hopeful route for a balanced and rights-respecting governance model, where the freedom to think or creatively innovate is preserved, with the promise of helping to achieve that.

5. RESPONSIBLE INNOVATION IN NEUROTECHNOLOGY

Responsible innovation in neurotechnology focuses on ethical, legal and societal aspects at the research and design stage, deployment and commercialization of all neurotechnology. Responsible innovation in the brain-data era is more than just a matter of risk management; it is about purposeful protection of the mental privacy, cognitive freedom and human dignity of users. It demands a complex interplay of protecting against harm, exploitation and rights abuses while simultaneously exploiting the great therapeutic and economic promise of Brain-Computer Interfaces (BCIs), neural implants and brain analytics powered by AI.

The four key principles of responsible innovation frameworks are anticipation of risks, inclusivity, reflexivity and responsiveness. The developers have to take into account the potential for dual-use – the application of medical technologies to a different purpose such as surveillance, military enhancement or coercive interrogation. The principles include, but are not limited to, safety, transparency, accountability, equity and public participation. UNESCO and the OECD, among other international organisations, have laid basic guidelines, encouraging the use of neuro-specific ethical impact assessments by states and companies (Hertz, 2025).

A proper understanding of responsible innovation in India is still in its infancy and currently there is no explicit law regarding the rights of a person with a disability. The DPPDA, 2023 and the oncoming AI regulations, however, provide entry points to incorporate responsible practices. Difficulties that exist include the lack of enforcement, lack of general awareness and pressure for fast commercialization. Cooperation across sectors is needed for responsible innovation, as is the development of autonomous oversight institutions, like National Neurotechnology Ethics Boards. Its ultimate goal is to make sure that the use of neurotechnologies fosters human flourishing more than they risk threatening autonomy, mental integrity or social justice. In this way, societies may reap the benefits of the neurotechnologies and safeguard the integrity of the human mind by institutionalizing responsible practices today.

5.1 Ethical Guidelines for Research and Commercial Development

To prevent exploitation and ensure alignment with human rights, ethical guidelines for research, and commercial development, in neurotechnology are necessary. The basic ethical principles of informed consent, specific consent and cancellable consent are followed, especially when involving vulnerable groups like patients with neurologic impairments and/or prisoners. Research procedures need to be carefully reviewed against ethical standards, taking care of possible long term psychological effects;(particularly) reversibility of interventions (Cabrera et al., 2026).

Commercial development is subject to further checks and considerations. Businesses need to carry out extended human rights due diligence, including neuro specific impact assessments of potential risks to mindful privacy, modifications of identities and cognitive manipulation. Transparency requirements include the transparent disclosure of the data collection process, the working of the algorithm, and possible dual-use applications. Equity in access is also a major emphasis of the guidelines, with the caution of forming a "neuro divide" between the wealthy and the marginalised.

UNESCO 2025 Recommendation on the Ethics of Neurotechnology and OECD principles are very supportive of these standards. They suggest that non-therapeutic forms of cognitive enhancement for children should never be allowed and that commercial use of any neurotechnologies that give people the ability to act upon one another without the consent of their subjects should be banned. The guidelines by the Indian Council of Medical Research (ICMR) take biomedical research into consideration but do not specifically encompass neurotechnology, Brain-Computer Interfaces (BCIs) and brain data commercialisation, which needs to be updated for India.

Prevention of epidemics entails, where possible, open practices, fair contractual channels for payment for services and products, and surveillance after the market. Businesses should have Ethics Committees within the business and Chief Neuroethics Officers. Ethical guidelines can help minimize legal and reputational harm, and foster trust among the public which is essential for the continued development and success of the neurotechnology industry. Ethical boundaries and constraints during the research and commercialization process are fundamental for ethical innovations in the brain-data era.

5.2 Privacy-Enhancing Technologies and Brain Data Protection

However, Privacy-Enhancing Technologies (PETs) play a crucial part in safeguarding human brain data and still supporting lawful applications of neurotechnology. Anonymisation methods are generally not enough for brain data, due to its specific qualities, associated with thoughts, intentions, emotions etc. only the brain contains this type of data. Sensitive technologies like differential privacy, homomorphic encryption, federated learning and secure multi-party computation enable the analysis of neural patterns without revealing original individual data. By processing on-device, sensitive brain signals need not be passed on to a central server.

Brain data protection calls for neural information to be a sub-class of personal data, or even therapeutic data—that is, genetic data from subjects being treated in accordance with particular medical plans, which is the broader category that encompasses personal data—and classified as a "special category" deserving more protection than other data. This includes a required encryption policy, limited intent in data use, data minimization rules and retention rules that have an expiration date. Synthetic brain data generation, among other techniques, can aid in research and powering AI training systems, while minimizing privacy risks. The blockchain technology can enable users to have fine-grained and revocable control over their neural information via consent management.

With commercial BCIs and wellness devices, the rule of "privacy by design" needs to be the rule. The principles of local neural processing, automatic deletion of data and user controlled sharing should be incorporated as part of the design upfront (Li, 2026). The regulatory regimes should require regular security testing and notifications of vulnerabilities.

PETs can be used to add a layer of security to balance the needs of security versus the rights, via warrant and audited access to processed not raw data for law enforcement and national security applications. Data protection laws in India must make specifically reference to brain data and facilitate the implementation of PETs by providing regulatory sandbox and compliance credits. Strategically important, also, is investment in indigenous technologies of privacy. While maintaining strong privacy and freedom of thought, stakeholders can still benefit from the innovation of PETs and the opportunities that neurotechnology presents.

5.3 Stakeholder Engagement: Industry, Academia and Civil Society

The responsible innovation in neurotechnology depends on a strong stakeholder engagement. A multi-stakeholder approach that incorporates different perspectives in the development and governance of neurotechnologies helps to avoid single stakeholder groups dominating. Industry offers technical knowledge and scalability;

academia offers in-depth scientific and ethical examination / evaluation and civil society organizations represents human rights, equity, and the public interest.

Coordinated platforms that include national neurotechnology ethics forums, multi-stakeholder advisory councils and public consultations are needed. To make ethics more of a part of the product design process, not as an add-on. To involve industry with ethicists and civil society at the point of product design, not as an afterthought (Berrera & Covarrubias, 2026). Academia is an important source for unbiased research into the longterm consequences of society, bias detection and standards of safety. Civil society allows the voices of people living with disabilities, mental health conditions and low incomes, and other marginalised groups, to be heard and safeguarded.

Engagement in India is not widespread and is confined to the expert circles. Having an Indian Neurotechnology Ethics Council having membership of all stakeholders would have a tremendous impact on the outcome. Societal trust requires open and accessible public reporting or communication of capabilities and risks of neurodevices. Involving UNESCO and OECD provides opportunities for additional contribution through international collaboration with national efforts.

6. CONCLUSION AND FUTURE PROSPECTS

Hybrid governance are key to solving the problems these arrangements pose. These involve binding national legislation and international collaboration, as well as principles for and technical requirements via independent ethics boards regarding safe handling of brain data. Judges have to create jurisprudence on the admissibility of neural evidence, while exercising high degree of caution with regard to reliability and voluntariness. Public engagement is improved and politically supervised by citizen assemblies.

The future directions of coercive use of neuro-technology should be focused on eliminating coercive use of neuro-technology without judicial warrants and proper security against its use. A world wide harmony by a UNESCO Declaration or a UN framework on minimum regulations on the global level, which could leave the room for a regulatory experiment. Leverage privacy-enhancing technologies, like on-device processing and federated learning, to reduce risks to data being exposed. The governance needs to be proactive and based on rights in the brain-data era. The international community can find guidance in Chile's innovative experience and benefit from the UNESCO and OECD parameters to guide the neurotechnology for a positive effect. Responsible innovation, security, justice and human flourishing need to be achieved, with the mind being the final frontier of personal freedom. To truly capitalise on the potential of neurotechnology, without sacrificing fundamental human values, it is necessary to bring the right systems in place and foster a sense of ethical accountability. The Societies must have systems in place and a spirit of responsible use, both in the policy making process and in practice, if they are to reap the benefits of neurotechnology without bringing the technology into conflict with the questions it raises about core human values.

REFERENCES

BUIATTI, F. (2025). Brain Computer Interfaces In The Medical Field: Legal And Ethical Considerations Surrounding The Global Protection Of Human Rights. *L'Europe Unie*, (23), 33–55.

Cabrera, L. Y., Evereteze, N., Shank, E. G., Wagner, J. K., Mekel, M., McCormick, J. B., & Wright, M. S. (2026). Neurotechnology Governance in the United States: Gaps and Opportunities. *Bioethics*, *40*(2), 225–235. DOI: 10.1111/bioe.70062 PMID: 41311287

Di Salvo, M. (2025). The protection of neural rights in the age of neurotechnologies and AI. The ethical challenge for law and neuroscience. *Russ. J. Econ. & L.*, *19*(1), 202–233. DOI: 10.21202/2782-2923.2025.1.202-233

Guterres, A., Martins, L. T., & de Carvalho, S. Q. (2026). Legal and Ethical Policies for Human Brain-Computer Interfaces Storage in The Cloud Era: Privacy Rights Protection and Neurological Data Treatment. *Indonesian Cyber Law Review*, *3*(1), 1–16. DOI: 10.59261/iclr.v3i1.37

Hertz, N. (2025). Workplace brain surveillance: The need for new approaches to protect mental privacy and neural data? *International Data Privacy Law*, *15*(2), 123–137. DOI: 10.1093/idpl/ipaf014

Johnson, W. G. (2026). Rights experimentalism under uncertainty: Transnational law and human rights for neurotechnologies. *Human Rights Law Review*, *26*(1), ngaf038. DOI: 10.1093/hrlr/ngaf038

Kritika. (2026). Ethical and Policy Considerations in Neuro-Integrated Security. In *Neuroscience Meets Cybersecurity: Applying Brain Science to Enhance Digital Protection* (pp. 311-354). Berkeley, CA: Apress.

Lee, A. (2026). Neurorights as Constitutional Rights: Enforcement Gaps in Chile and Lessons for Comparative Neurodata Governance. *Neurotechnology. Society & Governance*, *1*(1), 21–39.

Li, C. (2026). Governing Brain-Computer Interfaces: The Categorical Gap Hypothesis and a Five-Dimensional Global Typology of Neurotechnology Governance (2010-2026). *Neurotechnology. Society & Governance*, *1*(1), 1–20.

Mia, A. P. (2025). From Brain Evidence to Neurorights: Rethinking Criminal Responsibility in the Age of Neurotechnology. *Available at SSRN* 5588370. DOI: 10.2139/ssrn.5588370

Musole, E. (2026). Governing Neural Data in the Global South: Toward a Neuro-Responsible Business Framework for Zambia. *International Journal of Advanced Business Studies*, *5*(1), 47–61. DOI: 10.59857/g3bvjx74

Singh, P., Kumar, S., Singh, S. K., & Singh, H. (2026). Privacy in mental healthcare by data protection: Exploring AI-powered psychological assessment and identity crisis intervention with legal provisions. In *Imposter syndrome and AI: Navigating human identity in the age of intelligent machines* (pp. 327–346). IGI Global Scientific Publishing.

Sosa Navarro, M. (2026). Workplace Neurosurveillance: Is the Employee's Mental Privacy Protected Under International Law?. *BIOLAW JOURNAL*, (Special Issue 1/2026), 93-113.

Souza, J. D. N. (2025). Exploring New Frontiers in Personalized Criminal Responsibility through Neurotechnologies: Ethical Dilemmas and the Neuro-Rights Framework. *BioLaw Journal-Rivista di BioDiritto*, (4), 211–228.

Yang, H., & Jiang, L. (2025). Regulating neural data processing in the age of BCIs: Ethical concerns and legal approaches. *Digital Health*, *11*, 20552076251326123. DOI: 10.1177/20552076251326123 PMID: 40162168

Chapter 6

Legal Admissibility and Evidentiary Challenges:

Neural-Derived Evidence in Courts and Forensic Contexts

Pradip Kumar Kashyap
http://orcid.org/0009-0007-8156-2767
School of Legal Studies, CGC University, Mohali, India

Saurabh Chandra
http://orcid.org/0000-0003-4172-9968
Symbiosis Law School Noida, Symbiosis International (Deemed to be) University, Pune, India

ABSTRACT

Neural-derived evidence stems from the continued growth of neural networks and generative AI, which have opened a new category of evidence such as deepfakes, AI-generated documents, synthetic media and algorithmically-produced forensic reconstructions. This evidence, particularly in terms of legal admissibility, authenticity and reliability, poses new and formidable problems for both lawyers and the judiciary. The chapter explores both the technical aspects and the challenges of using the traditional legal criteria including Daubert, Frye and Section 65B of the Indian Evidence Act with materials fobtained from the brain. It reviews concerns regarding manipulation, algorithmic bias, need for explainability and associated concerns over fair trials. The chapter points out pressing requirements for the creation of new regulation, detection requirements; and judicial capacities in order to effectively answer this new frontier of digital forensics and criminal justice.

DOI: 10.4018/979-8-3373-9720-7.ch006

1. INTRODUCTION

Neural-derived evidence will undergo a paradigm shift in the future of judicial proceedings and forensic science and poses some of the most complicated evidentiary and admissibility issues of all time in the criminal justice system. Neural-derived evidence refers to all the material created, elaborated or greatly improved through artificial neural networks, and generative AI systems. Whether it's a synthetically edited video or audio, AI-seeking new criminally plausible answers from scenes, a phone bulletin designed by artificial intelligence, deep faux voice replication, deep fake facial reconstruction, predictive policing results, or algorithmic enhancement of forensic images and scenes (Roberts, 2018). Neural-derived evidence does not always come from a tangible original source and instead relies on probabilistic models based on large data sets that are often born digital like software, making notions of originality, authenticity and chain of custody more outdated.

The biggest challenge is the authentication issue. In the past evidence had to demonstrate itself to be evidence (or what it claims to be). This is very hard to do with neural-generated content as it is synthetic content and can be nearly indistinguishable from reality. With AI capabilities like GANs (Generative Adversarial Networks), diffusion models and large language models, a video can make a person look like they signed a document, committed a crime, etc. that they did not do in real life. Existing detection methods (based on artifact analysis, biological signals, or the frequency domain) will always be thwarted by new generation of STNs, with an accuracy of 80-95% at best, and much lower for newer generations and adversarial examples.

In the United States, neural evidence is subjected to heavy questioning in terms of its testability, peer-acceptability or review, error rates, and general acceptability per the Daubert standard. A majority of generative AI have either no open, peer-reviewed validation or have such high hallucination limits that are difficult to determine, and they also function as 'black boxes' and have a limited degree of explainability. It's unclear in India whether and who would issue such a certificate when AI-Model training spreads to computers located across the world's servers.In India, Section 65B of the Evidence Act calls for a proper working certificate, but when tied to cross-served distributed AI-model training this brings about serious questions as to who is going to issue them and how the integrity of systems will be certified. It is also difficult to adhere to the principles of electronic evidence due to the absence of a document of an "original".

The chain of custody issues and concerns are significant, too. With neural networks enhancing, reconstructing, or generating evidence, it is quite a challenge to track its provenance. The high algorithmic decisions, algorithmic biases from the training dataset, and algorithmic stochastic noise can only be recorded in as much detail as possible, even if the input data itself is forensically sound. Defenses can build a strong argument based on biased training data issues that impact the output of the AI and not the truth.Defendors could effectively raise the issue of the output of the AI reflecting its training biases, not truth.

A potential further layer of difficulty is bias and fair issues. Historical data used to train neural networks often contain racial, gender and socioeconomic biases. In such applications as face recognition, gait analysis or voice recognition, for instance, this can result in discrimination. Courts will now have to go to the next step of judging whether the evidence is authentic and whether the model underlying the evidence is fair and without bias a criterion that most judges and most lawyers are not trained to assess.

The thing that continues to be a serious obstacle is explainability. Modern deep learning models are often unable to give the expected explanation of their output, differing from the legal requirement that the evidence must be understandible and subject to cross-examination. By posing a "black box" problem, this raises due process concerns since there is a possibility that Defendants cannot effectively challenge the basis of the incriminating evidence derived from the brain (Bakhtiar, 2023).

1.1 Definition and Evolution of AI-Generated and Neural Evidence

The increasing number of neural data also presents worrying human rights and privacy concerns. With the help of deepfake technology, it is possible to alter even sophisticated witnesses, make up alibis, and slander characters. DeepFake technology allows for the manipulation of even the most sophisticated witness, for alibi manufacturing and character assassination. Synthetic evidence can easily be established as truth, thus endangering the very basis of fair trials and presumption of innocence in the name of "reality laundering."

Another key area of concern is Judicial capacity. Tech-neurology is under the technical literacy of very few judges, prosecutors, and investigators. This knowledge disparity is the potential for dependency on convincing AI produced outputs and excluding valuable evidence. In cross-border scenarios, biases and misunderstandings to evidence created by AI might be even more pronounced, primarily because the ways in which evidence is handled and used in legal practices across various jurisdictions vary greatly.

Some of these challenges have not descended in the end, however, and neural-derived evidence has clear, irrefutable merit. AI can improve current substandard surveillance video, reassemble broken footage, find patterns that the human eye cannot see, and speed the investigation process. It is not rejecting the technology that is the answer, it is creating strong protections. Some of these are required model auditing, watermarking and provenance (including C2PA), an adversarial and forensic testing regime, and unambiguous evidentiary tiering depending on how much AI was involved.

1.2 Emergence in Criminal Investigations and Forensics

A few jurisdictions are taking the first steps to respond. There is a high-risk category of AI systems in the EU AI Act subject to strict submission of transparency and oversight. States in the USA have implemented regulations that designate deepfakes as classifiable as evidence. Specific provisions for generative AI evidence may be required in future in the Indian digital framework. But altogether, there are no extensive global standards (Hussain, 2025).

Thus, the neural evidence is compelling only the rethinking of the century-old principles of evidence. The courts have a heavy duty to strike a balance between the significant investigative advantages that AI can offer and the concerns regarding manipulation, bias and opacity it poses. In the coming years, technologists, forensic experts, legal scholars, and policy-makers will have to work hand in hand to develop new admissibility models which balance the integrity of the justice system and technological progress. Unless a concerted effort is made, the judicial process may soon be flooded with ever-more complex and information dense synthetic evidence that will introduce doubt where previously there has been none.

2. TECHNICAL FOUNDATIONS AND RELIABILITY ISSUES

The evidence derived from a neural system is based on sophisticated architectures that are beyond traditional digital evidence. The essence of this type of evidence is that it does not come from the physical world and are the result of a large computation. A neural network, such as a deep learning model, can be used to analyze large amounts of data to find patterns, create or modify content. For these systems, the time-sequence recording of reality is not a mere observation of reality but rather a learning of statistical representations of reality and a extension to newer recorded sequences that can be indistinguishable from real ones.

The value of such evidence is open to question, however.The confidence in such evidence is probabilistic in nature. The outputs derived by the neural network are mathematical approximations and generative and do not have a direct causal connection to events as would a video off of a Surveillance Camera. This adds complexity in regards to the accuracy, origin and the possible manipulation. In forensics applications, investigators and courts will need to consider the final products but also the model's training data, parameters, architecture and operating environment.

The artifacts are significantly affected by the factors as Model version, Level setting during Generating processes, random Seed and Post Processing.

Training data biases, hallucination (models creating plausible yet incorrect information), output fluctuations and the "black box" nature of numerous deep learning models are examples of their sources of reliability problems. Algorithmic decisions applied to data as it passes through a neural network can also be hard to audit in ways that comprehensively prove the forensical soundness of the data.It gets more complicated when input data is forensically sound but the algorithmic decisions made with it at the neural network aren't fully audited and can't be reproduced comprehensively (Findlay & Grix, 2003). This poses problems in criminal investigations, where it is important to establish provenance, reproducibility and any margins for error for any findings to be admissible in court. However, the difference between creation and detection technologies is growing as much as the generative technologies advance and become increasingly powerful. What used to be evident from artifacts (blurring, lights that can't hold still, or unnatural blinking) has now become highly complex synthetic media which passes many traditional forensic tests.

2.1 Neural Networks, Generative AI and Synthetic Media

Neural networks are the building blocks of today's generations AI applications for generating synthetic media. These are multi layered computation constructs which are modeled after the structure of biological neurons that are capable of pattern recognition and the generation of new data. Some of the most important architectures are the Generative Adversarial Networks (GANs), Variational Autoencoders (VAEs) and newer diffusion models and transformer-based approaches. For example, in the case of GANs, two network are competing with one another; the generator attempting to create synthetic content and the discriminator to determine the difference between real and fake content, the output of which will progressively become more realistic, with adversarial training.

Generative AI involves building and training a model that learns from millions of images, video clips and audio recordings in a large dataset to generate synthetic media. As the models are leveled up, they can create all sorts of new material or manipulate existing content with tremendous fidelity. Face swapping, voice cloning, crime scene reconstruction, face aging/face de-aging and lip-sync manipulation are the applications in forensic area. In contrast, new methods called diffusion models have come to the fore recently and these are based on progressively adding noise to data and then removing it to create high quality images and videos which are frequently better than the previous generation of GAN-based models.

Forensics is not just limited to deepfake detection.Synthetic media is not limited to merely detecting deepfake videos. This encompasses computer-generated video with low resolution (AI), digitally pieced-together audio from small excerpts, computer-generated predictions for what happened, and fake alibi footage and videos. These tools have tremendous investigative value: they can make sense out of fuzzy surveillance information, or recreate lost evidence, but they also raise many questions of reliability.

2.2 Detection Challenges and Error Rates

Finding neural-derived evidence is difficult - and the percentage of error rates is still troubling for forensic and judicial settings with high consequences. With the latest detection systems (2026 and beyond), even the best ones are not very efficient from lab bench to real-world usage. While the best performing detectors can perform at up to 89-96% accuracy in ideal conditions, accuracy can be reduced by 45-50% in conditions of new generative models, adversarial inputs or when input content is compressed/re-encoded as found in investigations.

Methods of key detection encompass artifacts (blending boundaries, frequency domain inconsistencies, or biological signal inconsistencies such as changes in color that occur due to heartbeats) as well as machine learning classifiers trained on known sets of deepfake images and features, and multi-modal approaches, which look for inconsistencies in the visual, audio, and metadata features. But these techniques have difficulties adapting to fast technological changes in the production of generations (Grimm, 2017). The generation methods developed by the linear RNN and adversarial networks specifically target to defeat common generation fingerprints, making many of the previous technologies obsolete.

The accuracy rate for identifying a human with high quality video deepfakes is very low, 24.5% at best. Even professionals make marginally better results. In targeted environments, adversarial attacks requiring high visual fidelity but adding subtleties to the images, which are imperceptible to the human eye for the target, are typically successful rates are well above 80%. The type of errors creates more complexities for reliability. The greatest threat of false negatives in criminal trials is that of fabricating evidence or tampering with the actual media. False solutions (misidentifying real evidence as false) may compromise real cases & result in loss of trust.

2.3 Manipulation Risks and Deepfake Technology

Deepfake technology is one of the greatest threats to the criminal justice system that could be potentially used to alter images. The biggest manipulation dangers modern criminal justice systems contend with is deepfake technology. Whether animated videos, audio recordings, photos or even live interactive content, the possibilities with power of advanced artificial intelligence, Generative AI, deepfakes are endless and allow impersonation with an impressive degree of realism. These functions pose unprecedented dangers in the manner of evidence fabrication, victim intimidation, alibis and confession manufacturing, in the forensic and courtroom setting.

Manipulation techniques have gone well over face-swapping. Today's deepfakes allow complete body reconstruction, clone from just seconds of speech, real-time creation during a video conversation and add seamlessly to pre-recorded clips. Video can be altered and created to show a suspect at a crime scene, fake confessions can be made or fabricated exculpatory video created placing innocents away from the crime scene. Not only have these tools become generally available, but also through open-source models or "deepfake-as-a-service", they have created a new hybrid of sophisticated manipulation that is almost accessible to all orgaAnized crime or individual operators.

The dangers are far from exclusive to the process of making. The dangers are far from limited to the act of making. Even the possibility of deep fake technology has generated what feels like deep fake defense – as legitimate proof is now cast doubt on as possibly being a fake, there are increased verification requirements and reasonable doubt. The effect of this "liar's dividend" leads to the defeat of the probative value of genuine audio-visual evidence. On the technical side, today's generated deepfakes often have lower number of detectable artifacts, particularly with the latest state-of-the-art diffusion models and adversarial training. Can withstand compression, re-encoding and social media processing, while remaining perceptually high quality. When criminals are using more sophisticated methods like setting up a proxy or using VPNs, and/or laundered training data, in cross-border cases it becomes essentially unattainable.

3. LEGAL STANDARDS AND ADMISSIBILITY TESTS

The legal parameters and admissions rules for neural evidence are now being put to the test as courts roll out and develop a new class of language that is synthetically generated on computers. The conventional rules are only applicable in the instances of physical evidence or relatively simple electronic records with clear origins. Nearly all of the assumptions of evidence law are either contradicted or subverted by neural proof, which is proof created or heavily influenced by AI (Erbas, 2021).

Courts across jurisdictions use accepted standards like US Daubert v. REO (Daubert), US Frye test, Civil substantive and civil law standards of Section 65A/65B Indian Evidence Act, which allow the court to assess that specific standards of the given field of science are met. Most of the time, these standards core upon evidence that is relevant, reliable, and acquired through the correct means. Meeting these requirements for neural-derived evidence requires careful examination of the foundations of the underlying AI model(architecture, training data, validation processes, error rates and explainability). The decision-making process of neural networks is largely opaque and is, along with the finished product, subject to evaluation by the judges.

Some of the key aspects to be considered for admissibility are: Is the AI system scientificallyocumented, are the error rates found acceptable for forensic use, was the applied use of the system within the case justified and are there accepted rules and regulations governing the operation of the system (Wakili et al., 2025). Reproducibility is another issue that arises with probabilistic and stochastic generative AI, as is the main tenet of many admissibility tests. It is important to note that different outputs can be produced with given the same model with the same inputs, so that the results are not necessarily reliable and consistent.

Authentication requirements call for evidence that proves the evidence being presented is what the proponent alleges it is. In neural evidence cases, this is with respect to the output being accurate in the sense that it faithfully depicts facts—rather than invention—as algorithmic. The chain of custody becomes much more complicated when evidence goes through several AI enhancements or generation. Courts will have to determine if adequate supervision was provided and if all necessary steps were properly documented.

The tools for neural evidence are not standardized, leading to inconsistencies among cases and jurisdictions. There are some courts that have also authorized the enhanced evidence with extensive, well-founded validation, but a lot of doubts have been expressed regarding deepfakes and totally generative evidence in the other side. The changing legal landscape demands more technical skills for judges, prosecutors, and defense attorneys, as well as a new round of legal standards with special reference to AI-generated or AI-assisted evidence. Whether these technologies will be used in investigation while respecting the integrity of justice is a significant question that will have a tremendous impact over the next few years and the years ahead (Fry, 2014).

3.1 Authentication and Chain of Custody in Neural Evidence

Authentication and chain of custody of neural derived evidence are arguably the most challenging evidentiary problems of modern times. Traditional authentication involves establishing that the evidence is authentic and unaltered. Things become even more complicated with neural evidence, because the evidence itself may be synthetic, or very altered by AI, so that there is no clear "original" source in the usual meaning of the term.

Usually, several confirmations of neural evidence are needed. The first step involves demonstrating the reliability of the input AI model by documenting the model's architecture, training procedure, validation sets, and performance metrics. The first step is to establish the reliability of the underlying AI model with detailed documentation of its architecture, training procedure, validation datasets, and performance metrics (Bakhtiar, 2023). Secondly, they need to show that the particular case of evidence is a result of a controlled and auditable version of that model. Third, they have to show that the output matches actual facts with respect to the real world instead of being a hallucination or an imaginative reconstruction created by the AI. This frequently requires expert testimony to explain the technical process, with the help of logs, version control, input hashes for data and output verifications.

This is especially problematic when it comes to chain of custody. Traditional: Evidence goes from collection to analysis to presentation. The evidence of a neural step often experiences multiple transmutations labeled enhancement, reconstruction, generation, or refinement. Additional parameters of the AI, random generators, variables etc. are picked up in each processing step, adding to the possible biases. An uninterrupted chain depends on a detailed logging of each input, every modification of the models, every set-up of the inputs and all the output of each step; it also includes a record of any human activity. A comprehensive level of documentation is not always fully realised in investigative practices today. With existing deep learning systems, it can be difficult, if not impossible, to explain why the AI generated a specific outcome, given the inputs to its model. The opacity allows defense attorneys to challenge the evidence and declare that it may not represent facts but rather be an algorithmic artifact, a hallucination, or be biased.

Technical standards like cryptographic watermarking, provenance metadata (e.g., C2PA standards), a non-alterable audit log of AI processing activities, and third party review and validation of the model and specific evidence instance are being increasingly required by court. Some jurisdictions in progression are beginning to refine authentication strategies (less powerful evidence than true synthetic evidence). The lack of uniform procedures can help determine whether a test will be successful or not, and this relies on the expertise of the witnesses and how prepared the court is technically (DeMatteo & Olver, 2022). Without authenticating and providing chain of custody established by strong, court approved systems, neural evidence will still have substantial challenges to be submitted as evidence to help prosecute criminals, and it will be even more likely to be submitted to court for false identification and identify a perpetrator who did not commit the crime.

4. MAJOR EVIDENTIARY CHALLENGES IN COURT

Synthetic neural evidence creates significant evidentiary issues in court because of the core legal principles of 'truth', 'authenticity' and 'reliability' are undermined in the process. Neural evidence, which is algorithmically generated and/or transformed in relation to things physical, is inherently different from ordinary evidence that is directly associated with the physical world, with the resultant profound difficulties for judicial assessment.

The top problem is verification of authenticity. The courts will have to decide whether it was evidence of what actually happened or a "fly trap." The high-quality deepfakes and generative AI results are surprisingly adept at mimicking mannerisms, lighting, acoustics and micro-expressions. The authentication of a recorded confession to a crime, or of a damaging video recording, is now extraordinarily difficult, and the only weapons available are feeble detection methods and expert witnesses; aptly designed video equipment aside. Forcing the use of feeble detection devices and expert witnesses, the authentication of a recorded affirmation is extraordinarily difficult, as is a damaging video recording, particularly in the absence of expertly designed video equipment. Other important challenges are on the Explainability as many neural networks are unable to explain the cause of their output. This does not align with the legal obligations for knowledge to be supported by some kind of evidence which can be suitably challenged via cross examination. Judges and juries have trouble finding common ground in weighing evidence over which they have limited understanding, thereby posing an serious problem when it comes to due process (Ibrahim et al., 2025).

Admissibility is further fraught because of bias and hallucinating hazards. Biases in the training data can be reinforced by neural models. One direct threat to factual accuracy is hallucinations, where the AI logically, but inaccurately, compiles seemingly credible information. Flaws in this kind of work will result in wrongful convictions in a forensic reconstruction or identification.

Evaluation of probative value versus prejudicial is also difficult. Even if the evidence presented is not convincing, it can still have a deep emotional impact on jurors if it is synthetic evidence. At the other extreme, though, the fear that a person's images and voices could be replicated may result in courts placing too much weight on bogus evidence, which would be the "liar's dividend" effect. A chain of custody becomes ever more complicated if the evidence goes through several steps of AI processing (Lai, 2023). Every change results in introduction of new variables which are not easy to capture in detail. Further, questions of liability or responsibility come into existence who is at fault if evidence created by AI is used in a criminal trial to see someone convicted of a crime that they did not commit?

It is these issues that are exacerbated in cross-jurisdictional cases where legal principles vary from one jurisdiction to another as well as technology. There is currently a lack of technical expertise for many judges to deal with these matters effectively and clarity in legal practice, resulting in inconsistency in decisions of judges. Together these challenges undermine fundamental tenets of Justice, which include the presumption of innocence, fair trial and a clean and honest fact-finding process. To ensure that they are not tarnished by the removal of evidence that may prove to be accurate and important in court proceedings, or by their admission of evidence that is potentially inaccurate, courts will continue to grapple without effective options in place to ensure that this does not happen.

5. FUTURE DIRECTIONS AND REGULATORY RECOMMENDATIONS

The vision of neural evidence in the courts will rely on an urgent, coordinated effort throughout legal, technical and institutional areas. With the ongoing development of generative AI tools, it is crucial to take proactive steps to realize its potential and ensure the integrity of the judiciary system. Legislative Reform should be first on the list. Specific legislation is required in this area of neural and AI-generated evidence. These should encompass clear definitions, progressive levels of acceptability for the level of AI involvement (e.g. enhancement vs. full generation), compulsory disclosure conditions and trust only in systems certified. As in the case of electronic records, India could add specific provisions to the Indian Evidence Act about synthesised media.

Technical Safeguards and Standards need to be compulsory. It should become legal requirements for court-imputative evidence to include adoption of universal standards like C2PA (Content Credentials), a mandatory watermarking for AI-assisted content, as well as the recording of the Court-interpretable, immutable steps of AI processing of evidence. Prior to using AI forensic tools in investigations, these tools should be assessed and certified by independent entities. Judicial Capacity Building as well is very important. There should be courses in AI, neural networks, detecting deep fakes and digital forensics at judicial academies. Existing AI evidence benches or technical assessors be made available to major courts as an additional resource for judges handling complex cases.

Neural evidence handling should feature uniform processes, while its quality should be enhanced by multiple detection tools, a human-AI mixed verification procedure and a detailed record of model parameters and training data sources.Neural evidence handling protocols should be standardized, the number of detection tools should be set, the verification process should include a human-AI mix and a complete documentation of the model parameters as well as the sources of training data. There is scope to have a country-wide or international repository of validated Forensic AI models to secure reliability.

International Cooperation is a requirement to tackle the synthetic media's trans-border dimension. Forums such as the UN, INTERPOL or the Budapest Convention on Cybercrime should be established to develop harmonized standards, including cross-border approaches to responding to AI-generated deepfakes and mutual recognition of the methods of validation of evidence of such technologies.

Ethical and Human Rights Safeguards should be taken as part of all frameworks. This involves a regular bias audit of the forensic AI models, a Privacy impact assessment and measures for safeguarding vulnerable groups from deepfake abuse. In the long-term, a "reliability spectrum" approach could be taken, which takes the following into account: Whether neural evidence is transparent and validated, as well as the nature of the risks (447). Research into more effective detection technologies, and more explanatory AI (XAI) should be given more focus (Adinda et al., 2025). Over the next decade, these rules will be molded with critical actions. With careful consideration and cooperation among technologists, lawyers, law enforcement, and policy makers, evidence resulting from the brain can play a powerful role in the justice system. If a court, however, does not act decisively, the bedrock of the relation between weakening people and the court could be destroyed, thus undermining the pursuit of truth in courts across the world.

6. INTERNATIONAL COOPERATION AND JUDICIAL CAPACITY BUILDING

Thriving solutions to the problems neural evidence presents for criminal justice around the world require international cooperation and judicial capacity building. Since generative AI and deepfake are two technologies inextricably linked, a deepfake fraud produced in one jurisdiction may be utilized as proof in a different. The borderless nature of the generative AI and deepfake technology also can pose serious legal problems regarding jurisdiction and proof. Close cooperation on an international level is thus essential to form a uniform standard, exchange best practices and achieve uniform approaches to authentication and admissibility.

Currently there is no common philosophy or system for dealing with neural evidence. Although EU regulation under the AI Act sets standards for AI systems deemed to pose a high risk, and the United States has state-level laws against deepfakes, there is no widespread legislation anywhere else in the world that covers all types of AI. International body initiatives or model frameworks focused on AI-created evidence should be led by international organisations like INTERPOL, UNODC, and the Council of Europe (Budapest Convention). MRA for certified Forensic AI solutions, standardised procedures for AI deep fake detection, and cross-border solutions for proving provenance for deep fakes, such as C2PA.

Capacity building for judges is also highly needed. Neural evidence is presently not very useful for most judges, prosecutors, and lawyers because without basic technical proficiency, they can't assess information from the brain properly. It is important to establish international judicial training programmes, workshops, and certification courses on AI forensics, based on the cooperation between organisations such as the International Judicial Academy, the Commonwealth Judicial Training Institute or regional ones. The programs need to include technical basics of neural networks, detection methods, testing for bias, explainability problems, and test for admissibility in law (Santillan- Lima et al., 2025).

In developing countries, a significant problem exists in particular because of limited resources. International cooperation to involve technology transfer, financing of Forensic labs, validation of detection technology. It would be valuable to have a global collection of datasets, machine detection models, and precedents of past cases, to create a level playing field. Collaborate scross-border research efforts between academic institutions, forensic institutes and police forces can speed up the process of developing effective and reliable detection and authentication techniques.

Capacity building also needs to be enhanced with the law enforcement and forensic experts. There needs to be a set of standardized training curricula, simulation exercises with real world deep fake scenarios and certification programs for digital forensic examiners with specialisation in examining neural evidence. Defenders should be trained also in order to be able to defend the questionable neural evidence, maintain balance to a fair trial. Moreover, international coordinated action should be guided towards the establishment of swift conjunctive reaction procedures in the event of such incidents involving the deepfake technique, sharing information regarding new generation techniques and concerted enforcement actions against malicious AI tools. Steps must be taken diplomatically to tackle the state sponsored deepfake operations and misinformation campaigns which potentially can impact the judgment.

It is hoped that once this is achieved, an overall, global resilience will be achieved that will enable an inter-jurisdictional evaluation of neural-derived evidence with reasonable ease and reliability. If there is time and attention put into judging capacity building in the absence of strong international relations the justice system could be buried by fake evidence, leading to more convictions of the innocent, more acquittals of wrongful and unearning guilt, and a loss of confidence in the justice system. These 10-15 years are crucial for establishing this foundation (Oyedokm, 2026).

7. CONCLUSION

Neural derived evidence is something that could receive renewed attention as an important challenge to the fundamentals of the criminal justice system since the advent of the information technology revolution. However, as powerful new tools that significantly increase the ability to investigate, generative AI and deepfake technology have also presented new ethical issues for courts, such as the importance of authenticity, reliability, and even truth as the legal process moves forward. The chapter has explored in depth the 'evidentiary, legal and ethical challenges' that come with neural evidence, ranging from being technically difficult to detect, to being black-boxed and opaque, to exposing risks of bias, to having problems of authentication, and more fundamentally, the tension with core human rights.

There is a need for an evolutionary trail, a brush of changes that seemingly can keep classical concepts and rules that traditionally determined what would and would not count as evidence, such as the Daubert standard, the Frye test, and Section 65B of Indian Evidence Act, fit when dealing with synthetic evidence. The challenge for courts everywhere is how to make trade-offs between the strong points of using AI for forensics and the significant issues of manipulation, fabrication and algorithmic bias. Deepfakes can lead to public mistrust of the justice system, and the "liar's dividend" effect exacerbates this issue by suspicious fake evidence, should anyone seek to use such a tool to defraud.

There are what can only be described as: technical, legal, institutional and ethical. Solving them cannot be done merely by making half a step improvement to current legislation. A fundamental overhaul is required, involving new laws to regulate Artificial Intelligence-generated and AI-assisted 'evidence', technical standards to apply to AI evidence and training, and more rigorous evidence of provenance and watermarking, as well as much greater training programs for judges and forensicists.

In the future, further progress towards responsible integration of neural evidence will require the establishment of multiple requirements for admission depending on the extent of AI engagement, increased focus on developping explainable AI research and collaboration at the international level around protocols for detection and evidence. Managing technical capacity in judicious structures must be a top-priority issue for countries, and they must have strong protections for privacy and fairness, as well as due process.

The integration of neural evidence brings an unprecedented challenge to the robustness and adaptability of justice systems in a world rapidly changing with technology. When implemented collaboratively by the technologists, the legal community, policymakers and international organizations this technology can help to augment investigations, improve accuracy in complex cases and improve access to justice. But, where the regulatory and capacity gaps are not plugged, the opinions of the neurologists may be a game-changer and they can manipulate judicial decisions and undermine the basic judicial rule that judges are supposed to find truth. These decisions taken today on regulation, capacity building and international cooperation crucial will help neural-derived evidence to be a trusted partner of justice, or the worst threat to it. Balancing innovation with a steadfast commitment to upholding the integrity of judicial processes is not just about wanting to empower the judiciary, it is imperative for preserving the rule of law in a world inundated with AI.

REFERENCES

Adinda, F. A., Rahmawati, E., Suparman, E., Arifin, R., & Ezzerouali, S. (2025). The challenge of admitting electronic evidence in civil procedure law. *Jurnal IUS Kajian Hukum dan Keadilan, 13*(3), 656-680.

Bakhtiar, H. S. (2023). The role and nature of evidence: Forensic insight. *Human Rights (Chicago, Ill.), 8*(1), 81–100. DOI: 10.35586/jyur.v10i2.7072

DeMatteo, D., & Olver, M. E. (2022). Use of the Psychopathy Checklist-Revised in legal contexts: Validity, reliability, admissibility, and evidentiary issues. *Journal of Personality Assessment, 104*(2), 234–251. DOI: 10.1080/00223891.2021.1955693 PMID: 34357807

Erbas, R. (2021, December). Evidentiary challenges to an effective criminal investigation for domestic violence: an introduction. The 10th Anniversary of The Istanbul Convention: Italian–Turkish Conference, ed. by Valentina Bonini & Rahime Erbaş, Pisa University Press.

Findlay, M., & Grix, J. (2003). Challenging forensic evidence? Observations on the use of DNA in certain criminal trials. *Current Issues in Criminal Justice, 14*(3), 269–282. DOI: 10.1080/10345329.2003.12036267

Fry, E. (2014). The nature of international crimes and evidentiary challenges: Preserving quality while managing quantity. *Pluralism in International Criminal Law, Elies van Sliedregt and Sergey Vasiliev, eds (Oxford University Press, 2014).*

Grimm, P. W. (2017). Challenges facing judges regarding expert evidence in criminal cases. *Fordham Law Review, 86*, 1601.

Hussain, N. (2025). The Role of Forensic Evidence in Criminal Trials: Legal Reliability and Challenges. *Journal for Current Sign, 3*(4), 329–340.

Ibrahim, T. M. F. H. T., Muhamad, N. H. N., & Baharuddin, A. S. (2025). Maqasid Al-Shariʿah and Digital Forensics: Towards a Fiqh-Based Evidentiary Model in Syariah Criminal Justice. *Al-'Adalah, 22*(2).

Lai, M. (2023). Transcribing and translating forensic speech evidence containing foreign languages—An Australian perspective. *Frontiers in Communication, 8*, 1096639. DOI: 10.3389/fcomm.2023.1096639

Roberts, P. (2018). The forensic challenge. *Frontiers L. China, 13*, 43.

Santillan-Lima, J. C., Díaz, J. F., Piccirilli, D., Haro-Tufiño, K. A., Urgirles-Rodríguez, B., & Molina-Granja, F. T. (2025, October). Admissibility of digital evidence: integration of technical and legal standards in forensic and judicial contexts. In *International Conference on Advanced Research in Technologies, Information, Innovation and Sustainability* (pp. 252-266). Cham: Springer Nature Switzerland.

Wakili, S. A., Obisesan, O. O., Ekpenisi, C., Antai, G. O., & Umo, M. E. (2025). Legal framework and challenges concerning forensic evidence in Nigeria. *Trunojoyo Law Review*, *7*(1), 33–64. DOI: 10.21107/tlr.v7i1.28599

Chapter 7
Neural-Derived Evidence in Courts and Forensic Contexts: Case Studies

Hemant Singh
http://orcid.org/0000-0002-1258-5187
Amity University, Gwalior, India

Saurabh Kumar
http://orcid.org/0009-0005-4594-1597
Chanakya National Law University, Patna, India

Pragya Singh
http://orcid.org/0009-0003-5397-1492
The Neotia University, West Bengal, India

ABSTRACT

Evidence from some areas of the nervous system be it brain imaging or electrophysiological data has been increasingly used in the courts to substantiate allegations of mental state, deception, criminal responsibility, and injury, among other things. Technologies, such as fMRI, EEG, and PET scans, have advanced to a level that can provide information about brain structure and function, however, these technologies bring several challenges for the field of forensics with regard to reliability, admissibility and interpretability when it comes to psychiatric issues. In this paper, the focus is on critical technologies, here are some famous landmark products from the United States, India, and other parts of the world, and there are unsolved evidentiary issues.

DOI: 10.4018/979-8-3373-9720-7.ch007

1. INTRODUCTION

Embracing neuroscience in the courtroom is undoubtedly a revolution in legal practice that will shift the judgment-making power towards a more unified, scientific approach.This emerging field is on the verge of reshaping the way court decisions are made, essentially transforming the power balance in legal proceedings to something much more scientific and integrated. The term "neural-derived evidence" is used to describe data provided by brain imaging and electrophysiology methods which claim to provide information on cognitive function, mental state, deception, trauma or neurological defects. Its potential for objectively capturing subjective experiences of consciousness is a topic which continues to be debated in courts around the world, and it has critical reliability, generality and interpretability issues. This chapter discusses the case studies, admissibility to some degree and the justice system implications. It emphasizes the usefulness of neural evidence in reducing sentence and/or making it clear that the person may be unfit to stand trial, but also warns against the danger of too much reliance as scientific evidence has its limitations and may be biased (KAN, 2025). Setting a high standard for responsible integration is necessary to train and equip judges, and to provide ethical safeguards to ensure that evidence derived from the nervous system that supports the administration of justice does not lead to its impairment.

United States v. Semrau was a key precedent in the United States in 2010 which established an accurate standard for the evaluation of functional Magnetic Resonance Imaging (fMRI) lie detection, and was affirmed by the sixth Circuit in 2012. In a healthcare fraud case, the defense wanted to present the findings from an fMRI Examination, which it argued represented a generally truthful statement on the defendant's intent. The court refused to admit the evidence under the Daubert standard, which it noted is that some studies reported a rate of 60-70% for false-positive results; the ecological validity of the evidence was difficult (because the evidence was from a laboratory setting, and not from a natural setting where deception occurs); and general acceptance in the scientific community did not exist. The decision showed that using fMRI, researchers can see the difference in blood flow between mental effort and different thoughts, but don't have a reliable method for determining which thoughts in particular are untrue or dishonest for a particular person. The ruling has played a significant role in controlling other cases, and it has restricted the use of fMRI mainly as a mitigating device – not as an accurate way to prove a person is telling the truth.

The other famous American case was that of Herbert Weinstein in 1992 when defence lawyers provided evidence of a large subarachnoid cyst in his frontal lobe, which was captured from CT imagery. Weinstein has been charged with strangifying his wife and tossing her body out of a window (Darby et al., 2023). The photos were received for an insanity/diminished capacity defense but the expert was not allowed to make a direct connection to the crime scene and having the cyst. The case became the basis for a plea of manslaughter because of "humane" brain defects, which sentencing is believed to have touched, as well as effecting verdicts in other cases. If a murder appeal happens, the evidence can be seen on the brain scans in about 5% of cases and even as high as 25% in death penalty cases, and these results lead to a change of the sentence towards a more lenient indicating neurological damage or disorders.

1.1 Scope of Neuroscientific Evidence

The most politically charged instances of such testing in India was the person who faced a conviction in the 2008 murder case in Pune, in which part of the case was foreshadowed with the use of a "Brain Electrical Oscillation Signature" (BEOS). BEOS, developed by Dr. Champadi Raman Mukundan detects cognitive reactions in the brain when the person is given a set of questions related to the crime picture, which allegedly differentiates the "experiential knowledge" (if the person had participated in it) from simply being aware of it. The judge referenced the scan as evidence the suspect had that the only person with would be the perpetrator. The method did, however, come under much criticism because it was not rigorously peer-reviewed to validate the technique and because it involved self-incrimination. Later the Supreme Court of India doubted the feasibility of compulsory brain testing and weighed it against presuming the right to innovate.

Neuroimaging has also been used to determine criminal responsibility. For a juvenile defendant accused of serious crime, structural MRI scans were submitted in Commonwealth v. Chism that revealed volumetric abnormalities that suggested schizophrenia. The court cited the multidisciplinary consensus reports which warn of the temporal disconnect to and from the scan after the crime and the issue of comparison groups (Darby et al., 2024). However, this evidence often tips the scales in sentencing toward treatment rather than just punishment. PET and fMRI machines have been used to designate brain injury in foreign civil litigation, especially PTSD cases, and have provided evidence for physical changes in brain activity, the blurred lines of the brain between physical and emotional injury. In this latter context, neuroscience can be more readily admitted in the sentencing stage, where its value will be in helping frame the case for a lower level of blame arising from injury to the frontal lobes, impacting on a person's ability to control their impulses.

1.2 Historical Development in Forensic Applications

Challenges remain profound. Neural evidence has problems with daubert.The daubert criteria testability, peer review, error rates, general acceptance, these are problems for neural evidence. Essentially most reviews assume the group means and thus risk inferences at the individual level the "group-to-individual" inference problem. Brain activity is correlated, not causal, and can be affected by other factors such as medication, anxiety or the social and economic environment. The images can give jurors the sense of certainty and preference that distracts them from the other evidence, and are often in colorful depictions of the brain. Rights against self-incrimination give rise to privacy concerns that might be raised given the possibility that forcing the scans might potentially uncover more information than was meant to be.

1.3 Intersection of Neuroscience and Legal Systems

While these obstacles exist, the evidence from the brain can be helpful in a few ways, of course, but not predominantly as exonerating or conclusive; for now it is more of a not-guilty piece of evidence. Development of standardized protocols, sophistication of AI analysis to improve the ecological validity, and to formulate interdisciplinary guidelines are future directions. A more basic understanding of neuroscience principles is needed for judiciary training to ensure that the concepts are not misinterpreted. With the development of technology, the legal systems should become more grapcious to the advantages that the technology brings to equity and keep the evidence of neural activity contributing toward justice and not toward sensationalism. If integrated in a responsible manner, more complex and better understandings of human behavior, better rehabilitation outcomes, and equitable adjudication may result (Call et al., 2025).

2. TECHNOLOGIES BEHIND NEURAL-DERIVED EVIDENCE

Neural-derived evidence utilizes advanced technology which records the structure, functioning and electrical communication in the brain to discern mental imagery, emotions, deceptive or traumatic events, and neurological irregularities in cognitive processes. Such tools have moved from the clinical and research venues to forensics and legal application (Bakhtiary et al., 2026). These tools are now in use not just in clinical or research situations, but in the forensics and legal environments as well where traditional evidence is subjective or lacking.

The central and yet predominant research technique of this area is structural and functional neuroimaging. Magnetic Resonance Imaging (MRI) provides high-resolution pictures of brain structure, which can be detection evidence for abnormalities such as a tumor, lesion, cyst, or developmental abnormality. In forensic contexts, SMI has been employed to reveal frontal lobe damage or frontal lobe atrophy which can result in alterations to impulsive control and/or decision-making. fMRI is a type of MRI that detects changes in blood oxygenation, as human brains process different tasks. Can observe areas that are activated when deception, remembering or processing memories are related to emotions (Marchant, 2026). Promising for the study of lie detection, but has limitations of ecological validity, fMRI is unlikely to be a representation of real-world situations. Positron Emission Tomography (PET) and Single-Photon Emission Computed Tomography (SPECT) can help to evaluate metabolic activity and blood flow, which can be valuable in the evaluation of a traumatic brain injury or dementia or psychiatric conditions that are associated with criminal responsibility.

Electrophysiological techniques provide very good temporal resolution. EEG detects the electrical activity produced by using electrodes placed on the scalp of the person which measure event-related potentials (ERP) including the P300 wave evoked when a familiar stimulus is encountered. Dr. C.R. Mukundan of India has developed a technique known as Brain Electrical Oscillation Signature (BEOS) profiling which is based on the EEG techniques to detect the "experiential knowledge" of the crime, which is either from the direct participation or through a second awareness from the victim or witness. BEOS has been used in a number hundred of Indian cases, but has received a number of restrictions when it comes to court admissibility. A complementary approach that combines high temporal and spatial resolution can be achieved by measuring the magnetic fields resulted from neural currents as measured by magnetoencephalography (MEG).

New tools and the future innovations are broadening the opportunities. The functional near-infrared spectroscopy (fNIRS) is a portable, inexpensive system for measuring neural activity in the brain. Using so called multimodal data, combined fMRI with EEG data is now analysed by more advanced AI and machine learning algorithms, thus providing better pattern recognition (Reddy, 2025). Progress along with brain-computer interfaces and real-time decoding procedures makes it possible that we will be able to recreate thoughts or visual images from neural patterns. TDI involves a brain mapping technique, Diffusion Tensor Imaging, which is used to determine white matter connectivity, which can be helpful in assessing traumatic brain injury.

Although technology is advancing day by day, there are still issues to be faced. The majority of techniques give correlational data not causal data. There are limitations to forensic reliability due to individual variability, confounding factors (medication, anxiety or countermeasures) and the "group-to-individual" inference problem. Brain scans are not necessarily timely, either, which means that what is seen now does not necessarily depict a person's mental state when the crime was committed. Relibility advances critically with integration of multimodal data, and standardization of protocols. The technologies will bring us ever deeper understandings of people as they develop, but have to be used wisely to avoid exaggeration or mis-use of law. The use of RUD must be accompanied by synergies of interdisciplinary cooperation between neuroscientists, forensic specialists and the legal field.

3. ADMISSIBILITY STANDARDS AND LEGAL FRAMEWORKS

The admission of evidence derived from the nervous system in the courts depends on the requirements contained in the respective jurisdictions for scientific reliability, relevance and prejudice. There are two standards that prevail in the United States, namely the Daubert test and the Frye test. To be considered generally accepted in the field in question, as will be required under the Frye test, if it is a scientific technique, the technique must be generally accepted within the scientific community. The modifications of Frye that are used for novel scientific evidence remain in use in many states. Federal judges are gatekeepers, however, under the tougher standard set forth by Daubert v. Merrell Dow Pharmaceuticals (1993). Multiple factors are taken into account: Testability/Falsifiability, Peer review and publication, Known or possible error rates, General acceptance, Standards-driven techniques. Daubert has been used to render an fMRI lie detection analysis unreliable and/or invalid, as in United States v. Semrau (2010), where the expert testified insufficient reliability and error rates, and lack of ecological validity were cited against the fMRI.

However, globally, methods of teaching and learning are quite different. Brain Electrical Oscillation Signature (BEOS) testing was early in public discussion - in the case of Pune murder in 2008 - but raised the Supreme Court's gaze in Selvi v. State of Karnataka (2010). The Court has held that use of neuroscientific tests in criminal proceedings is incompatible with Article 20 (3) against self-incrimination, but is allowed if the use is voluntary, with modifications. While in the UK and other European jurisdictions there is a softer, case by case approach to assessment with a focus on reliability and fairness, in some countries neuroscientific evidence is used more readily at sentencing. In the context of mitigation, however, increasing acceptance is evident in both Canada and Australia, while in the context of guilt phase there seems to be a continued cautious approach (Albright et al., 2023).

It complicates and adds to the ethical and constitutional issues. Issues of concern include the right against self-incrimination, privacy of mental condition, and possible infringement of the subjects' body and/or mind. Coercive brain scanning is a huge issue of freedom of thought. There also are potential "seductive allure" in colorful brain images that can affect juries beyond the merit of the case, blying them to the point of taking undue importance of potentially "inaccurate" evidence. Issues of inequality occur when use of costly MRI scans is biased towards the better-off defendant. With the advent of big data, new challenges arise concerning the protection of data, data storing and potential misuse of neural profiles.

In most jurisdictions, training of judges is still deficient. Neuroscientists and the public face legal professionals with limited knowledge on how to interpret the experts' claims.Judge and lawyers have an inadequate level of neuroscience literacy to be critical of the experts' claims. This lack of information can lead to cynical rejection, or credulous endorsement of information. Many courts will allow neural evidence for what they call "mitigation" cases or civil damages cases (for instance, establishing traumatic brain injury) but they will not be used for establishing mens rea or deception.

Two further recommendations are that future frameworks should include specific evidentiary guidance for neurolaw or the obligation to certify experts who testify as such; and that there needs to be a protocol for the acquisition of scans and a protocol for interpreting scans. Incorporating neuroscientists, ethicists and jurists in interdisciplinary panels could offer a basis for best practices to evolve (Hefetz, 2025). However, with the proliferation of emerging technologies, the law needs to harmonise innovation with protection to guarantee that evidence based on the brain promotes justice through a non-arbitrary, reliable and non-violation of fundamental rights. International efforts and more research on how the standards can be applied in practice are needed to achieve harmonisation of standards at the jurisdiction level.

4. APPLICATIONS IN CRIMINAL AND CIVIL CONTEXTS: LIE DETECTION AND DECEPTION ASSESSMENT; MITIGATION IN SENTENCING AND RESPONSIBILITY DETERMINATIONS

The neural-derived evidence has been widely utilized in criminal and civil actions, most notably in lie detection and deception evaluation, and in sentencing and responsibility calculations. Sneak detection methods, including MRI and EEG, are used to detect brain activity patterns indicating lying, such as persons lying exhibiting greater activation in the frontal lobe, specifically the prefrontal cortex and anterior cingulate cortex, are being explored in cases of criminal offenses. The tools were designed to help overcome the shortcomings of current polygraph tests, which focus on peripheral physiological indicators, by using tools that measure cognitive effort. But courts are wary because of the number of errors and lesser validity in the real world. In real life, it's not usually the kind of evidence that can be used in court to prove someone's guilty or not guilty, but it might be used to reinforce or destroy witness credibility.

A more accepted use is in mitigation when determining a sentence and criminal responsibility. Structural MRI (and PET) can show abnormalities in the brain, that may include damage to the frontal lobe, tumor, cysts or brain atrophy, associated with impaired impulse control, emotional regulation or decision-making. Prosecutors often suppress, and defense attorneys introduce these scans, as evidence that reduces the defendant's culpability, argues for the possibility of diminished capacity and/or insanity, and can lead to lighter sentences, the possibility of treatment, or not going to death. In juvenile cases, for whom evidence has identified immature brain regions, those influences have cropped up in U.S. Supreme Court decisions on sentencing.

It is widely accepted in civil cases that neural evidence is valid to establish the occurrence of a traumatic brain injury (TBI), post traumatic stress disorder (PTSD) or cognitive impairment. Plaintiffs provide fMRI or DTI scans showing that the brain is physically damaged or changed in structure and/or function or that they have limited earning capacity and/or lost pain and suffering because of it. Neuroimaging provides an objective way of quantifying psychological injuries that can otherwise be subjective (Fabian, 2026). Scans can be used to show signs of dementia or neurological impairments in disputes over mental capacity in contracts.

5. CASE STUDIES

5.1 Landmark U.S. Cases on Lie Detection and Brain Abnormalities

Neural evidence has been a strong influence on judicial interpretation across the U.S. in the context of lie detection and also brain abnormality.The landmark U.S. cases have greatly influenced judicial attitudes toward neural evidence in lie detection and brain abnormality claims. In the case of United States v. Semrau (2010), the defense representation sought to offer fMRI lie-detection evidence in the context of a fraud trial, in an effort to show the defendant's truthfulness. The court rejected the evidence as a result of its error rates, lack of standardization and the lack of scientific acceptance for actual use in forensic science practice, and excluded the evidence. This has set a high standard for using fMRI as evidence of deception in federal courts.

In 1992, the case of People v. Weinstein came down that was one of the earliest influential cases that dealt with abnormalities of the brain. Charges of murder read against Herbert Weinstein for the murdering of his wife. Defense experts showed a series of CT and MRI scans, depicting a large arachnoid cyst in his front lobe, which they said made him more impulsive and unreasonable. While the judge forbade linking the evidence directly to the cause of death, the neuro imaging evidence is a factor in a plea agreement for manslaughter, instead of murder. This case ushered in "neurolaw" defenses.

In Roper v. Simmons (2005), Graham v. Florida (2010), and Miller v. Alabama (2012), the U.S. Supreme Court cited advances in neuroscience on the issue of adolescent brain maturation specifically the underdeveloped prefrontal lobe to prevent or reduce severe punishment for youth. Individual scans were not being used, but these decisions were based on neurodevelopmental evidence, which was made legitimate (Zheng et al., 2024).

Recently, brain imaging has been seen in many death penalty mitigation cases. In State v. Stanko and other cases, brain injuries – caused by trauma or sickness seen on MRIs – have been cited in securing life sentences, instead of execution. During the penalty phase, such evidence is growing to be accepted in court; during guilt, it is growing to be doubted.

5.2 Indian Experience with Brain Electrical Oscillation Signature (BEOS)

Although the use of Brain Electrical Oscillation Signature (BEOS) profiling in forensics has come in for a lot of controversy, India has been using it for years in court cases. Developed by Dr Champadi Raman Mukundan, the BEOS is an EEG-based method which measure brain responses to probes related to crime. It distinguishes between semantic knowledge (from second hand sources) and experiential (personal knowledge from having participated in an event).

The most notable case was in 2008 in Pune, in Maharashtra where a woman named Aditi Sharma was convicted of murder in large part thanks to BEOS test results. The fact that it was a scan that could only have been obtained by the perpetrator was accepted as evidence by the court. Neural evidence was involved in one of the first worldwide cases where it was directly presented as evidence at trial. In several other such high profile cases, police in Maharashtra and other states used the BEOS as a part of their investigations and took charge of hundreds of cases.

This method was, however, criticized by the scientific community due to the lack of validation in peer-review journals and its uncertainty and unspecificity. The landmark case of Selvi v. State of Karnataka (2010) before the Supreme Court of India declared that compulsory administration of BEOS, narco-analysis or polygraph tests were unconstitutional and infringed upon Article 20(3) of the Constitution (which deals with self-incrimination) and Article 21 (which deals with right to go further in life but not beyond the law). The Court said these tests will have to be done, if at all possible, by informed consent alone and not as compulsory tests.

5.3 International Forensic Applications

Neural derived evidence used in internationally forensics applications reflects innovation and prudence in different jurisdictions. Neuroimaging evidence is widely introduced in the United Kingdom at sentencing and in cases of diminished responsibility, as set out in the Homicide Act. In cases of brain injury, psychopathy, or neurological disorder that would affect culpability, British courts have considered the fMRI and structural MRI.

The use of neuroscientific evidence has been increasing in the justice and mental health systems in Canada. PET and SPECT scans have been accepted in Courts in Australia in cases relating to traumatic brain injury and behavioural effects. Neuroscientists routinely provide expert evidence on, for instance, criminal responsibility and parole or rehabilitation in some European countries, e.g. in the Netherlands and Germany.

While details of some cases have leaked to the public, it is said that China has successfully employed brain imaging and a technique similar to a polygraph on numerous investigations. The R v. Albert case (2011) was brought into public attention in Italy, where the testimony of fMRI to evaluate the defendant's mentality was presented (Jalava et al., 2023). Neuroimaging is now being used in high-profile cases of violence in South Africa and other African countries, especially cases involving witchcraft or cultural defences and neurological problems. International criminal courts including the International Criminal Court have been interested in the use of neuroscientific evidence for the determination of command responsibility and mental capacity - albeit not extensively at present.

6. CHALLENGES AND LIMITATIONS

Often, neural-derived evidence is not particularly reliable and easy to accept in courts and forensic contexts to address some of the formidable challenges that scientists, lawyers, ethicists and practitioners must overcome. The group-to-individual inference problem is one of the scientific challenges. Most studies using neuro-imaging techniques use group averages but the courts make judgments about an individual.

This uncertainty is increased when trying to extrapolate data on population level to an individual defendant. Secondly, there are largely correlating instead of causal relationships in the neural data. Even the increased activity in some parts of the brain when people are lying doesn't necessarily mean they are lying, though other cognitively similar tasks, like anxiety, conflict monitoring or decision making, produce the same results.

One of the main limitations of ecological validity is still a significant issue. While lie detection fMRI in the lab typically involves a controlled and low-stakes situation, most situations involved in crime and deception is so emotionally charged, life-threatening, and countermeasures sophisticated that it can never be replicated in a lab experiment. Frequently false-positive errors are encountered in fMRI-based deception detection, with rates between 10-40% unavailable for forensic use. Some newer techniques, such as Brain Electrical Oscillation Signature (BEOS), have been criticized for the lack of independence in the tests used to validate those methods and replicability. Brain structure issues (e.g., frontal lobe damage) also pose challenges of interpretation — there are many people who have large brain lesions who don't commit crimes, and many people with normal brain scans who do,

It seems that incorporating neuroimages in the "seductive allure" of brain-based judgments carries a considerable risk of bias in cognition (Kadir & Mappaselleng, 2026). The vivid computer-generated images of brain scans that senators and jurors see during trials can be misleading and can cause them to give too much credibility to the testimony and so devalue the eyewitness testimony or circumstantial evidence presented to them. Research has demonstrated that the use of psychological testimony and/or neuroimages can boost perceived credibility for even when the images contribute no substantive evidence.

Likewise, important legal and ethical issues arise. Forced testing of the nervous system poses significant safeguards issues in terms of freedom of thought, mental privacy and the right against self-incrimination. The issues raised by the Selvi judgement in India and similar concerns in other jurisdictions raise constitutional issues. Concerns regarding data privacy, the storage over time of neural profiles and unauthorized access for non-forensic use of these types of data have also been raised. Expensive technology in the brain (neurology) works in favor of more affluent defendants – which can, in turn, result in inequality: that of the defendant in poverty versus the wealthy defendant.

Standardization is lacking. In a forensic environment, there are no fixed rules to follow when scanning: no fixed rules on the scan analysis, no rules for the expertise qualifications, etc. There are additional temporal uncertainties that make it difficult to properly evaluate the criminal's state of mind at the time of the crime several months, if not years, before — a brain scan right now can't tell how the brain was functioning at their time of crime. Other factors that can influence the results, like medication use, substance abuse, psychiatric disorders, age and socioeconomic status, are hard to control.

Last, but not least, those who work in the liberal arts field struggle with cross-disciplinary issues. Few legal professionals are as knowledgeable in neuroscience as they are about legal evidence and/or burden of proof, and few neuroscientists are as knowledgeable about neuroscience as they are about legal evidence and/or burden of proof. These problems are many faceted and indicate that the evidence provided by the nervous system is promising, but is fraught with limitations which necessitate both careful and limited use these days in particular, in order to corroborate or mitigate; not as proof. To rectify these weaknesses, substantial research efforts, uniform rules and constant education of the judiciary are necessary (Aggarwal & Jain, 2024).

7. CONCLUSION AND FUTURE DIRECTIONS

Neural-derived evidence is a fascinating junction between neuroscience and law, and could provide new insights into human cognition, human behavior, and human responsibility as the crossroads of these two fields. A collection of case studies, from the United States, India and elsewhere, illustrates the capacity and the difficulties of using brain imaging and electrophysiology in judicial proceedings. Techniques like fMRI, EEG/BEOS, PET and structural MRI have shown good results with respect to influencing sentencing processes, mitigation and/or assessing damages for civil actions, but have yet to withstand rigorously set admissibility requirements with respect to establishing guilt or deceptiveness.

Overall, it is a message of guarded optimism. Evidence from the brain can humanise accused persons, show the impact of injuries which might not be readily apparent, and inform more sophisticated justice processes; including sentencing and the assessment of mental competence. The fact that scientific limitations on reliability, interpretation, and possible bias, require that it be relied on as additional and not instead of evidence, however. Excessive use of newly developed neurotechnologies may lead to violations of basic standards of fair trial rights and the integrity of the evidence.

The following areas should be focused on in future directions. The need to build clear judicial guidelines and admissibility frameworks specific to neurolaw are first. Possibly develop specific standards of evidence to reflect the specific features of neuroscientific evidence. Second, while much investment is required for interdisciplinary research, it is of ecological value, accuracy, and that individual-level inference models may be established. The addition of artificial intelligence and multimodal imaging (combination of the fMRI and EEG and behavioral data) has great potential to increase the extent of accuracy.

Third, comprehensive educational initiatives in the fields of judiciary and legal education must be undertaken to ensure that judges, lawyers and forensic professionals have adequate neuroscience literacy. Fourth, there is a need to create legal and international solutions to issues of mental privacy, consent and data protection and equitable access. Standards of forensic neuroscientists should be maintained by the establishment of an independent oversight body or certification system.

Applications in the next 10 years will likely be extended by new developments like portable fNIRS, decoding brain activity in real time, and powerful pattern recognition algorithms. But these of progress must be matched by increased protections. Strategies to pilot the programs in some jurisdictions, carefully designed research to establish validity and reliability, and effective reports of the percentage of errors and limitations should be common practice.

So, well-informed use of evidence from the nervous system can help create a more scientific, compassionate and fair justice system. It provides the opportunity to go beyond simply retributive models and consider models that include rehabilitation, proper culpability determination and improved mental health interventions. However, maintaining a careful balance between the adoptions of science and the upholding fundamental legal principles of fairness, reliability and human rights will have to be carefully carried out for success. The evolution of both the law and the technologies used in their administration has lagged behind the rapid progress of neuroscience. The law and its administration cannot keep pace with the rapid development of neuroscience, and must adapt in a proactive manner. Any near future events will decide if there will be more supporting evidence to justice or more lessons to learn in cautious use of technology. Policy creation, scientific research, and ethical oversight can play a crucial role in advancing truth and justice in contemporary legal frameworks when handled with a thoughtful approach to addressing issues of neurolaw.

REFERENCES

Aggarwal, N. K., & Jain, A. (2024). Neuroethics and neurolaw in forensic neuropsychiatry: A guide for clinicians. *Behavioral Sciences & the Law*, *42*(1), 11–19. DOI: 10.1002/bsl.2638 PMID: 37983666

Albright, T. D., Baltimore, D., Mazza, A. M., Mnookin, J. L., & Tatel, D. S. (2023). Science, evidence, law, and justice. *Proceedings of the National Academy of Sciences of the United States of America*, *120*(41), e2312529120. DOI: 10.1073/pnas.2312529120 PMID: 37782804

Bakhtiary, H., Eslamitabar, S., Shiarzian, S., & Lame, E. (2026). Challenges of the Application of Emerging Neuroscience Technologies in Courts. *Avicenna Journal of Medical Biotechnology*, *18*(1), 32. DOI: 10.18502/ajmb.v18i1.21043 PMID: 42080114

Call, A. A., Wilson, L., & Wingrove, T. (2025). Neuroscience Evidence and Legal Decision-Making. In *Decision-Making in Life and Work: Foundations, Strategies, and Current Neuroscience* (pp. 209–256). Springer Nature Switzerland. DOI: 10.1007/978-3-031-88415-3_10

Darby, R. R., Considine, C., Weinstock, R., & Darby, W. C. (2024). Forensic neurology: A distinct subspecialty at the intersection of neurology, neuroscience and law. *Nature Reviews. Neurology*, *20*(3), 183–193. DOI: 10.1038/s41582-023-00920-0 PMID: 38228905

Darby, W. C., MacIntyre, M., Cockerill, R. G., Stephens, D. B., Weinstock, R., & Darby, R. R. (2023). In the courts: Ethical and legal implications of emerging neuroscience technologies used for forensic purposes. In *Ethics and Clinical Neuroinnovation: Fundamentals, Stakeholders, Case Studies, and Emerging Issues* (pp. 173–193). Springer International Publishing. DOI: 10.1007/978-3-031-14339-7_10

Fabian, J. M. (2026). Forensic Neuroscience and the Law: The Brain on Trial. *Forensic Neuroscience and Violence*, 678-696.

Hefetz, I. (2025). Integrating AI systems in criminal justice: The forensic expert as a corridor between algorithms and courtroom evidence. *Forensic Science*, *5*(4), 53. DOI: 10.3390/forensicsci5040053

Jalava, J., Griffiths, S., & Larsen, R. R. (2023). How to keep unreproducible neuroimaging evidence out of court: A case study in fMRI and psychopathy. *Psychology, Public Policy, and Law*, *29*(1), 1–18. DOI: 10.1037/law0000383

Kadir, Z. K., & Mappaselleng, N. F. (2026). Neurocriminology and evidentiary standards in Indonesian courts. *Priviet Social Sciences Journal*, *6*(1), 579–588. DOI: 10.55942/pssj.v6i1.786

KAN, C. H. (2025). The examination of neuroscientific evidence in the criminal trial process: The importance of collaboration between criminal law and neuroscience. *International Journal of Eurasia Social Sciences/Uluslararasi Avrasya Sosyal Bilimler Dergisi, 16*(59).

Marchant, G. E. (2026). Applications of Forensic Neuroscience and the Law. *Forensic Neuroscience and Violence*, 643-654.

Reddy, K. J. (2025). Neuroscientific Evidence in Legal Proceedings. In *Foundations of Criminal Forensic Neuropsychology: Bridging Mind, Law, and Criminal Justice* (pp. 213–238). Springer Nature Switzerland. DOI: 10.1007/978-3-031-83771-5_9

Zheng, D., Considine, C. M., Weinstock, R., Darby, W. C., & Darby, R. R. (2024). Forensic neurology: Practice considerations and training opportunities. *Neurology*, *103*(1), e209560. DOI: 10.1212/WNL.0000000000209560 PMID: 38833660

Chapter 8
Neurorights Legislation and Responsible Innovation in the Brain Data Era

Arunima Shastri
http://orcid.org/0000-0002-6260-1253
Christ University, Bangalore, India

Laeeq R. Janjua
http://orcid.org/0000-0002-1948-5859
WSB University, Poland

Saurabh Chandra
http://orcid.org/0000-0003-4172-9968
Symbiosis Law School, Symbiosis International (Deemed to be) University, Pune, India

ABSTRACT

Neurorights law has become an important field to protect human dignity, mental privacy, cognitive freedom, and other fundamental rights and freedoms of every person in the Brain Data Era, where excessive amounts of intimate brain data generated by advanced neurotech including brain-computer interfaces (BCIs), neural implants, wearables EEG, AI-assisted neuroimage systems and is collected through thought decoding, revealing thoughts, emotions, intentions and cognitive state. Led by some neuroscientists are proposed rights that address mental privacy as the right not to be subjected to gathering or decoding of neural data without consent, cognitive liberty as the freedom from the possibility of coercive manipulation of one's

DOI: 10.4018/979-8-3373-9720-7.ch008

mind, personal identity as the right not to have one's sense of self, or the right to one's identity, altered, equal access to neuroenhancement, and protection against algorithmic bias and discrimination.

1. INTRODUCTION

The Brain Data Era exacerbates risks of privacy and intimacy as neural data is available and can be used to provide "brain surveillance", decoding of the contents of one's thoughts, or subtle orientation of one's thought by closed-loop systems and this is not possible with genetic data (Robertson et al., 2025). Current regulations such as HIPAA in the U.S. and GDPR in Europe provide some protection to cover clinical situations and fall short in terms of consumer neuros. Neurorights law can close these loopholes by treating neural data like genetic information under the existing GINA, including by requiring the administration of neural data to obtain explicit, revocable consent; purpose limitation; and rights to explanation and to have one's neural data erased when lawfully granted. But, excessive regulation, in the extreme, could inhibit innovation that could change the lives of the more than 3 billion people worldwide who suffer from a neurological disorder, whether that means restoring mobility with a BCI, alleviating depression through precise stimulation or improving communication for people with locked-in syndrome. Responsible innovation resolves this tension through two concepts: 'sandbox regimes to test innovativeness requirements', 'ethical review boards embedded in the corporate governance framework', continuous assessment and reporting on the effects, and international coordination to prevent 'mosaics of different regulations that will harm ethical innovation' (Mia, 2025).

1.1 Defining Neurorights

These rights are geared toward special susceptibilities experienced by neurotech and may have been overlooked or inadequately addressed by existing human rights regimes–which were conceived for the analog era. In 2021, Chile passed its constitution to include protection for brain activity and mental integrity from neurotechnologies; a landmark Supreme Court decision in 2023 confirmed neural data as a highly sensitive personal identifier by ruling that a U.S. company (Emotiv) must delete neural data it had collected from a previous senator.

1.2 The Rise of Brain-Computer Interfaces and Neurotechnology

This surge of Latin America has spread. Neurorights and neurotechnologies regulations have progressed to the level of proposals of a national council on neuroethics, whether in the context of a constitutional or legislative framework, in countries such as Mexico (with the General Law on Neurorights and Neurotechnologies of 2024), Uruguay, Brazil, Colombia, Argentina and the Cantabria region of Spain. The OECD's 2019 Recommendation on Responsible Innovation in Neurotechnology advocates for a framework that emphasizes the 9 principles of responsible innovation including assessing safety, protecting data, making sure it is accessible to everyone, engaging in work collaborative with stakeholders, and considering it could be misused; and UNESCO has worked through its International Bioethics Committee reports for ethical governance. Neurotech aspects have been included in the EU AI Act, though various parts of the system have either high-risk or low-risk classifications, and GDPR enhancements for neural information have been considered, yet there still are requests for specific neurorights declarations. The approach of Privacy laws taking incremental steps in US states is unevenly concentrated but growing, with Colorado's HB24-1058 (2024) being among the first to recognize neural data as protected biological data, and California's SB 1223 (2024) (effective 2025) updating the CCPA to add neural data as a new category of sensitive personal data that brings rights for consumers to access, delete, and opt out of sale/sharing. At the federal level, Congress has now taken initial action when, in 2025, Senators Schumer, Cantwell and Markey introduced the MIND Act of 2025, which calls on the FTC to conduct a study on how to manage neural data.

1.3 Ethical Imperatives for Human Brain Data Protection

These advancements are centered on responsible innovation, highlighting the need to advance these technologies while maintaining respectful levels of ethics, law, and societal protections. It calls for the incidence of values such as beneficence and non-maleficence, respectability for autonomy, and fairness and justice in the R&D process from its early stages to its final commercial use. Companies working on BCIs (such as Neuralink) must place a greater emphasis on developing systems for robust informed consent that extend beyond medical ethics, taking into account the nature of neural data – interpretive, predictive, and potentially permanent. Technical Best Practice recommendations to avoid the commodification or weaponization of brain signals include data minimization, on-device processing, encryption and strict use restriction practices as outlined by OECD guidelines. It is important for neuroscientists, ethicists, lawyers, policymakers, industry and civil society groups to work together and for the public to have the opportunity to discuss among themselves how to establish the public's trust in the development of these technologies (Di Salvo, 2025). The problems are plentiful: clarifying what is considered "neural data" under one jurisdiction and not the next (for example, distinguishing neural signals vs. inner thoughts), enforcing compliance across jurisdictions while diffusion of new technologies continues, privacy concerns from a point of view with therapeutic uses as opposed to those being used for surveillance or enhancement purposes, the possibility of inequitable access in a population to harm them a population neuro-divide (wealthy vs. marginalized populations), and the danger of inequities in AI algorithms trained on neural data and applied to populations in employment, insurance, or justice systems.

2. GLOBAL LEGISLATIVE DEVELOPMENTS

Legislative changes globally speak of an increasing awareness of the need for a broader awareness of the human rights issues in the Brain Data Era brought about by neurotechnologies. The fact that these developments reflect a new approach to governance – a proactive one that anticipates harms via the use of a risk-based approach, through partnerships with the public and with adaptive processes, is significant. The momentum is a sign of the growing international agreement that the data of the brain should be afforded high-level protection on par with the genetic data, and that favourable conditions for sharing and using should be promoted. Finally, how well these measures are achieved at the legislative level will shape whether neurotechnology will improve individual flourishing or invade the inner temple of human consciousness.

2.1 Key International Frameworks and Declarations

Normative principles for ethical governance of neurotechnology have been provided by key international laws and declarations concerning neurorights. The OECD's 2019 Recommendation on Responsible Innovation in Neurotechnology is fundamental, and has been adopted by 39 countries. It defines nine principles that favour safety evaluations, privacy protection, inclusiveness, engagement with stakeholders and scientific co-operation, open deliberation within society, protection of data, anticipation of misuse and stewardship cultures. It is a soft-law instrument which drives policy-makers and innovators in a human-centered development. In November 2025, UNESCO undertook a comprehensive but first-of-its-kind global normative framework, the Recommendation on the Ethics of Neurotechnology, that builds on this. It takes a rights approach that spans the entire life cycle of neurotechnologies while focusing on mental privacy, cognitive liberty, personal identity, transparency, consent, protection of vulnerable groups and convergence with AI ethics. The recommendation calls on the member States to promote their incorporation into the national legislations, taking into account cultural contexts.

These are complemented by regional efforts. The Declaration and Principles (2021 and 2023) on Neurosciences and Human Rights (NHR) provided by the Organization of American States (OAS) has had an impact on local projects in the region. The Latin American Parliament (Parlatino) endorsed in 2023 a Model Law on Neurorights which offers a framework for constitutional amendments and laws in the member countries. Neurotech features are built into many relevant EU regulations, such as the EU AI Act (which considers some emotion recognition and biometric technologies as "high-risk" and prohibited) and GDP (where they will consider neural data as sensitive health data in many cases). Other contributions are from Council of Europe concerning human rights implications and national charters such as the Spanish Digital Rights Charter (Rudroff, 2025).

2.2 National Initiatives (Chile, EU, US, and Others)

Neurorights policies at the national level show also different conceptions that reflect legal traditions and technological settings. Chile has led the way in international protection of mental integrity, brain activity and resulting neural data via the constitutional amendment of 2021 (Law 21.383). In a historic 2023 land mark Supreme Court ruling, Emotiv, a U.S. company, was ordered to destroy a senator's brain data on a precedent-setting basis. Passage of legislation (Bill 13.828-19) continues to progress in Congress as of 2026, with a number of outstanding issues in the debates regarding the language of inferred data and commercial applications. This model has been adopted in Latin America: The general law on neurorights and neurotechnologies in Mexico (GNN) proposes the creation of a national neuroethics council, and Brazil, Argentina, Colombia and Uruguay have developed similar legislation which has been boosted by the Parlatino Model Law.

By contrast, there are no neurorights laws in the European Union but rather protections exist as part of other laws. Much of the neural data is sensitive under the GDPR, and the AI Act not only broadly applies to AI systems related to the identification or analysis of emotions or biometric categorisation of persons, but also prohibits manipulative uses of such systems. Ministers from several countries have signed the León Declaration following the 2023 principles on their digital rights. España has its Cantabria region and national digital rights charters, which reflect some of the ideas of the neurorights. In early 2026, nef federal protection in Canada was achieved by updates to the privacy commissioner that classified neural data as a sensitive data type.In 2026, for the first time, the federal protection of neural data was achieved in Canada by the inclusion of neural data as a sensitive data type in updates to the privacy commissioner.

2.3 Comparative Analysis of Existing Laws

To achieve convergence, existing neurorights laws are analysed in a comparative manner, identifying their strengths and weaknesses and areas for convergence. A judicial basis for protection of the mental integrity exists in Chile through the constitutional model, which explicitly protects neural data and neural integrity, and allows it to be enforced against a third-party use. As exemplified in the Emotiv case, this is the strongest rights-based protection available (Muravieva, 2025). It emphasises the concept of human dignity, has established a precedent symbolically worldwide but faces implementation issues such as mental states and innovation versus restrictions. The Latin American approaches through the Parlatino Model Law place a strong focus on comprehensive surveillance, consent, and redress mechanisms, which promotes harmonization at the regional level.

The horizontal approach of the European Union's regulation strategy incorporates elements of neurorights in the GDPR (when it comes to the sensitive use of data), the AI Act (at the level of high-risk classification and harm prohibition in using AI), and the Medical Device Regulation (in the context of sensitive data). Offers effective, internationally applicable protections based on a risk analysis framework; places focus on impact assessment of fundamental rights, transparency and accountability. It does not contain dedicated neurerights language, however, but instead has overarching language that covers data protection and AI governance, which may create a vacuum for anything that will not use AI but rather non-AI-based devices or consumer wellness apps. The federal government's decision to consider neural data a sensitive information is an important milestone toward a national norm.

The U.S. laws are broken and consumers are the focus. California, Colorado, Montana, and Connecticut have state statutes that grant privacy rights (access, deletion, opt-out/consent) to neural data, which have somewhat different definitions (e.g., does it include data from the peripheral nervous system or would inferred information qualify) and means of enforcing such privacy rights. The federal MIND Act is dedicated to study and gap analysis, embodying the best of both federalism: experiment and lack of uniformity. In contrast, U.S. rights' protections emphasize the market-based protection and innovation, which could generate a less rigorous level of protections outside the jurisprudence of court cases than other approaches such as Chilean Dignity or EU Systemic Risk, which emphasize dignity as the basis for rights. Chile is strong on symbolic and constitutional aspects; the EU on comprehensive aspects and enforcement; and the U.S. on agility and sectoral adaptations.

3. CHALLENGES IN BRAIN DATA GOVERNANCE

The data governance challenges to brain data in the era of neurotechnology are vast and complex, surpassing the scope of present day legal, ethical and technical frameworks. Brain-computer interfaces, wearable EEG caps and advanced brain imaging technologies through AI yield unprecedented amounts of private neural data that can unveil thoughts, feelings, intentions, subconscious states and brain patterns. The "Brain Data Era" poses special dangers, in addition to personal data, genetic information, or biometrics, because brain data is directly tied to many aspects of human identity, autonomy and mental life. Governance should encompass both collection and storage, interpretation, inference, real-time modulation, as well as impacts on individuals and society in the long run.

Some difficulties are that the brain signals are only partially interpretable: as AI technologies improve, mental states can be deduced from brain signals—fuzzy semantic distinctions between observation and mindreading. There are power differentials in workplaces, clinical settings and in consumer markets that mean that there is a lack of true consent; commercial interests bias the maximization of data, not minimization. Ensuring compliance becomes a challenge in a worldwide tech landscape dominated by a handful of strong competitors. In addition, there are dual use issues, for which therapeutic applications of a product vs. surveillance or manipulation is another concern that adds further confusion to regulation. Current regulations (e.g., GDPR, CCPA) provide some protection and typically can't account for the special sensitivity of neural data or non-clinical consumer use case.

Technology is progressing faster than policy: Definitions of "neural data" can't be standardised, devices are undergoing constant evolution and there are gaps in the protection of them from hacking, backdoors or algorithmic bias. Societies' challenges include equal access (the threat of a 'neuro-divide'), discrimination based on assumed mental characteristics, and a narrowing of 'cognitive liberty' through subtle influence. In the name of ethics, there is a need to give a weight to innovation, for treating neurological disorders, as well as mental privacy and integrity safeguards.

3.1 Privacy, Mental Integrity, and Cognitive Liberty Risks

The biggest existential threats in brain data governance include privacy risks, mental integrity risks and cognitive liberty risks. Neural signals provide direct access to the mind by decoding thoughts, emotions, memories and intentions without the subject necessarily being conscious. In addition to privacy of action, privacy of mind, mindfulness and access to neural data (such as subconscious states), is compromised by unexpected data collection, hacking and the intrusion of third parties who can draw highly personal conclusions on the basis of this information and cannot be ‘hidden' or retracted by the individual (Lopes, 2026).

The use of neurotechnologies and their potential for interfering with mental integrity, including for inducing undesired emotions, personalities, decisions and beyond with unintended stimuli through BCIs, is a risk. There are worries that the closed-loop systems which affect brain activity in order to improve or treat positive conditions could cause some form of psychological damage, changes in identity or loss of psychological continuity. Subtle behavioral manipulations, targeted ads based on emotional states or coercive applications in employment, education, or law enforcement threaten cognitive liberty: freedom of thought not influenced by others.

Consumers' neurodevices are not as secure as they should be and many companies in the data processing system accessing raw brain data stored in the cloud are subject to security breaches. There are reports of practices that allow very little or no access to neural data beyond broad access by 96%+ of the firms reviewed. Issues are aggravated by power imbalance, workers/patients might be forced to give up data without it being their choice of giving up. Biased inferences generated with AI can bring new risks, such as the possibility of discrimination during the recruitment process, insurance or judicial procedures, concerning mental characteristics predicted by the analysis (Mukherjee, 2025).

Current frameworks fall short since they are based on identifiability rather than the close, predictive power of a neural inference. If devices are not used in a healthcare setting such as a hospital or clinic, or the properties are not specified as medical devices, they will not be subject to medical laws such as HIPAA, thus resulting in a regulatory grey zone. Long term effects not known – may become addicted to enhancements, or may cause a loss of basic intelligence. Arising from these hazards is a world of surveillance, in which the refuge within the mind vanishes leaving individuals to become conformist or enhanced.

3.2 Data Ownership, Consent, and Commercial Exploitation

Owning, consenting to, and commercial exploitation of brain data are key governance issues in the brain data landscape. Ownership on neural data is unclear: Private companies create the data, extract rights on the terms of service, considering it as their property to use for training their models, monetize, and share among others. This may cause a product to be many users' worst nightmare because they become many consumers' victims: the loss of meaningful control of their most intimate contents.

Consent processes don't meet the needs of neurodata. Current notice and consent frameworks are inadequate since people often do not have awareness of what inferences AI might be able to make from their brain signals, they do not know how to prevent subconscious data from being shared, and there are power dynamics in workplaces or in clinical trials. With a continuous stream, Consent may in practice not be consent free or with full and informed consent and certainly cannot be revoked. Fewer than 20% of the companies reviewed actually have strictly defined conditions regarding data sales.Less than 20% of all consumer neurotech reviewed policies have a distinct policy surrounding potential third-party transfers of data strictly under terms broadly defined for companies (Bariffi, 2026).

These problems are exacerbated when commercial use is taken up. Brain data is being turned into revenue for publishers for advertising, behavioural profiling, or resale, bringing up dystopian speculations of mental commodification. With these gadgets for wellness and productivity, data will create addictive loops, or disciplinary code. lines are increasingly becoming blurred between therapeutic applications of the technology and enhancement/marketing ones and data maximization over data minimization and data security takes precedence for maximum profits. Most companies report allowing "hands on" and transference access, and weak deletion.

3.3 Technological and Enforcement Gaps

Reportedly, technological and enforcement gaps are major challenges in the effort for good governance in brain data. Definitions, standards and tools are outdated due to the fact that the field of BCIs and AI decoding is rapidly evolving, while regulatory adaption lags behind. Protecting is technically and legally tricky since it can be difficult to separate out signals from inferred states of mind. The processing, encryption and hacking resistance are variable from device to device.

Enforcement is fragmented: cross border data flows are out of reach of enforcement regimes, and there are dominant tech-companies operating across the globe while laws are national or regional. Consumers devices are frequently outside of medical regulations (HIPAA gaps), and many consumers devices do not have any meaningful audit trails or impact assessment. Very hard to prove harm from manipulation or probabilistic inferences in judicial systems. There is limited international harmonization, in the form of soft law instruments such as OECD and UNESCO recommendations, which are not given deadlines.

Data minimization challenges with streams, explainability of AI models developed from neural data and risks for long-term storage are all areas of technical difficulty. Algorithms can bias and lead to the perpetuation of discrimination, and states or private sectors can use the dual use technologies to conduct surveillance and monitoring. In smaller jurisdictions, and due to resource constraints generally, there is less oversight. The gaps need to be addressed by adapting the regulatory framework, such as through regulatory sandboxes, mandatory ethical review committees, standardizing technical rules and procedures (such as neurosecurity-by-design), and international cooperation for mutual recognition. Research spending on secure architectures and public information on risk need to be spent (Musole, 2026).

4. RESPONSIBLE INNOVATION PRINCIPLES

The key concepts of responsible innovation are to move away from reactive regulation to proactive, value-sensitive design, including ethics at the design stage. It requires interdisciplinary contributions, accountability and transparency in aligning the neurotech with fundamental rights and the values of society. In actual implementation, these transform into a "privacy by design" approach, in-depth evaluation of impact and a stewardship culture to make sure that companies are not simply the owners of neural data, but stewards who act as a trustee for neural data. The issues are how to maintain the therapeutic promise, whether your mobility is restored, a depression is treated or whether you are able to communicate, but how to ensure there's no enhancement divide, and mental surveillance or unintended identity changes. Principles promote open science and public engagement as well as regulatory sandboxes and ethical review boards for adaptive governance. Responsible innovation, by creating trust and collaboration among Governments, Industry, academia and civil society, will avoid a race to the bottom and speed up positive uses. In the final instance, adherence to these principles will help to carve out a way on which neurotechnology contributes to the improvement of human dignity and human flourishing, instead of human expression being reduced to a commodity (Cornejo-Plaza & Cippitani, 2025). On the whole, these principles will support neurorights laws and sustainable development in the Brain Data Era to ensure that neurotech benefits humanity and is not used to monetize human minds.

4.1 Ethical Design and Human-Centered Neurotechnology

So, responsible innovation is ethical design and human centred neurotechnology, covering the design of innovative neurotechnologies all the way from conceptual stage to deployment, with a deep respect for human values, autonomy and well being. It is important to focus on human factors engineering, user needs, capabilities and context in human-centred design, which aims to develop user-friendly, safe and accessible BCIs and neurodevices. This is not just 'usability considerations', but an approach that considers the psychological, social and identity impacts of chronic use – for example, what might be a consideration when thinking about sense of self and agency over the period of chronic use?

Four core ethical principles are beneficence (maximising benefits), non-maleficence (minimising harm), respect for informed choice (autonomy) and equal opportunity (justice). Designers need to see the need to create "neurosecurity-by-design," features such as the ability to perform calculations on the device, the granular option for consent, hard on/off buttons and robust encryption to prevent access points for hacking and unauthorized decoding. Value sensitive design embeds aspects of the mental privacy, cognitive liberty and personal identity of neurorights into architectures, while excluding architecture features that could allow for subtle-level manipulation or allow for enhancement of socioeconomic bias in inferences drawn by an Ai system. Additional protections are needed for the children, the elderly, and the disabled, who are among the populations susceptible to causing.

These include iterative user testing with diverse groups, ethical impact assessments of the whole lifecycle and transparency in capabilities and limitations. Open interoperable standards should be used with data minimization education for companies working on said projects such as Neuralink, and for consumer EEG wearables like this. Ethical design also calls for considering dual-use risks and issues, so that therapeutic technologies are not misapplied or repurposed to be used in surveillance or enhancement and to amplify inequalities. Implementing the ideals of training neuroethics developers, and setting up internal review boards according to OECD and UNESCO guidelines support them. Ethical design shows us that while enhancing humans is certainly part of the vision behind most innovative technologies, it is not about profit, but rather about people and the power they can harness; it is about those beneficial societal effects and impacts that last for generations, but could be reduced or eliminated if humans were at the forefront of the technology. When humans—not profit or speed—are at the center, the technology fosters public trust and societal benefits and reduces long-run harms to society; when humans are at the center, the technology really liberates individuals and empowers them to harness their tools responsibly and maintain the sanctity of the mind.

4.2 Stakeholder Collaboration and Transparency Standards

The public-private partnerships and open standards for trust are essential in the development of trustworthy neurotechnology ecosystems. A successful governance process needs to be ongoing, with the ability to listen and hear diasagenda breaking inter-sectoral conversations involving neuroscientists, ethicists, policy makers, industry, civil society, patients and the public, with a view to anticipating and co-creating solutions (Souza, 2025). At both OECD and UNESCO, scientific co-operation is clearly mentioned, as is societal consultation and engaging in an inclusive way.

Transparency requirements call for open dialogue about the way data is used, algorithmic decision-making, and associated risks and restrictions. Companies should ensure they make complete privacy policies available regarding neural data available, offer easy-to-understand explanations of neural inferences and inform customers about changes to policy or breaches promptly. Efforts towards accountability through open reporting of Safety Assessments, Bias audits, and impact assessments. Shared best practices, harmonized standards and procedures can be promoted through multi-stakeholder initiatives like industry codes of conduct, international forums, or data trusts.

By adding end-user input to the design and policy-making process, empowering independent watchdogs to monitor and report, and helping to make cross-border inter-agency cooperation more effective and efficient to manage global data flows, collaboration helps to offset power imbalances. Examples include collaboration projects and public hearings on neurorights bills or joint regulatory and developer collaborations to undertake experimentation in the so-called "sandboxes. Transparency also applies to the chains linked to it and data sharing with third parties, which curtails a black market of economic exploitation. There are some issues to reconcile proprietary interests with openness and ensure proper participation that is beyond tokenism.

4.3 Balancing Innovation with Safety and Accountability

Safety and accountability, along with suppleness, are certainly among the most tricky and essential elements of responsible governance of neurotechnology. Too strict regulations can undermine solutions for the treatment of neurological conditions impacting billions of people, too lax regulations can bring about mental privacy breaches, discrimination and unintended social issues. The idea is to allow progress without infringing on the core of the human rights, while regulating in an adaptive and risk-proportionate way.

Strict preclinical and clinical trial standards, rigorous post-market surveillance and the appropriate security measures are essential to tracking it to ensure safety, given its sensitivity. Mechanisms of accountability, including: explicit liability structures; mandatory auditing; and rights of redress, are in place for developers and deployers for harms. Focusing on "controlled testing" to make sure findings don't worsen poverty or lead to unforeseen negative effects, and "guardrails" with ethical review boards, impact assessments. There are international (OECD and UNESCO) frameworks that call for anticipatory governance – considering how the materials may be used out of their intended design, and designing them to be inclusive rather than leading to neuro-divides; and designing them to be socially useful and for stewardship by companies (Ding, 2026).

Practical measures encompass tiered regulation according to risk (higher monitoring for systems that pose more risks or are closed-loop systems), incentives for ethical innovation (flexibility and tax credits for products that comply with them, rapid approval mechanisms), and international harmonization, thus avoiding forum-shopping. There are important implications for industry self-regulation which, with the incorporation of binding neurorights elements, can speed up the process of best practices. Transparency is also a key component of accountability, with clear success measures beyond increased profits – such as enhanced quality of life, equity and trust. They need to constantly learn and adapt to the everyday shift in technology to maintain this balance.

5. CONCLUSION AND FUTURE DIRECTIONS

The problem comes in the fact that there is a need to achieve a level of universal standards, but cultural sensitivity needs to be taken into consideration, which means that concepts of privacy and autonomy may vary across cultures. Its key components may be adapted suitably to a possible UN or expanded OECD Framework proffered by the OAS Inter-American Principles on Neurosciences and Human Rights, and the Chilean model. In addition, industry self-regulation is available where stewardship cultures have established codes of conduct that individual companies agree to follow, such as user trust in companies' responsible stewardship over neural information, which can add to the amount of trust.

There is a need for an ongoing awareness of possible unforeseen side effects such as changes in identity after extended use of such devices (chronic) or pressure to improve cognition in society. Neuroethics education must be popularized and made the norm to arm citizens and individuals as "consumers". These are not debates about responsible "smart," or intelligent, attack on invention that leads to the development of new brains new human brains and increasingly seamless human-machine integration; this is not a debate about the assault of human autonomy and dignity as equal members of the human race by new technologies, but the protection of this inner sanctuary of the mind and the ongoing autonomy and dignity of its owners: human inventors. The potential for a transformative future driven by neurotechnology in the field of health, social and human wellbeing exists; it may be realised through responsible governance processes – and we must be proactive in having a say in shaping the future of this rather than let it be the dystopian future where mental products are sold or shaped. The future of the Brain Data Era will depend upon the laws, business models and global initiatives that are taken today.

REFERENCES

Bariffi, F. (2026). Mind, machine, and the law: Reimagining neurotechnology governance through disability rights. *Journal of Law and the Biosciences, 13*(1), lsag011. DOI: 10.1093/jlb/lsag011 PMID: 42147125

Cornejo-Plaza, I., & Cippitani, R. (2025). Principles of Research with Neurotechnologies and Artificial Intelligence: A Comparative Analysis of Latin American and European Laws. In *Contextualizing Neuroprotection: Latin American Perspectives on the Impact of Neurotechnological Development in Life and Society* (pp. 205–220). Springer Nature Switzerland. DOI: 10.1007/978-3-031-96055-0_14

Di Salvo, M. (2025). The protection of neural rights in the age of neurotechnologies and AI. The ethical challenge for law and neuroscience. *Russian Journal of Economics and Law, 19*(1), 202–233. DOI: 10.21202/2782-2923.2025.1.202-233

Ding, Y. (2026). From Ethics to Governance: Why Neurotechnology Requires Institutionally Actionable Concepts. *Neurotechnology. Society & Governance, 1*(1), 93–119.

Lopes, A. M. D. A. (2026). *Challenges for the regulation of neurotechnology companies*. Livraria do Advogado.

Mia, A. P. (2025). From Brain Evidence to Neurorights: Rethinking Criminal Responsibility in the Age of Neurotechnology. *Available at SSRN* 5588370. DOI: 10.2139/ssrn.5588370

Mukherjee, S. (2025). Neuro-Law and Brain–Machine Interfaces: Emerging Frontiers of Legal Responsibility, Rights, and Regulation. *AIJFR-Advanced International Journal for Research, 6*(5).

Muravieva, L. (2025). Regulating Neurotechnologies and AI-driven neural implants in the European Union: Legal and ethical challenges.

Musole, E. (2026). Governing Neural Data in the Global South: Toward a Neuro-Responsible Business Framework for Zambia. *International Journal of Advanced Business Studies, 5*(1), 47–61. DOI: 10.59857/g3bvjx74

Robertson, L. J., Higgins, N. L., Maier, M. J., Carter, A., & Gardner, J. G. (2025). Ethical Governance Strategies for the Responsible Innovation of Neurotechnologies: A Scoping Review. *Journal of Bioethical Inquiry, 22*(4), 1–18. DOI: 10.1007/s11673-025-10440-9 PMID: 41217705

Rudroff, T. (2025). A Framework for Responsible Innovation. In *AI for the Healthy Brain and Neurological Disorders: Neuroscience Innovation in an Anti-Science Era* (pp. 405–420). Springer Nature Switzerland. DOI: 10.1007/978-3-032-11596-6_18

Souza, J. D. N. (2025). Exploring New Frontiers in Personalized Criminal Responsibility through Neurotechnologies: Ethical Dilemmas and the Neuro-Rights Framework. *BioLaw Journal-Rivista di BioDiritto*, (4), 211–228.

Chapter 9
Neurorights Legislation in the Brain Data Era:
Forging Comprehensive Legal Frameworks to Safeguard Cognitive Liberty and Mental Privacy

Sukhwinder Singh
http://orcid.org/0009-0004-9025-2355
School of Legal Studies, CGC University, Mohali, India

Swarnima Gorani
http://orcid.org/0009-0004-2052-6891
Sharda University, India

ABSTRACT

The unprecedented threats to cognitive liberty and mental privacy posed by the rapid development and maturing of neurotechnology in the brain data era. This chapter reviews the development of laws that protect individuals against unauthorized access, manipulation and/or the commodification of brain generated information. Attempts are accelerating to form more far-reaching frameworks, from Chile's constitutional amendment through state constitutional bans in California and Colorado, and from UNESCO's Ethical Recommendations. However, there are clearly shortcomings with respect to the perceived mental data and regulatory convergence and enforcement. Enhancing existing laws is crucial to accommodate innovation and human right principles to protect human beings' personal autonomy, identity and freedom of thought in this world of connectivity and communication.

DOI: 10.4018/979-8-3373-9720-7.ch009

1. INTRODUCTION

With all those mood-enhancing brain-tech devices being popularised, like EEG headsets, cloth-on-head BCIs, and mental wellness accessories, mental privacy and cognitive liberty have emerged as hot topics in legal and ethical debates around consumer brain technologies. Neural data, which capture the activity of the brain's central or peripheral nervous systems, can provide intimate insights into thoughts, feelings, intentions, and more. Unlike other biometrics, the data is directly related to the substrate of thought and identity in the living organism, requiring special legal safeguards. Addressing such vulnerabilities, neurorights laws attempt to effectively present strong frameworks in the context of rapid advances in technology with a focus on prioritizing human dignity, autonomy and mental integrity (Farahany, 2023).

Chile was the first country to include protection for mental integrity and brain activity in its 2021 constitutional amendment, creating the first protection of neurorights. A groundbreaking reform, driven by the Neurorights Foundation and other experts such as Rafael Yuste, that brings about legal oversight of neurodata while guaranteeing that there will be no damages against physical and mental integrity. Subsequent applications for enforcement showed how it works in practice, such as in a U.S. company's 2023 Supreme Court case for the removal of improperly collected brain data (Yuste et al., 2021). These rights are further invioled and operationalized in the case of Chile, under the on-going law for the protection of the nervous system which handles consent, research ethics and non-discrimination issues. These rights are further contextualised and operationalised in the case of the Chilean law on-going “Nervous System Protection”, dealing with consent, research ethics and non-discrimination in access to enhancement.

Throughout Latin America, similar protections have gained traction as some countries, such as Mexico and Brazil, are looking into creating protections. At the international level, UNESCO's 2025 Recommendation on the Ethics of Neurotechnology is a non-binding but influential document that sets out principles of human rights-oriented governance, mental privacy, and preventing abuse, including manipulation, for this emerging technology. The changes bring an emerging agreement that current human rights (HR) instruments are not fit for purpose to tackle the challenges of neurotech.

The United States has taken a development-centric approach. The HB 24-1058 requiring neuroprivacy protections and heightened consent (in effect in 2024) was passed in Colorado.In Colorado, HB 24-1058 classified neural data as sensitive biological data within its privacy act, and has placed special protections and consent requirements on such data. SB 1223 (effective 2025) amended the CCPA to explicitly define neural data as sensitive personal information and provide consumers with rights to access, delete, correct and opt-out from sharing this type of data. Analogous measures were taken in Montana and Connecticut. These represent a real step forward and are quite disjoined and inconsistently applied between jurisdictions. In the federal arena, the proposed MIND Act (2025) would provide the FTC with jurisdiction to study and address a range of neural data issues could offer additional scope for federal oversight.

As progress has been made, so too have problems emerged. According to an audit of 30 consumer neurotech companies by the Neurorights Foundation in 2024, there are systemic gaps: the majority of firms provide broad access to neural data, often with little restriction, have unclear policies on the handling of neural data, and give wide-ranging sharing rights to third parties. Many companies consider devices a wellness device to avoid more stringent medical regulations, which continue the opacity of the devices. Data that is impossible to measure is called inferred data, and no clear laws define the protection of such data.

The principles of protecting mental privacy (from unauthorised access), mental cognitive liberty (freedom from mental manipulation and the right to exclude manipulation to control mental states), mental integrity (preventing harmful alterations to mental states) and equitable access to the use of these technologies are some key core principles. Good laws must include privacy features built-in, informational consent, data reduction, strong security, and independent, regulatory oversight. International harmonization is important, as well to limit forum shopping and to have uniform standards throughout the world.

The balance between innovation and protecting involves moving on multiple levels. Too narrow definitions could prevent medical advances like restoring BCIs for people who have suffered a stroke, paralysis, or mental health treatments based on brain signals. On the other hand, lack of protection has the potential of undermining autonomy: by surveillance, by discrimination, by neuromarketing. One has confirmed path forward that is based on adaptive, technology neutral legislation with a mechanism for review. Legitimacy and compliance building is essential and requires public education and collaborative activities between governments, industry, ethicists and the civil society.

For the future, neurorights should adapt to the new technologies that develop, such as closed-loop systems, inferences derived from AI, and consumer uptake in general. Future attempts to create a framework should equate the subject with the algorithm itself and include clauses banning non-consensual mental manipulation, as well as omens concerning the development of privacy-enhancing algorithms like on-device processing. Co-operation between States, perhaps at greater scale under UNESCO or new treaties will be important (Yuste et al., 2023).

In effect, the act of building overarching legal arrangements in the new age of the brain is not only about regulatory work, it's about a fundamental defence of what we know as a human being. Neurorights laws can promote mental privacy and cognitive freedom, enabling neurotechnology to help people flourish—for now as consumers, and ultimately as creators—rather than control them. The deeper into the society the technology burrows, the more it is the question of proactive rights-based governance ensuring that the "brain" will not be the final bastion of freedom and expression but more like another stream of data. While the work in Chile and in the U.S. states and international forums is going well, the necessary innovation and commitment of lawmakers is still needed to continue to confront challenges.

2. CONCEPTUAL FOUNDATIONS OF NEURORIGHTS

The neurorights are grounded in concepts respecting the ability of neurotechnology to offer new and unprecedented strains of problems relating to autonomy, identity and privacy of human beings. Neurorights" are new human rights that are tailored to make sure that people are not subject to the special dangers that technologies that directly connect with the brain and the nervous system present. Any such rights have as their purpose to ensure the rights to control one's mental processes and states of consciousness—the freedom to control one's mind, or mental privacy—freedom from someone else tapping into one's mind, coercing one to change a thought or amply affecting ones thinking with information that they do not endorse or agree with.

These form the pillars on which traditional human rights frameworks (including in the Universal Declaration of Human Rights) are developed and expanded but need to become applicable to the human brain as the birthplace of personhood, consciousness and self-determination. The growing market of consumer brain technologies, such as the EEG wearable, brain-computer interfaces (BCIs), and neural implants has created the urgent requirement for specially tailored protections. Neural signals can get much richer than these conventional data elements; they can determine in real-time what people are feeling, what they are thinking, what they are hoping to do, and even what thoughts and ideas are present out of consciousness.Traditional data is not nearly as revealing as these neural signals, which can alert to real-time emotional feelings, intentions, cognitive patterns and even subconscious biases, posing serious, ethical and legal dilemmas.

The main conceptual frameworks are mental integrity (prevention of adverse changes of psychological states), psychological continuity (maintenance of personality) and the equal accessibility of neuroenhancements. The Neurorights Foundation and theorists such as Rafaël Yuste have helped to define these rights and declared that current privacy regulations aren't referring to what's really occurring in the mind. The constitutional amendment of 2021 was Chile's first new law formally acknowledging that mental integrity is a protected right and thus establishing a precedent for the international community.

In a conceptual sense, neurorights are about proactive governance not the restrictive "letmercely," ingestive "regulate," or regulatory "inhibit" of movement. They believe in privacy by design, consent based privacy laws specifically for neural applications, and bans on non-consensual neuromodulation (and on manipulative applications, where appropriate). With the brain data revolution in the making, these bases highlight the importance of integrating between humanity and technology (Feitzen, 2023). The absence of robust concepts leads to the derogation of laws and lawmaking, which could result in more fragmented or insufficient laws, as people become increasingly target in the fields of wellness/entertainment, healthcare, and workplaces with the continual implementation of neurotechnology.

2.1 Distinctions between Neural Data and Other Biometrics

Unlike biometric data like fingerprints, facial recognition, DNA or even heart beat information, neural information is unique in that it is directly related to the inner workings of the mind. Recently, biometrics have been commonly used for identifying humans and monitoring physiological functions, whereas neural biometrics, based on EEG, fNIRS or BCI, now allows us to decode high-level cognitive and emotional information, intentions, attention item, etc. and even to predict future behaviors. It makes it uniquely personal and expository of personal traits, experiences or aspects of personhood that the person may want to be kept in private.

A major difference is about its dynamic and inferential aspects. Neural Patterns are not static like Finger prints or DNA markers, are context dependent and can show the "live" state of a mind. Even from rhetorical gestures such as those offered by seemingly friendly, obvious clues, such as a person's posture, such as a gesture. Even from rhetorical gestures, as seemingly friendly as it may be, or as obvious as a clue may turn out to be, such as gesture is something that can be revealed by advanced AI as being related to sensitive data, such as mental health conditions, political inclinations, or subconscious preferences. This increases the probability of "mind reading" and of predictive profiling, but beyond identification.

A second big difference between them is their ability to be cheated. Biometric information such as a person's iris is generally used for authentication, while neural information is used in closed-loop systems that can manipulate brain activity, thereby raising concerns about the respective notions of cognitive liberty and mental integrity. Identification risks are also greater: True anonymisation with advanced techniques is extremely difficult because the richness and the uniqueness of brain signatures.

These differences are further echoed in the approach of the regulations to the subject. Laws such as California's SB 1223 and Colorado's privacy amendments make explicit the existence of an added level of sensitivity in neural data that gives it greater privacy protection than ordinary "biometrics. There are other current frameworks, like GDPR or HIPAA, which are not suitable because they did not cater to current thinking where data touches the biological substrate of thought.

A Neurorights Foundation audit of consumer neurotech firms highlighted some of these gaps in 2024, showing there was hardly enough to do about neural-specific risks. To appropriately address these differences, there is a need for a more nuanced approach to how brains should be protected in the age of brain data, where distinct, customizable legal tools should be drawn on to prevent brain data breach affecting mental privacy and autonomy.

2.2 Ethical and Philosophical Underpinnings

The underlying foundations of neurorights are rooted in ethical, moral principles and human rights theory that have deep backgrounds. To treat individuals as ends in themselves, not data from which to extract data, is Central, which is the Kantian imperative. Brain is the centre of one's personality, awareness and volition and therefore any interference with the brain without permission crosses basic concepts of decency and freedom of the person (Sharp, 2025).

The idea of cognitive liberty is a philosophical expansion of John Stuart Mill's harm principle and freedom of thought to the realm of neurotechnologies. It is an assertion of "mental self determination" without the intrusion of another person in their mental process and without another person to be able to eye them when they are using it. The concept of mental privacy evolves from that of the right to be let alone as put by Warren and Brandeis, in keeping with the times when it is conceivable that one's thoughts can be observed or be for sale.

Other principles from bioethics that support are beneficence, the principle of doing good; nonmaleficence principle of doing no harm; the principle of justice, or fairness; and the principle of respecting persons. Justice issues with equality of access to neuroenhancing treatments must be taken into account alongside the risks of discrimination and/or social control which require non-maleficence protections. Psychological continuity (the thought that personal identity extends over time, and needs not be meddled with by neurotechnologies without permission) is emphasized.

Four fundamental neurorights mental privacy, cognitive liberty, mental integrity and 'psychological continuity have been proposed by influential thinkers such as Rafael Yuste and the Neurorights Foundation. These ideas have spread internationally, and the UNESCO Ethics of Neurotechnology Recommendation, for example, emphasises the human-centred approach to control over governance and bans manipulative uses of the technology.

In terms of ethics, neurorights are the balancing of the potential of neural technology for treating neurological disorders with the potential for surveillance capitalism and authoritarian control. Theoretically, they dispute reasons that hold that the mind is composed of information that can be measured, reinforcing the subjective, irreducibleness of conscious experience. During the brain data era, these foundations call on legislators to shift away from 'utilitarian cost/bene' analysis, and turn to a rights-based approach focused on human flourishing. Educating these ethical and philosophical concepts in law gives societies the power to ensure that technological advancements uphold and strengthen, instead of detract, from those values that define humanity.

3. GLOBAL AND REGIONAL NEURORIGHTS INITIATIVES

Since the beginning of the 21st century there has been an unprecedented amount of activity in international and regional neurorights initiatives, in part due to the rapid pace of development of the neurotechnologies that research preserves and enhance, and in part due to an increasing awareness of dangers to mental privacy and the various aspects of cognitive liberty. Chile was the first country to reform its constitutional system, modelling the process for other Latin American countries and Globally (Alonso, 2021). They are meant to be measures establishing specific protections over brain data, different from those of other privacy laws and protecting against specific risks of brain signals sharing emotional states, intentions or mental processes.

The Neurorights Foundation has been a major contributor to advocacy and aided legislative work around the globe. The momentum has infiltrated Latin America, given that constitutional amendments were proposed in Mexico, Brazil and other countries there. The Recommendation on the Ethics of Neurotechnology, adopted in November 2025, is the first international framework in its broadness: recommended by UNESCO at the global level. It focuses on governance that is rooted in human rights, transparency, informed consent and bans manipulative use of neural data.

Such changes signal a sea change towards proactive rights-based approaches, away from the reactive regulatory regime. But, there's work to do in implementing, enforcing and dealing with portrays that are not overt data from AI analysis. In the era of brain-based data, neurorights efforts are ongoing as they continue to develop and balance on the edges of on innovation and protecting foundational human attributes in the brain.

3.1 Chile's Pioneering Constitutional Framework

In the year 2021, the constitution of Chile was amended to incorporate neurorights as the first country in the world to do so, in Article 19. A particular part of the reform concerns the protection of mental integrity, and, respectively, the scientific and technological developments must respect physical and mental indemnity. It ensures there is a regulatory framework on the requirements, conditions and restrictions regarding neurodata and specific protection for brain activity and derived information.

This revolutionary clause, inspired by the Neurorights Foundation and neuroscientist Rafael Yuste, allowed to ensure that the privacy of mental state, free will, personal identity, and non-discrimination in relation to access to neurotechnology would be protected. In practice, in 2023, the Chilean Supreme Court implemented this framework to order that a collection of brain data by a US company (Emotiv) for a former senator be deleted because it was done in violation of their rights; this precedent was important for enforcement purposes.

The enactment of legislation (Bill 13.828-19) has come a long way since 2026, and continues to be discussed in the Chamber of Deputies. This bill aims to implement constitutional principles by providing specific procedure and guidelines for obtaining consent, conducting research, regulating neurotechnology, and fines for breach of the guidelines (Helbing & Mahajan, 2025). The healthcare-harmonia, human rights-based perspective on neurotechnologies is a Chilean model that is taught around the world, while exposing the many regulatory gaps and future challenges, especially for technologies involving drawdown of data from the mind. The framework proves itself a model that can be emulated by other countries, whilst at the same time highlighting the need for ongoing development within its application, as technology advances.

3.2 Latin American Developments

The introduction of neurorights laws in Latin America – a region which has become a global leader – has been influenced directly by Chile's pioneering work. In several countries initiatives have been undertaken to safeguard mental privacy through constitutional changes and bills in support of the protection of brain activity. Ryo seined the idea with the constitutionality of amending Article 5, which protects neural data, in 2023, Senator Randolfe Rodrigues, and the state of Rio Grande do Sul approved an amendment that does exactly that. In 2023, Mexico made strides with constitutional proposals through advocacy, and soon after, bills were introduced.

The Latin American Parliament (Parlatino) has been very active in creating a Model Law on Neurorights for guidance of its members (Splichal, 2022). Often these campaigns focus on mental privacy, cognitive freedom, informed consent and fair access to brain and mind technologies. The technological feasibility of neurotech to facilitate surveillance, discrimination or manipulation forms a shared concern in the region, and was evident in calls for regional cooperation.Joint calls for regional cooperation on surveillance, discrimination and manipulation issues due to the technological feasibility of neurotech in environments of different degrees of data protection maturity.

Countries too such as Uruguay, which has ratified the Council of Europe's AI treaty, also cross-fertilise with the issues related to neurorights. But it hasn't been consistent, and many proposals are yet to go through legislative approval as of 2026. Implementing capacity, harmonization across borders and dealing with new issues like "inferred data" given by AI systems are considered as challenges. The way Latin America has embraced the concept makes it an interesting site for the development of neurorights protections: valuable insights into how decisions are made around the world, and the need to tailor protections to the local context and technological realities.

3.3 UNESCO and International Efforts

The UN is leading the way in international neurorights initiatives with the adoption of the Recommendation on the Ethics of Neurotechnology in November 2025. UNESCO has been a major player in international neurorights activities with the adoption of the Recommendation on the Ethics of Neurotechnology in November 2025. This is the first worldwide norm which offers guidance to Member States regarding ethical development and use of neurotechnologies. It emphasizes human rights-based solutions, mental privacy, consent, transparency and bans manipulative use like non-consensual influencing or neuromarketing.

Major issues discussed in the Recommendation are data governance, protection of vulnerable groups – particularly children, equity in welfare distribution and safeguarding against discrimination or biases in the processing of neural data. It stresses on privacy by design, independent oversight and international cooperation, and on being technology neutral, which means that it can accommodate innovations down the road.

In addition to UNESCO, there are international initiatives at the advocacy level spearheaded by the Neurorights Foundation, and platforms of academic networks in favor of key principles—mental privacy, cognitive liberty, mental integrity, and psychological continuity. Global discussion continues through events such as forums like World Economic Forum and a variety of bioethics organizations (Sommaggio, 2024).

The UNESCO Recommendation is not binding but does have an impact on national policies and make for harmonising. It further aligns with the regional but also with the calls for a more robust enforcement system and standards across countries. As markets expand in the world of neurotechnologies, these international efforts seek to avoid an 'arms race' toward the bottom and to make sure technological advances are in line with universal human dignity and mental autonomy. Collaboration will be key to solving new problems such as making inferences using AI and international data transfers.

4. CHALLENGES IN FORGING COMPREHENSIVE FRAMEWORKS

The problems are tremendous in the spirit of the brain data era with the formation of full legislation on the topic of neurorights including regulatory, technological, ethical and practical issues. With the rapid development of technologies targeting the information found in the brain, such as personal EEG, to the creation of advanced BCI, the concern for the preservation of cognitive liberty and mental privacy is becoming increasingly critical, but not all lawmakers have dared to make the right steps towards effective and flexible legislation. There are significant regional and jurisdictional differences in regulation, as well as the challenge of finding a balance between innovation and robust protections, and the complexity of issues relating to inferred neural data and emerging technology.

Despite all that, the most frequently recurring discrepancies revealed by the Neurorights Foundation 2024 audit and subsequent analysis are: Consumer Neurotech companies continue to have ambiguous policies regarding how neural data is handled, third-party data sharing rights remain wide ranging, and lack of users' control over data. Even with the ground-breaking actions such as the Chilean constitutional change, there are unshaded areas in regard to data being implied. From an ethical perspective, the initiative to reach the 2025 Recommendations of the International Union for Conservation of Nature (IUCN) is of valuable guidance, however, in the absence of enforceable provisions. State legislation and initiatives in the U.S. are a tangle, and plans for a federal measure, such as the Bipartisan Winn Disaster Payroll and Innovation Disaster Research Act on Mental Illness and Recovery (MIND Act), are still in progress.

Such difficulties could lead to regulatory creep and regulatory arbitrage, with much of the innovation in medical neurotechnology being exploited by firms in weaker jurisdictions, while limiting its extent of consumer exploitation (George, 2024). Further complicating progress is the capacity for enforcement, the difficulty of finding clarity on definitions (particularly regarding inferred data), public awareness, and international harmonization. Flexibility to technology, collaboration between stakeholders, and technology-neutral mechanisms as they come are needed to tackle these. If these challenges are not addressed, neurorights frameworks could reduce progress on the implementation of technology, or they could be too weak, undermining basic concepts of human dignity and autonomy.

4.1 Regulatory Fragmentation and Enforcement Issues

Fragmentation is one of the issues most pressing with comprehensive neurorights frameworks that continue to be underdevelopment. The amendment to the constitution adopted by Chile during the 2021 elections established a precedent, especially at the international level, but its implementation will have different shapes and features in various countries. A state led approach has also generated some key laws for the United States in recent years, including California's SB1223, which recognizes neural data as sensitive, and Colorado's HB24-1058, which calls for increased consent around neural data; however, the disparate nature of these different laws has created compliance challenges for companies that are nationwide, leaving some citizens with uneven protection. To date, there have been no uniform standards as a result of federal efforts, such as the proposed MIND Act.

Internationally, the UNESCO 'Recommendation' 2025 is a very good ethical guideline to take but it is not binding, which results in a widely variable uptake across countries. Utilizing Chile's approach, there are bills on the table at parliament in a number of countries in the LAC region, with varying degrees of progress (Bublitz & Blitz, 2026). Fragmentation both allows data regulatory arbitrage and makes cross-border data flows and enforcement difficult.

Problems are exacerbated by enforcement issues. There are numerous laws that do not have specific agencies to oversee them, funding to support them or penalties for non-compliance. It is only technically and legally challenging to define exactly what neural data means, also at sorting out when the raw data matches the AI-created interpretation. Companies marketing these devices as neurotech products for consumers frequently label them as wellness products – avoiding the toughest medical regulations and lessening responsibilities. There are issues of public awareness and few exercise of rights to further weaken enforcement. Even Chilean's framework remains struggling to develop operational measures to guarantee safeguards for inferred data in non-medical settings as of 2026.

An increased need for model laws and capacity building for regulators and greater international coordination is needed to overcome fragmentation. If there is no greater harmonisation and enforcement, then it is possible that neurorights could turn out to be only aspirational and not protect cognitive liberty and mental privacy.

4.2 Balancing Innovation with Protection

A key issue of neurorights legislation is to strike the right balance between the need to enable innovation of "new technologies of the mind" and the assurance of "cognitive liberty" and the protection of "mental privacy (Blitz, 2026). Too "aggressive" a set of rules could deter progress in medical uses, including those for restoring the function of a paralyzed brain or helping those who suffer from neurological diseases, while too relaxed could leave people vulnerable to mental spying, manipulation and discrimination.

The ambivalent issue of the use of neurotech as improved cognitive functions and information about mental health and illness can be put to work across many other applications, including neuromarketing, monitoring employees at work, or influencing behaviour in the most sophisticated ways. What Chile has tried to do is balance this with the inclusion of protections for sensitive data and consent in its framework, while the state laws in the U.S. introduce some of the same concepts and restrictions. But, critics say, these laws and protections could cause compliance costs for smaller innovators. The MIND Act's approach is also a cautious one in terms of heavy regulation, which might affect U.S. competitiveness, before they get to the point of studying.

It is the UNESCO 2025 Recommendation that calls for human centred governance that promotes responsible innovation, emphasizing and enabling privacy by design and ethics (O'Callaghan & Shiner, 2026). But these principles will be hard to put into practice. There is a need for technology-neutral and adaptive AI regulations which reflect frequent developments in AI technology and closed-loop systems.

Being overly risk averse means that the adoption of useful technologies will be delayed and so will the achievement of equity of access, especially in lower-middle-income countries, while poor protection will mean that mental autonomy will become the norm. Balancing needs to include engagement of stakeholders (researchers, civil society, industry and ethicists) to create proportionate and risk-based frameworks. Incentivizing PWTs and providing sandboxes for testing can help facilitate innovation while maintaining other protections. Finally, a stroke of legislation should look at robust neurorights as drivers of trustworthy, sustainable innovation in the brain data age.

4.3 Addressing Inferred Data and Emerging Technologies

Inferred data and emerging technologies are one of the most challenging issues to resolve in the field of neurorights (RoA) frameworks. Inferred data (information about emotions, intentions, or thoughts based on the analysis by AI) is sometimes considered data in the legal gray area, unlike raw neural data. Chile's constitutional language in this regard is expansive – implementation is difficult because of the difficulty of defining what is "information derived from" brain activity, highlighted in the debates to date on the bill.

The original privacy laws such as GDPR or CCPA are not intended for these changes and the nature of predictive data, so there are still some lapses in protection from profiling, discrimination and manipulation. The use of new technologies like advanced BCIs, closed-loop systems and multimodal AI further muddies the waters by providing live feedback into the brain. These can bring new threats to cognitive freedom for which there is a lack of adequate infrastructure (Spinello, 2026).

Capsim has recognized that the inferences that are encountered in many of these consumer neurotech privacy policies are not discussed as thoroughly with regards to inferences.The analyses for the 2024-2026 point to consumer neurotech privacy policies that are not adequate to discuss inferences anywhere but chapter on inferences. The Recommendation of UNESCO requires protection against "manipulative application", but this is difficult to enforce because of lack of transparency and rapid change of techniques. Regulators have difficulty in defining the scope without being too broad and/or too quickly "out there.

The solutions need to account for flexible, risk-based approaches: establishing clear definitions for "raw" data, "processed data" and "derived data" and presenting the consequences of the algorithm as an impact assessment; and denying access of high risk uses, unless explicitly consented. Lighthouses need to be reviewed regularly by law and in collaboration with technologists. A proactive approach through to such problems can make or break whether neurorights can protect mental privacy in the age of constant technological progress or will fall behind the curve, leaving people exposed in the era of brain data.

5. PRINCIPLES FOR EFFECTIVE LEGAL FRAMEWORKS

A sound set of principles, based on respect for cognitive liberty and mental privacy, must form the foundation of neurorights legislation in the brain data era; ones that are accessible and effective, and flexible and responsive to technological change. Informed consent should be granular (specific), revocable, and ongoing (Di Ieva et al., 2026). Clear multi-layered information for consumers on what types of neural data is being collected, the potential inferences that could be made, how it is being saved, shared and/or profiled, including opt-in options for applications that are sensitive to such information. This not only involves generic privacy information but also visual representation of data flow and real-time controls.

Second, Privacy by design and transparency is basic. Government laws should ensure that by default all neurotechnologies will feature data minimization, processing on the device, robust encryption and pseudonymization. Businesses should have transparent privacy policies that include details about neural data, have periodic algorithmic impact assessments and should give annual transparency reports. Both of these laws make helpful parallel reading models: SB 1223 in California classifies neural data as sensitive, and Colorado has laws which call for explicit disclosures.

Third, there should be solid rights to access, rectification, deletion, portability and red Flag the objection to automated decision making should be exercised. Mental integrity protections should ban all uses other than what is meant to bring about this improvement to the mind, such as subliminal influence via consumer products, and nonconsensual neuromodulations or similar use of non-generic solvents. Fourthly, independent oversight and accountability mechanisms are necessary (Dixon et al., 2026). Enforcement powers of regulatory bodies or ethics committees, like the bodies along the lines of the data protection authorities, should be given powers to be able to audit, to fine and to order deletion of data as it is the case in Chile.

Finally, an international draft and technology neutral regulation do not facilitate regulatory arbitrage. Priorities should take inspiration from the UNESCO 2025 Recommendation, with a scope for periodic review that takes into account opportunities for new and evolving capabilities, such as highly sophisticated BCI interfaces or inferences using AI tools. Equity measures will need to be incorporated to ensure that the protection measures do not widen the gap between different groups of people in this context, thus enabling inclusive access to useful neurotechnologies.

There is an element of risk-based and proportionate regulation that strikes the balance between innovation and protection. Companies that use AI to monitor workers at their place of work or for neuromarketing or other similar applications, which are sensitive to privacy concerns, should be subject to much more restrictive regulations; meanwhile, less sensitive wellness applications could be subject to less stringent, but still transparent, regulation. Denials of such discriminatory uses of neural data, for example, in hiring, insuring, or educating, are essential to avoiding harm to society.

Third, by engaging the public and ethical integration, legitimacy is enhanced. Legislation needs to be inclusive of stakeholder perspective from the neuroscientists, ethicists, civil society and impacted communities (Damani, 2026). These principles, in turn, can be woven into the fabric of neurorights frameworks, shaping them from reactive guards, battling the infringement of human rights into proactive monitors of human dignity. Enabling elements for such comprehensive systems exist in Chile, in the U.S. state innovations and in UNESCO guidelines. Scaling up these principles globally and keeping pace with enforcement in line with innovation remains the challenge as of 2026, and the importance is the last personal freedom that remains: the mind.

6. CONCLUSION AND FUTURE DIRECTIONS

"Neurorights law" is an essential reaction to the enormous challenges of the era of data on the brain. As the regulatory landscape is expanding in scope and new laws are being introduced since more and more neurotechnologies become integral parts of the most intimate experiences of humanity, an all-encompassing framework is needed to protect cognitive liberty and mental privacy. Examples from various countries around the world show an increasing realisation of the need for new forms of privacy regulation, such as pioneering initiatives in Chile, progressive state laws in California and Colorado, and the UNESCO's ethical recommendations for 2025. In the context of these schemes, the imperative arises to look upon the neural data as a different sensitive category, and pass the highest protection against unauthorized access, inference, manipulation and becoming a commodity.

Achievement towards robust frameworks has been dotted with progress and remained areas of persisting gaps. The challenge of inferred data and the enforcement difficulties and regulatory fragmentation still prevent managing on a fully protective basis. However, there is a clear path to follow in this regard: the four pillars of informed consent, privacy-by-design, transparency and user rights as well as the presence of international cooperation. If they're applied right they can reduce risks and help to construct public trust around these devices and promote responsible innovation for the potential societal advantages that neuroscience could bring to healthcare, wellness, and human augmentation.

For the future there are some priorities. One way in which this is recommended is for countries to aim at harmonized model laws, for which extension could be UNESCO's Recommendation, which could be transformed into binding international instruments or region-specific treaties. Second, if State legislation in the United States were to build on the MIND Act, it could set a national standard without inhibiting or dampening State innovation. Third, there needs to be investment in research to complement regulation for issues of privacy enhancing technologies (on-device AI, homomorphic encryption, explainable systems), so as to achieve the goal of compliance in a practical and effective way.

Equity and global justice should also be included in future frameworks, with developing countries' interests not being ignored in either its protection process or in its technologies for protection. Evidence-based refinement of the neurorights law would be beneficial from longitudinal studies of real-world consequences on innovation, consumer usage and privacy violations from mental mechanisms. New applications like neural data in immersive metaverses, brain monitoring while at work and brain monitoring for military use need to be addressed proactively.

The ultimate test of the success of neurorights legislation will be its ability to ensure equal human rights in the age of technology. Societies have the ability to create thorough, flexible and rights-based policies to create neurotechnology that empowers instead of controlling. In an era of brain data, it is wisdom and creativity in the law that will be needed.Wisdom and creativity in the law is needed in an era defined by brain data and centuries-old values of autonomy, privacy and freedom of thought. It is essential to bring together in immediate action policymakers, industry leaders and civil society, to harness the momentum to a lasting protection of cognitive liberty for both past and future generations.

REFERENCES

Alonso, L. E. E. (2021). From Neuroethics to Neo-romanticism. Aldous Huxley in response to current proposals for ethical and legal regulation of neuroscience. *Scio*, (21), 113–148. DOI: 10.46583/scio_2021.21.783

Blitz, M. J. (2026). Cognitive Liberty and Rights to (and Against) Cultural and Chemical Transformations of the Mind. In *The Law and Ethics of Freedom of Thought, Volume 2: Cognitive Liberty, Mental Privacy, and International Law* (pp. 151-189). Cham: Springer Nature Switzerland.

Bublitz, J. C., & Blitz, M. J. (Eds.). (2026). The Law and Ethics of Freedom of Thought: Vol. 2. *Cognitive Liberty, Mental Privacy, and International Law*. Springer Nature.

Damani, D. N. (2026). Social Media, Algorithms and Children's Human Rights: Institutional Accountability in the Digital Age. *Algorithms and Children's Human Rights: Institutional Accountability in the Digital Age (January 18, 2026).*

Di Ieva, A., Tavallaii, A., Somerville, M. A., Suero Molina, E., DeGaetano, A., Mc-Cay, A., ... & Rosenfeld, J. (2026). The Declaration of Sydney: Ethical, Legal, and Professional Foundations of Computational Neurosurgery. *Legal, and Professional Foundations of Computational Neurosurgery (February 08, 2026).*

Dixon, J., Bark, H., Fang, C., Laing, J., & Patsios, D. (2026). The use of mental capacity and mental health laws in the care of people living with dementia in residential and hospital settings: A systematic review of the literature. *Dementia (London)*, *25*(3), 654–673. DOI: 10.1177/14713012251367810 PMID: 40816887

Farahany, N. A. (2023). *The battle for your brain: defending the right to think freely in the age of neurotechnology*. St. Martin's Press.

George, A. S. (2024). Protecting Brain Privacy in the Age of Neurotechnology: Policy Responses and Remaining Challenges. *Partners Universal Innovative Research Publication*, 2(5), 18–33.

Helbing, D., & Mahajan, S. (2025). Repairing, Reviving, and Upgrading Democracies in the Age of AI. *ResearchGate preprint.* https://www. researchgate. net/ publication/394105855. *Accessed, 18.*

O'Callaghan, P., & Shiner, B. (2026). Privacy 6.0: Privacy as Mental Integrity. In *The Law and Ethics of Freedom of Thought, Volume 2: Cognitive Liberty, Mental Privacy, and International Law* (pp. 93-115). Cham: Springer Nature Switzerland.

Sharp, D. N. (2025). Comparative frameworks for a human rights-based approach to psychedelics. *Human Rights Quarterly*, *47*(1), 63–86. DOI: 10.1353/hrq.2025.a951572

Sommaggio, P. (2024). Protecting my mind: Cognitive liberty, commons, and neurorights. In *The Discourse of Biorights: European Perspectives* (pp. 133–145). Springer International Publishing. DOI: 10.1007/978-3-031-66804-3_9

Spinello, R. A. (2026). *Cyberethics: Morality and law in cyberspace*. Jones & Bartlett Learning.

Splichal, S. (2022). *Datafication of public opinion and the public sphere: How extraction replaced expression of opinion*. Anthem Press. DOI: 10.2307/j.ctv2s2pp3n

Yuste, R., De La Quadra-Salcedo, T., & Fernández, M. G. (2023). Neuro-rights and new charts of digital rights: A dialogue beyond the limits of the law. *Indiana Journal of Global Legal Studies*, *30*(1), 15–37. DOI: 10.2979/gls.2023.a886161

Yuste, R., Genser, J., & Herrmann, S. (2021). It's time for neuro-rights. *Horizons*, *18*, 154–164.

Chapter 10
Neurotechnology, Mental Health, and Gender-Neutral Justice:
Brain-Computer Interface as a Tool for Addressing Cruelty Against Men

Yash Saxena
Amity University, Gwalior, India

Hemant Singh
http://orcid.org/0000-0002-1258-5187
Amity University, Gwalior, India

Radha Naruka
High Court of Rajasthan, Jaipur, India

ABSTRACT

In the field of mental health, public policy and a gender-neutral justice-for-all are where Brain-Computer Interfaces (BCIs) come into play as emerging neurotechnological means. This chapter discusses the potential of BCIs to mitigate experience of cruelty and abuse by the male population such as psychological trauma, and Domestic violence victimization, but also certain biases in legal approaches. BCIs provide opportunities for evidence in the legal system, personalized rehabilitation of mental health and objective assessment of trauma, as well as real-time monitoring and management of neural signals, states of mind, and therapeutic interventions. Although there has been a push to implement gender neutral approaches, privacy,

DOI: 10.4018/979-8-3373-9720-7.ch010

ethical consent, and access to services are key issues to be resolved. The chapter calls for a legal intersectionality of neurotechnology to achieve greater fairness and inclusion, as is required in mental health approaches in the modern world.

1. INTRODUCTION

Brain-Computer Interfaces (BCIs) represent much of the cutting edge technologies that unite neurotechnology, mental health intervention and emerging notions of gender-neutral justice, providing novel avenues to tackle the rarely reported problem domain of male cruelty and abuse in today's society. Evidence consistently shows that there are disparities in the rates of awareness and reporting of domestic violence and psychological cruelty for male victims, although the rates of such victimisation are not higher than those for women. Research suggests that 25%–40% of all survivors of domestic abuse are male, and that 1 in 7 men in the U.S. have experienced severe physical violence by an intimate partner, but that few men turn to formal help services because of stigma, expectations for male resiliency, and biases of services and legal systems. BCIs can be used to decode and modulate neural activity, facilitating a reduction in the dependency on subjective histories of traumatic experiences, which are often dismissed; furthermore they could provide a largely more objective way of documenting trauma, aiding therapeutic recovery and giving veridical evidence in gender neutral legal proceedings. It also provide some support for male victims of cruel treatment. Key to this is interdisciplinary collaboration between neuroscientists, legal and policy analysts who will need to work together to implement it responsibly.

BCIs have the promise of revolutionizing the field of mental health by treating trauma-related conditions, like PTSD, depression, anxiety, and emotional dysregulation that are widely associated with male victims of psychological, emotional, and physical cruelty. New non-invasive EEG-based and the still to-be seen invasive device platforms like the ones developed by Neuralink, or Synchron, will allow real time monitoring of brain state; and neurofeedback therapies can be offered to individuals in order to help them to self-regulate abnormal neural patterns in hypervigilance, intrusive memories, and mood disorders. Compared to conventional talk therapy, the feedback or stimulation for managing symptoms provided by a closed-loop BCI can be more precise and targeted and can potentially provide a more personalized response. The different technologies could give men identification of trauma from an experience of being treated with cruelty, from controlling behaviors to gaslighting, from physical violence; technologies that would be kindred markers when cultural norms portray men as victims rather than perpetrators of the violence. This objective information may help decrease a delay in diagnosis and enhance a person's outcome, helping to combat the stark difference in rates of suicide among men and women, where men have recently been four times more likely than women to have an untreated mental health problem secondary to abuse.

In terms of justice, BCIs could support gender-neutral legal systems by providing input from the neuroscientific evidence of psychological harm. Patterns of stress or trauma that the neural recordings show could support claims of family violence, including in cases of a custody dispute or for a sexual assault prosecution or for a restraining order. Emerging extensions to neurorights campaigns (which call for mental privacy, cognitive liberty, and blocking unauthorized use of neural data) are a basis for integrating some of that evidence while protecting rights (Koecke, 2025). In the U.S. state legislation has been enacted in California and Colorado to safeguard neural data, and the protection granted by GDPR and AI Act across the EU could also be applied to justice BCI. This way equity is how the rights of male incidents is seen as equal to others and challenging male victimisation biases in systems where male numbers claiming to be victimised (usually below 10-20%) are afraid of being found real incidents or even the perception of loss of manhood.

The technology in patents for BCI, or companies such as Neuralink (high bandwidth implants), Synchron (minimally invasive endovascular ways in which to implant), and more, seem to be steering all the innovation in the field toward mental health uses like treatment for PTSD and depression. However, equitable access under the strong IP protections is an issue as is cost, for both justice and health systems. Indeed, a range of potential measures, including licensing, public-private partnerships and ethical patent pooling, might facilitate greater accessibility for programs of victim support.

1.1 Evolution and Applications in Mental Health

There are some legal considerations that are complex. The reliability and validity of BCI-derived evidence must be carefully investigated to ensure that it meets the requirements outlined in the Daubert case in the USA, including algorithms and potential biases, and risks of over-interpretation of BCI-derived neural data (Said, 2025). This means privacy safeguards need to be in place to stop this misuse, including the potentially powerful tools of neural scanning and data exploitation, consistent with the approaches suggested by the declaration of neurorights, in which mental integrity is considered a fundamental human right. Informed consent becomes essential, especially with vulnerable populations, and the liability aspects will be hard to clarify in the courts in case of a malfunction or erroneous interpretation.

Opportunities continue in rehabilitation, and prevention. Neurotherapy, mandated by the courts or voluntarily participated in through BCI, can help achieve offender accountability and victim recovery in gender neutral programs, which can support the development of restorative justice models. Integrating public health could more broadly extend mental health support, helping to lower the burden of untreated trauma, lost productivity, and cycles of violence in the broader society. To build equitable standards, it is important that inter-disciplinary partnerships work between neuroscientists, lawyers, policy makers and mental health workers.

Issues remain, such as technical constraints such as signal stability and biocompatibility in addition to potential moral concerns like autonomy being undermined by neuro-surveillance and a risk of re-normalizing gender-typed roles if not carefully designed. Excessive reliance on technology may cause the lack of recognition or awareness of social factors of abuse and high costs may worsen disparities. Educational requirements and resistance from the cultural environment within justice systems need to be addressed through education and policy reform.

2. MENTAL HEALTH IMPACTS OF CRUELTY ON MEN IN MODERN SOCIETY

Psychological, emotional, physical and coerced control types of intimate partner violence (IPV), work-related harassment, and societal expectations, have significant mental health costs that are often not recognised or reported in modern society. Population-based studies suggest that IPV is a significant problem among men, with figures suggesting that physical, sexual, or psychological abuse rates are comparable to that of women, with up to 22.9% in large samples in the U.S., although the experiences of physical abuse may not be as extensive among men. Men face stigma, or the perception that they are stoic and perpetrators of violence, deterring them from seeking assistance, and in some jurisdictions, seeking assistance is less than 10-20%. This can result in untreated depression, anxiety, post-traumatic stress disorder (PTSD), substance abuse and higher risk of suicide.

Bullying or assault may not be as strongly associated to mental health damage as psychological cruelty, like "gaslighting," isolation, monetary control, or verbal degradation. Medium-to-large effect sizes are found in male victims for psychological IPV and related to PTSD, depression, and anxiety, confirmed by meta-analyses (Wallana et al., 2025). A common pattern among men who are experiencing this kind of abuse is emotional regulation, low self-esteem, social isolation, and a lack of trusting relationships. Chronic exposure reinforces a compounding effect in which a person's mental health problems create a greater risk for doing more harm and make him or her more vulnerable to doing harm.

Data from the public health system show that men who are victims are more likely to develop chronic mental illness, poor physical health and impaired ability to work and/or maintain family roles. In the UK, each year around 700,000 men are victims of domestic violence, with resulting social and economic impacts such as lost working time, use of health services and intergenerational effects. Neutral approaches to justice are necessary, but they can be exacerbated by other systemic barriers to empowerment for male survivors – such as lack of support and unequal access to justice.

Intervention opportunities encompass mental health-specific services, customized measures to counter stereotypes, and the incorporation of neurotechnology such as Brain-Computer Interfaces (BCIs) for non-subjective evaluation and treatment. If these impacts are not addressed, societies will inevitably suffer not only the individual, but also undetected suffering that will impact mental health overall, without fairness.Failing to address these impacts leaves societies vulnerable to unexplored suffering – resulting in imbalanced mental health. To validate and reduce the stigma and promote recovery in male victims, an interdisciplinary plane comprising of neuroscientific, psychological and policy perspectives is essential (Rustamov et al., 2025). Long-term unmitigated acts of hatred affect both the health and strength of individuals and communities, and a failure to address them in the modern-day healthcare and justice sectors leaves people more vulnerable.

2.1 Psychological Trauma and Neurobiological Effects

Psychological trauma as a result of cruel treatment of men elicits qualitatively different forms and expressions of neurobiological shifts as seen in other trauma groups but also has some distinct gender-specific characteristics. Prolonged exposure to emotional abuse, coercive control and/or physical violence triggers the brain's stress response systems including the hypothalamic-pituitary-adrenal (HPA) axis, resulting in disregulated levels of cortisol. For survivors, this can also take the form of hyperarousal, emotional numbing or hypoarousal, resulting in PTSD symptoms that are often experienced by males just as much as by females in some studies.

Regions of the brain that are affected include the amygdala which is overactive and responsible for increased fear responses and hypervigilance, the hippocampus, which may be underactive or reduced in volume, causing poor contextualisation of memories and intrusive recollections or dissociation, and the prefrontal cortex, which has reduced regulatory capacity, leading to reduced emotional regulation and impaired decision making. Such changes reflect chronic exposure to glucocorticoids and inflammation, and may give rise to structural changes including integrity of the corpus callosum and/or enlargement of the ventricles – some of which indicate greater susceptibility in males to some of the neurotoxic effects of maltreatment.

According to the science of neurobiology, an adverse event damages the ability of these systems to develop themselves and reorganized the neurotransmitter pathways (serotonin, dopamine) and epigenetic tags which can impact stress response from generation to generation. Male victims are often affected by depressive and/or anxious disorders, which also have strong associations (mediam effects) with psychological IPV. Trauma responses are associated with other symptoms such as erectile dysfunction, intimacy avoidance, substance abuse and impairment of work performance, which further increase burden and integrate with trauma responses.

These effects are not fixed, meaning that there are various factors such as resilience, social support networks, and intervention time that can help to modulate outcomes. Reporting is, however, under reported and that leads to delayed treatment times, resulting in the establishment of "fired" neural network changes that make it more difficult to recover. With the advent of emerging neuro-technologies such as BCIs, real-time monitoring of such dysregulated patterns and targeted neurofeedback to restore balance to affective circuits is possible, thus providing promise for an innovative future (Istace, 2025).

Recognizing these neurobiological signatures from a gender neutral justice perspective can give credibility to descriptions of psychological cruelty with objective evidence during a trial, while maintaining privacy and consent, leading to increased evidentiary standards in lawsuits. Further studies should focus on the longitudinal course of boys' development and at intersectionalities. It is essential to draw on the strengths of integrated care and the mental health and/or legal frameworks to mitigate the impact of long-term consequences, to heal and to respond equitably to trauma experienced by every victimiser and victim.

3. LEGAL FRAMEWORKS FOR GENDER-NEUTRAL JUSTICE

The legal responses to gender injustice within gender based domestic violence and domestic cruelty have also changed immensely, from gender-specific laws focused primarily on the protection of women to more dynamic, gender-inclusive and recognizing gender as an irrelevance, treating abuse regardless of the victim or perpetrator. Domestic laws in many places—such as the United States, United Kingdom, Canada, Australia, and some parts of Europe—are becoming gender neutral, emphasizing previous patterns of coercive behavior, psychological abuse, physical violence, and power imbalance toward women, instead of the assumption that these activities are carried out by men and directed at women. For example, some definitions in the U.S. Violence Against Women Act (VAWA) and those in reauthorization clauses extend to cover services for all victims; and state laws are also interpreted differently with regard to neutral definitions. In the same way, nations such as Canada and Australia have enacted policies that allow individuals a right to restraining orders, legal services and services of all kinds, on an equal basis with women.

This shift is in line with international human rights law, including the Istanbul Convention of the Council of Europe, which frequently focuses on violence against women, but contains articles that are general and relevant to violence against both genders, with a number of signatories expanding the scope of the Convention's definition of violence to cover acts against men.The evolution reflects international human rights law, specifically the Council of Europe's Istanbul Convention, which frequently addresses violence against women, but many of its articles apply to both men and women (Perez-Sales, 2026). By encouraging the use of gender-neutral models, gender recognition services will create an awareness of the experiences of male victims as a significant and under-served share of cases (ranging from 25 to 40% of intimate partner violence (IPV) as reflected in a number of different surveys). These frameworks may be further improved with the use of objective neural imaging data related to trauma, like pattern of chronic stress, emotional dysregulation, that could be provided by Neurotechnology, such as Brain-Computer Interfaces (BCIs), to support one party's claim in a family court or in a case involving protection orders or criminal charges.

Gender-neutral justice can be achieved through BCIs's integration in the legal system because to provide biomarkers that are readily accepted that go beyond bias. In cases where there is no physical evidence, neural data may be used to prove the effects of psychological cruelty, such as "gaslighting," isolation or threats, by using neural changes—such as amygdala activity, prefrontal regulation or stress-related biomarkers. Ethical use of neural data in the justice realm is supportable by emerging neurorights laws such as Colorado and California's which explicitly classify neural data as sensitive. This may help to maintain a restorative justice process, advance mandatory neurofeedback treatment of the victim and perpetrator, and improve risk assessment.

But there are obstacles to implementation. The historical mindset of IPV as a "women's issue" has an organic part in many legal structures, and this mindset leads to different kinds of reactions from police, the interpretation of laws, and different allocations of resources. While the patent-driven BCI innovations found in the companies (e.g., Neuralink and Synchron) offer an acceleration of abilities, they also have usability questions which are of greater concern in the public legal aid or less resource-rich environment because they are expensive. Harmonizing policies and/or laws internationally is not uniform, with some countries progressing with inclusive laws, others possessing gender-specific laws which exclude male victims.

There is a clear case for reform because of health and mental health intersections.Public health/mental health intersections support the argument for health reform. Untreated trauma in males also causes increased costs in society such as suicide rates, productivity loss and violence. Neurotechnology-based assessments in IPV cases may be required or purely voluntary (and thus potentially incentivized) by law, but the overall framework will need to ensure that such measures are cognitively sound, respect cognitive liberty and mental privacy, and enhance equity. Policymakers should work on creating policies to establish admissibility standards (similar to Daubertlike standards), data protection standards and informed consent standards that involve multiple disciplines, including neuroscientists, lawyers and victim advocates.

Patent licensing for humanitarian uses, public-private partnerships to support the use of BCI tools in courts, and training for judges and law enforcement on the interpretation of neuroevidence are just a few opportunities available. A strong, gender-inclusive legal framework, backed by compassionate neurotechnology, can do this much better, alleviate systemic biases, recognise the experiences of those affected by it and create a system of justice that is based on human dignity and 'truth' as determined by the evidence. As BCI capabilities develop, proactively reforming is crucial to realize this potential (Urbaite, 2025).

3.1 Challenges in Addressing Male Victimization

Although social and legal recognition of the principles of treating male survivors equitably has been rising, the issue of male victimization in cases of domestic violence for male victims of cruelty and intimate partner violence (IPV) remains difficult. Stigma and fear of ridicule and a sense that men should be resilient and strong all contribute to underreporting, which is evidenced by studies of 40-50% or more of male victims not reporting the nature of their experiences. Men make up 25-35% of reported domestic abuse cases, but may not access formal help, or they may only be classed as a perpetrator when they are convicted, as often the rates of service by victim are lower than by men (typically <5-10% of supported victims).

Policyming and judicial reactions often are a reflection of ingrained bias. In this, officers might assume the directing male being the initial aggressor in both cases of a bidirectional or female perpetrated violence resulting in further arterialization of only males or in situational hesitation to charge a female perpetrator. Tools for risk assessment, like some ODARAs examples, frequently employ a gendered language with assumptions that women are the victims, limiting their usefulness and effectiveness with men. Male allegations of psychological attack, or pressure and intimidation, in court are sometimes discounted, especially where there is no physical evidence, reinforcing a vicious cycle of disbelief or possible counterclaims by the victim.

Lack of services can worsen the situation. The majority of domestic violence shelters/hotlines and domestic violence advocates continue to be geared toward female survivors with few customized resources for men. Practical obstacles like the absence of safe homes, counselling responding to males experience (such as dealing with emasculation, economic manage or parental alienation issues by children) and legal assistance responsive to male dynamics, such as fabricated accusations of abuse or parental alienation also get in the way. The cultural narratives that largely depict IPV as violence targeted at women affect both policy and resources, and they further shore up IPV divides (Blitz, 2026).

Some difficulties might be addressed through neurotechnology; for example, Brain-Computer Interfaces (BCIs) would provide a concrete, factual record of neurobiological effects that would include measurement of disturbances in the HPA axis, hyperactivity in the amygdala, or disturbances to the prefrontal cortex, legally respecting psychological trauma. But it presents some new challenges, such as the issue of admissibility of neural data, mental privacy under new governing neurorights laws, informed consent in trauma situations and the prevention of misuse (such as compelled scanning, or data breaches). BCI decoding algorithms may result in an imbalance of victimular responses if their neural responses are under-represented in the training data, especially for males.

There are some other legal challenges such as fragmentation from different jurisdictions. Some jurisdictions are adopting gender neutral laws, whereas others use precepts that block male survivors from obtaining a protection order or "fair" parenting decisions. Along with vulnerabilities, intersectional factors – race, sexuality, socioeconomic status and disability – exacerbate this sense of disbelieve or lack of support, with marginalized men experiencing more disbelieve or less support. High costs for advanced BCIs could lead to a two-tiered system, with only beacons with enough resources taking part.Advanced BCIs may create the risk of a landscape where only well-off victims will have access to neuroevidence.

4. BRAIN-COMPUTER INTERFACES AS TOOLS FOR JUSTICE AND REHABILITATION

Brain-Computer Interfaces (BCI) are developing to become insightful, real-time, neurotechnological tools that could revolutionise the ways justice and rehabilitation systems work, by offering objective information about mental state, especially when addressing cases of cruelty against men in gender-neutral justice and rehabilitation systems (Musole, 2026). They not only decode and modulate this neural activity to enable us to do more than just treat the illness, they can also be used in other ways, things like evidential, rehabilitative, and restorative justice. BCIs provide objective and quantifiable markers of trauma that can alleviate the systematic distrust and severity experienced by male victims of psychological, emotional or physical violence, and directly support equitable legal processes as well as customized recovery journeys.

In the context of justice, BCIs can reinforce gender neutral justice by capturing measurable patterns of brain activity related to neurobiological effects of coerced and/or chronically stressful experiences, such as increased amygdala response or a dysfunction of the prefrontal cortex, which could be evidence of gaslighting / coercive control. By providing objective information, this objective data reinforces claims in situations where there are few or no physical pieces of evidence with supporting information to back up the male victim's experience, whether it be in a family court context, criminal trials, or hearing a protection order. BCIs can be integrated in rehabilitation programs for court mandated or voluntary neurofeedback therapies, which can aid survivors to control emotional reactions and to diminish the symptoms of post-traumatic stress disorder (PTSD) and restore cognitive functions that may have been damaged as a result of the extended abuse.

Public health advantage of BCIs lie in the shift away from in punitive models and the creation of a closed-loop system that can detect signs of distress and dispense a targeted intervention, such as an intervention to stabilize mood using neurostimulation or intervention for attention, has been suggested. This is particularly important for male survivors who have experienced the effects of trauma, stigma, isolation, substance abuse, and/or suicidal thinking. organizations such as Neuralink and Synchron are developing implantable and less-invasive technologies that could be a key element of community mental health and justice programs, thereby reducing the societal cost tied to the myriad cycles of mental health treatment and incarceration for which these technologies could improve outcomes and rates of recidivism.

The development of patent landscapes is extremely important and the key holders are trying to concentrate on therapeutic applications that can be licensed for humanitarian justice uses. Law must change to include BCI data, and be compatible with the current evidence standards. Pilot programs are available that integrate BCI-supported assessments with counselling; opportunities to support restorative justice dialogues based on common neural insights (with consent). Challenges include access to, and cost of, infrastructure and the need for equipment too expensive for or inappropriate in low resource systems.

BCIs are, overall, the most transformative shift in perspective to evidence-based, healing, and equitable justice that's truly neuro-informed. These tools, when used in an integrated and thoughtful manner, will further help societies to respond to the often-understated forms of violence suffered by men, facilitate holistic rehabilitation and foster gender-inclusive, safe environments with the aim of ensuring mental health and human dignity. But the implementation of such applications will require collaboration across disciplines, between neuroscientists, lawyers, policymakers and victim-support groups, if they are to be successfully and responsibly implemented on a large scale (Cuk & Batarelo Kokic, 2026).

4.1 Neuroevidence in Legal Proceedings and Therapy

Neuroevidence derived from Brain-Computer Interfaces (BCIs) has great potential to improve not only the legal administration of cases of male on male sexual violence, but also therapeutic measures in cases of sexual violence against men. BCI provides objective evidence, which can complement existing stated evidence in a gender neutral justice system and which has the potential to improve not only the legal administration of cases of male on male sexual violence but also therapeutic efforts in cases of sexual violence against men. BCIs record actual neural changes associated with emotional responses, past trauma, and cognitive deficits, and generate a biomarker like a change in event-related potentials, a change in power in a specific frequency band of EEG, or a pattern of activity in a specific brain area. Professionally, this neuroevidence could support allegations of psychological abuse, such as when there is prolonged victimization, emotional dysregulation and/or a signature of chronic stress, as certain psychological aspects can go under-recognized and are impacted by gender biases.

BCI data when used in court environments, may satisfy evidentiary requirements, such as Daubert requirements in USA, when supported by evidence of reliability, relevance and absence from prejudice. For men who have been victims of abuse, such evidence may rebut statements that condone or discount a victim's experience of abuse, be used to initiate a restraining order, custody proceedings and civil action for damages. Admissibility of neural data is tempered by emerging laws in jurisdictions such as California and Colorado that treat neural data as a sensitive data.The admissibility of neural data is circumscribed by the emerging laws, which protect neural data as “sensitive information”, with requirements for obtaining informed consent and safeguarding privacy. This integration helps to make things fairer since it is based on actions rather than on feelings or interpretations, which may be biased.

5. ETHICAL CONSIDERATIONS AND OPPORTUNITIES

There are complex ethical debates related to the potential use of brain-computer interfaces (BCIs) to help remedy abuse of men in gender-neutral justice and mental health systems, with concerns about autonomy, privacy, equity, and potential abuse. In order to ensure that BCIs are not used as devices of surveillance or coercion, a set of core principles of neuroethics must be taken into consideration in their implementation: those of cognitive liberty, mental privacy, and mental integrity.

Ensuring that voluntary and informed consent is a central component to protecting male victims is critically important, especially when there are power differentials involved, such as in legal or therapeutic contexts in which the victim might already feel vulnerable and stigmatised. If these thoughts, feelings, and memories could be accessed without consent, it could cause further harm, or to discriminate.

Equity issues stand out and include prohibitive expenses and lack of access to high-tech systems for BCI that could result in a stratified form of BCI in which only certain high-income, color, or geographical types of victims would benefit. Whether due to the nature of the data it is trained on, algorithmic biases in decoding neural signals might misinterpret trauma expressions commonly expressed by males as unfair legal or clinical consequences. The risks associated with civilians using neurotechnologies confront additional complexities in the military arena and the commercial sphere as well, especially regarding potential uses for these technologies in military or civilian prosecution settings.

The opportunities are certainly good and quite significant. BCIs provide unique means to effectively document psychological cruelty, empowering a gender-equality justice system to transcend gender stereotyping and supply evidence-based resources for all perpetrators of psychological violence. Through neurofeedback and closed loop stimulation, mental health healing is a much more achievable process, and suicidal ideation, trauma and cycles can break. Public-private partnerships and ethical patent licensing could help to make access wide open, incorporating both BCIs into sources of public health and legal aid, for the good of society.

New, emerging neural rights frameworks and laws (such as state neural data protection, EU AI Act) offer opportunities for policy integration of ethical safeguards. Responsible innovation guidelines can be elaborated by interdisciplinary oversight bodies composed of neuroscientists, ethists, legal experts and representatives from the affected communities (including survivors). There are opportunities in prevention areas as well—such as early detection of abusive relationships and community systems for mental health monitoring, which does not include consent.

Such considerations must be balanced – and be conducted in a proactive manner – through governance: by setting standards for data use transparently; in having ethics processes reviewed by an independent body; and through ongoing monitoring for the long-term impacts on identities and agency. BCIs can serve as tools for justice and healing without creating new injustices by focusing on human dignity and inclusivity (Turner et al., 2026). The way we approach the ethical issues will determine if we are promoting a compassionate, just, move toward taking action against male cruelty and all victims of cruelty in contemporary society using neurotechnology or exacerbating it (Rys & Gorska, 2026).

6. CONCLUSION AND FUTURE DIRECTIONS

In a gender neutral Justice arena the BCI can be put into place as a mechanism to address and end brutality towards men without compromising the attention of the rest of the victims (Sarkar, 2026). A combination of the objective insight into the human mind that neurotechnology offers and powerful legal protections would help to improve mental health equity, recognize the unclaimed experience of mental anguish and create more sensible, research-informed solutions to interpersonal suffering. This has to be achieved through proactive governance, ethical innovation and attention to universal human dignity, so that the potential of technology for the brain is used for justice – not division (Rituraj, 2026). It remains to be seen over the next few years whether this interaction is truly inclusive – whether BCI trials continue to be advanced and neurorights evolve to bring about the advancement of true inclusive perspectives on the role of emotions in addressing all aspects of cruelty in modern society.

REFERENCES

Blitz, M. J. (2026). Cognitive Liberty and Rights to (and Against) Cultural and Chemical Transformations of the Mind. In *The Law and Ethics of Freedom of Thought, Volume 2: Cognitive Liberty, Mental Privacy, and International Law* (pp. 151-189). Cham: Springer Nature Switzerland.

Cuk, M., & Batarelo Kokic, I. (2026). Techno-optimism or Thoughtful Scepticism? Demographic and Academic Differences in Student Views on Human Enhancement Technologies. *Nova prisutnost: časopis za intelektualna i duhovna pitanja, 24*(1), 89-110.

Istace, T. (2025). Exploring the Essence of the Freedom of Thought–A Normative Framework for Identifying Undue Mind Interventions. *Neuroethics, 18*(1), 10. DOI: 10.1007/s12152-025-09582-9

Koecke, D. (2025). Merging man and machine: A legal assessment of brain–computer interfaces in armed conflict. *International Review of the Red Cross, 107*(928), 176–199. DOI: 10.1017/S1816383125000098

Musole, E. (2026, April). Cognitive Extraction and the Neuro-Chilimba Framework: An Indigenous ROSCA-Based Governance Architecture for Neural Data in Zambia. In *International Journal of Applied Research in Business and Management.*

Perez-Sales, P. (2026). Coercion without contact: New technologies and the boundaries of torture. *Torture Journal, 36*(1).

Rituraj, A. (2026, March). Achieving child-friendly justice through the integration of artificial intelligence in healthcare systems for victims of child sexual abuse. In. AIP Conference Proceedings: Vol. 3386. *No. 1* (p. 020084). AIP Publishing LLC. DOI: 10.1063/5.0322628

Rustamov, N., Souders, L., Sheehan, L., Carter, A., & Leuthardt, E. C. (2025). IpsiHand Brain–Computer Interface Therapy Induces Broad Upper Extremity Motor Rehabilitation in Chronic Stroke. *Neurorehabilitation and Neural Repair, 39*(1), 74–86. DOI: 10.1177/15459683241287731 PMID: 39345118

Rys, M., & Gorska, A. M. (2026). Inclusive innovation: Balancing gender equality and gender neutrality in hackathons. *Equality, Diversity and Inclusion, 45*(2), 292–309. DOI: 10.1108/EDI-08-2024-0344

Said, G. (2025). Brain-Computer Interface 5.0: Potential threats, computational law and protection of digital rights. *Legal Issues in the digital. The Age (Melbourne, Vic.)*, (2), 134–160.

Sarkar, R. (2026). Policy Regression, Mental Health, and the Lived Experience of LGBTQ+ Students in Anti-DEI Times: Queer Futures Denied. In *Impacts of Anti-DEI Initiatives on Educational Institutions and Policy* (pp. 119-146). IGI Global Scientific Publishing.

Turner, S., Yadav, P., Morrin, H., & Bhat, A. (2026). The future of psychiatry: Clinical practice, diagnosis, and treatment. *International Review of Psychiatry (Abingdon, England)*, *38*(1-3), 314–335. DOI: 10.1080/09540261.2025.2594523 PMID: 41295901

Urbaite, G. (2025). Advancements in Neural Implants: A Systematic Review of Neuralink-Enabled Brain-Machine Communication. *Luminis Applied Science and Engineering*, *2*(3), 46–65.

Wallana, T., Banitsas, K., & Balachandran, W. (2025). Reviewing Breakthroughs and Limitations of Implantable and External Medical Device Treatments for Spinal Cord Injury. *Applied Sciences (Basel, Switzerland)*, *15*(15), 8488. DOI: 10.3390/app15158488

Chapter 11
Public Health, Patents, and Neuroscience:
Legal Implications and Opportunities of Brain-Computer Interfaces in Modern Healthcare

Swati Mehra
http://orcid.org/0009-0004-5384-0051
Amity University, Gwalior, India

Abhijay Chakraborty
http://orcid.org/0000-0003-4228-1931
Amity Law School, Amity University, Jaipur, India

Priyansh Samadhiya
http://orcid.org/0009-0008-4901-3677
Amity University, Gwalior, India

ABSTRACT

Brain-Computer Interfaces (BCIs) are a promising multidisciplinary field that combines interdisciplinary areas of neuroscience and engineering and healthcare that provides unparalleled opportunities to restore motor and sensory functions to patients suffering from neurological disorders. This chapter examines the various legal aspects of patents, informed consent, data privacy and regulation in regards to public health. Although BCIs have their merits, there are several difficulties with them including the security of intellectual property rights, ethical uses of neural data and access for people in health systems. There are opportunities to speed up

DOI: 10.4018/979-8-3373-9720-7.ch011

innovation, such as with patent incentives, as well as opportunities to integrate into precision medicine. Politically strong instruments are essential to securing the rights of the patients, risk minimisation and proper interaction with the patient.

1. INTRODUCTION

Brain-Computer Interfaces (BCIs) are at the forefront of an exciting nexus of neuroscience, public health, and intellectual property, and have the potential to transform the healthcare landscape by allowing the brain to interact directly with machines and technology. These systems translate neural activity to enable recovery of human function and extend human cognition and motor skills, with tremendous potential promise for those suffering from neurological disease including amyotrophic lateral sclerosis (ALS), spinal cord injuries, stroke, epilepsy and locked-in syndrome. In terms of public health, the potential of adaptive and effective BCIs technology is enormous to potentially greatly reduce the social burden of disability, enhance quality of life and lower expenses for long-term healthcare, by enabling enhanced rehab, independent living and customized treatments. The advancement of companies like Neuralink, Synchron, and Precision Neuroscience with implantable and non-invasive technologies such as a new device by Synchron called the Stentrode that is currently in its way to the FDA for digital communication and motor control is rapidly increasing.

BCIs in neuroscience make use of the latest in electrode array development, signal processing methods, AI technologies, and neuroimaging to gain a deeper understanding of and enhance brain function with stunning accuracy. Non-invasive EEG-based systems can offer more convenient research and consumer applications whereas invasive systems, such as the Neuralink neural threads and Synchron's endovascular stents can be of higher resolution for clinical use. Beyond enhancing sight and movement as with Neuralink's breakthrough device, Blindsight – these technologies have the promise to treat psychiatric disorders, foresee and prevent seizures, and for cognitive enhancement (Zhu et al., 2025). Public health systems can reap great rewards: if they can be widely adopted they could help meet older citizen healthcare needs in developed countries and protect against the vacuum in health coverage that exists in low- and middle-income countries (LMICs), contingent on surmounting cost, infrastructure, and training hurdles. Yet equity must not be overlooked or the risk of disparity arises that only those wealthier patients benefit.

The patent landscape prompts innovation and is a source of complexity in respect of patent laws. More than 2,000 patent families have been identified worldwide, with many of the top candidates in academia such as Stanford, or with companies working on improving the electrodes and their placement into the body or on its surfaces, as well as on algorithms to decode what takes place there or on wireless technologies. Patents promote huge private capital investments and the companies are doing just that: Neuralink with tremendous amounts of funding and Synchron with their extensive IP portfolio in various jurisdictions. However, patent thickets do have some negative side effects because they might further drive monopolisation, cost increase, and a hampering on competition, thereby limiting the impact of the public health. While IP protection has been beneficial to FDA-regulated pathways in the United States, inventorship issues develop when BCIs improve the human mind: ownership of inventions and creative works is an issue. While some are becoming more interested, barriers to the commercialization of BCI are seen across the globe in the segments (3(k) and 3(i) of the Patent Act India, which limit software patent and medical method patent).

Legal concerns are informed consent, liability, regulation and data privacy. Neural data is specifically meaningful, and can be used to identify thoughts, feelings, intentions and health state conditions which are not possible with traditional biometrics. If wherewithall systems are not consolidated, businesses can certainly exploit this information, which can lead to mishandling, hacking and even unauthorized commercial exploitation. HIPAA is only applicable to medical BCIs, with states bylaws calling for more protections for consumer neurotech products and needs being emphasized by the pressures from at least one U.S. senator calling on the FTC to make specific steps to protect consumers. The EU has worked towards mental privacy and cognitive liberty, in both GDPR and in new neurorights initiatives. In situations where AI decoding goes wrong due to some problems or bias there must be clear rules. In instances of BCI problems and/or biases, there must be clear rules of accountability over whose actions it is. Ethics become more complex with the application; there are, under the international humanitarian law (IHL), dual-use issues.

1.1 Applications of Public Health, Patents and Neuroscience

There are many possible applications in precision medicine and public health that could be created in collaboration with BCIs. To gain quicker access for unmet needs, FDA fast tracks such as Breakthrough Device status are introduced. LIC can be harnessed by licensing or partnership between public and private sector which can enable scale up manufacturing and costs down. To establish standards of safety, effectiveness, and equity, interdisciplinary work between neuroscientists, ethicists, public health and policy makers is critical. At a more global scale, over the long term BCIs would revolutionize the rehabilitation centres, allow for long-distance monitoring, and make it possible for neurorehabilitation at scale, potentially saving time and money because of the reduced amount of care required and allowing more people to become part of the workforce (Varughese et al., 2025).

There remain different problems, such as high costs, surgical risks (infection and rejection), biocompatibility, algorithmic bias, and psychological impact on identity and autonomy. In deciding on ethical frameworks, considerations of the differences between enhancement and therapy cannot be ignored, nor can the question of the possible coercion in working or insurance settings.Ethical frameworks have to include writers on the difference between enhancement and therapy, a potential for coercion in the work market or insurance coverage market, and the tale of the cultural acceptance. The models are data ownership, offering user control of local data in need of balancing with innovation and rights, or cloud processing.

In preparation for AI's future, policy makers should consider the development of a general uniform protection framework for neural data, the creation of patent laws that are more ethical such as, in some instances, granting patents to persons rather than businesses who created their images, and the development of regulations prohibiting the use of people in ways that benefit someone other than themselves.

The elements of promise and danger that exist in healthcare with the use of neurotechnology were seen in BCIs which, in conclusion, provided a good example of both. The public health sector can make good use of the developments of neuroscience research, all while balancing the incentives with increased legal safeguards of patents. The number of opportunities that can be used for restoration and enhancement should provide positive global governance – the dignity of people, the rights to rest, privacy and equity as well as risk reduction. The next ten years will see more trials and adoption/expansion, and this technology will be a challenge to make inclusive and ethical steps forward.

2. PATENT LANDSCAPE IN BCI TECHNOLOGY

The patent landscape of Brain-Computer Interface (BCI) technology is dynamic and constantly changing and highlights both the competition and global interest in the field of BCI at the intersection of neuroscience, engineering and IP law. More than 2160 unique patent families have been filed by more than 664 organizations worldwide as of recent analyses, thus ample investments in this transformative area (Lavazza et al., 2025). The number of patent applications has almost doubled from 2018 to 2025, with improvements proposed in neural recording and processing, implanting techniques, and AI algorithms to decode information from the brain.

The surge reflects the shift from research prototypes to clinical application of the technology, both in the invasive (implanted) and the non-invasive systems.

This area sees the bolstering of patents for electrode designs (such as flexible threads, stent-like endovascular arrays, and high-density Utah-style arrays), wireless data transmission, biocompatible materials, and surgical robotics for the implantation process, along with models of machine learning for real-time interpretation of neural signals. At the core level, fundamental technologies can come from academic institutions, and commercial firms will be more interested in system integration and scalability. While the United States is leading in high impact filings, China, Europe and other jurisdictions are displaying aggressive growth and in particular for non-invasive BCIs and wearable BCIs with strong IP protection under USPTO.

One of the special features of the BCI patent landscape is that of " Patent Thickets," where there are multiple patents in a single cluster that relate to the same innovation and could potentially bar freedom to operate and make litigation more likely. For example, there are important core innovations in neural signal acquisition and processing that are well protected so that new technology companies must license around existing claims or design around existing technology. While fostering innovation, it also leaves questions about potential abuse of monopoly power that may limit wider uptake of medically important products as their price rises or due to slower availability of generic/based-lines (Cavanaugh, 2026).

As far as public health benefits are concerned, robust patent is also crucial for the necessary private investment financing, as Class III medical devices require a significant investment in R&D and a long regulatory review process. As evidenced by the FDA Breakthrough Device designation, which for many companies goes hand-in-hand with the device's patent strength, companies use patents to attract funding rounds and partnerships. But the question is the patient or provider has access or not? Patently priced products might be able to be purchased by only a select few people, creating global inequalities in neurological care and diseases such as paralysis, epilepsy, and neurodegenerative diseases.

Legal ramifications are vast. The involvement of teams, particularly in academia–industry collaboration, can lead to inventorship conflict; the evolving nature of BCI-human cognition interactions can introduce ownership complexities into thought-to-text outputs (where AI extracts something from what humans say and/or think). The process of international harmonization is still difficult, though the Patent Cooperation Treaty (PCT) allows for international filing of patents, there are regional differences in the criteria on the patentability of products, including some of them being exempt from protection for their medical uses.

Strategic licensing, cross-border partnerships and patent pooling opportunities are available for humanitarian uses. Patents can be utilized to facilitate treatment of poor people in public health services through public private partnership. With the evolution of BCI technology, patent analytics will be a key enabler in anticipating convergence with AI, 5G/6G connectivity and precision medicine. In addition, regulatory authorities, such as the FDA or EMA, gradually begin to incorporate IP strength into their pathways, and new legislation under the rise in the spirit of new neurorights may have new disclosure or ethical review requirements for patented neurotechnologies.

Main issues are evergreen strategies (extending the protection by minor tweacs), patent trolls on startups and the conflicts between IP protection and open innovation for rapid clinical translation (Said, 2025). However, patent activity looks like it reached its maximum point in a number of the subsectors, indicating a change in focus from invention to enforcement and commercialization.

2.1 Key Patent Holders and Strategies

The players in the Brain-Computer Interface (BCI) arena include some pioneering companies, mature medical device companies, and academic giants who use various approaches to create competitive moats and achieve fast commercialization. Neuralink, Synchron, Blackrock Neurotech, Precision Neuroscince, and academic institutions like Stanford University and Tianjin University are among the predominant actors in the IP sphere (Ng, 2025).

With high-profile investing, Neuralink has applied for approximately 67 international patents some of which have been granted all of which center on "high-bandwidth implantable systems with connectivity threads as thin as possible and with robotic implementations, and innovative signal compression." It aims to use vertical integration and intensive filings in its core technologies such as wireless power transmission, hermetic sealing, and AI decoding, with a vision to create a broader user-centric platform that's not limited to medical applications. The strategy of neuralink is to get to market quickly and claim the widest possible product scope, but with problems along the way of having to deal with the prior art in a way that avoids competitors.

Synchron truly distinguishes itself with its targeted, high quality portfolio comprised of around 25-118 documents with up to 6-16 families and filed in up to 10 jurisdictions. Its flagship Stentrode™ an endovascular stent-electrode array holds patents in the minimally invasive delivery of particles via blood vessels, long-term biocompatibility and compatibility with external devices. Like being developed by Synchron with global partnerships (such as Nvidia for AI) and built around defensible IP, application-specific methods that enable quicker regulatory clearance and greater patient access with non-open craniotomy. This focus makes it different from the others and offers great licensing opportunities.

Blackrock Neurotech (formerly Blackrock Microsystems) has an extensive estate of ~65 patent documents in about 27 patent families and have had several decades of experience in the Utah Array. It focuses on achieving long-term stability of the implant, robust recording of many channels and its clinical translation, and is the foundation for many clinical research applications and early clinical use (Lewis, 2025). Patents include those for electrode materials, chronic reliability and advanced arrays such as Neuralace (10,000+ channels). Blackrock focuses on core technology licensing to the academic and industrial community and generates revenue for growth of their ecosystems.

Other companies that hold are Precision Neuroscence (surface arrays), INBRAIN Neuroelectronics (Graphene based), Paradromics, Kernel, NeuroPace and Neurable. Consumer and non-invasive segments are extended all the way to the corporate level, with media giants such as Panasonic and Snap (through NextMind). Key IP around signal processing and interface architectures have been owned by academic institutions like Stanford, University of California and Tianjin University, which frequently license it to startups or spin them out.

3. LEGAL AND REGULATORY FRAMEWORKS

Brain-Computer Interfaces (BCIs) are currently subject to a complex and inadequate legal and regulatory landscape, far removed from the fast pace of technological development in the field of neuroscience and healthcare applications. Most invasive BCIs are classified by the FDA as Class III medical devices and must undergo extensive premarket approval processes such as Investigational Device Exemptions (IDEs), clinical trials, and post-market surveillance. In 2021 the FDA published guidance on the requirements for implanted BCI devices used for paralysis or amputation, outlining generally non-binding requirements applicable to non-clinical testing and study design that focus on safety, biocompatibility and efficacy. Rocket fuel is offered for novel technologies such as Neuralink and Synchron where the company has received Breakthrough Device Designation from FDA. But BCIs found in the mass market and not those used in a medical setting, are generally considered in the gray area of the regulatory process and subject to limited supervision (Sanders, 2025).

In the EU, BCIs are mainly subject of the conformity assessments, clinical evaluations and CE marking requirements of the Medical Devices Regulation (MDR 2017/745) which also contains strict requirements for clinical evaluations. Some non-medical devices that present similar risks are covered by the framework. At the EU level, the AI Act focuses on high-risk AI elements in BCI, such as those that rely on biometric or neural data processing, including risk assessments, transparency, and human oversight. A few new developments in the field of neurorights, which continue to be promoted by the Council of Europe, as well as proposals for cognitive liberty, mental privacy and mental integrity go beyond and populate the gaps left by existing human rights paradigms.

Food safety implications are great. While regulation is essential for patient safety and access to care, it must be properly balanced to prevent uncontrollable innovation and spend. rules that are too strict also place a greater barrier in the way of deployment in a resource-limited health system (Vasiliu-Feltes, 2025). Worldwide, the differences create barriers to world-wide trials and commercialization, such as in India, where patent protection is hampered by medical method protection and by strong IP protection in the United States. An added difficulty in the use of International humanitarian law is whether goods are being used in civil or military fashion ("dual use").

Legal hurdles include problems with malfunctioning devices, algorithmic errors in the decoding of signals, informed consent (when cognitively impaired) and the question of responsibility in decisions made or taken away through the use of BCIs. Here patent law comes in, as well, with uncertainties regarding inventorship in AI-generated neural outputs. The adaptive regulation topic provides us with the opportunity to apply public-private partnerships, WHO/OECD harmonization or incorporate the topic of neuroethics into ethical review boards. Policymakers need to strike a balance between incentive for developing new innovations and protection of the interests of those who might exploit BCIs while also maintaining integrity of the rights of individuals which may safeguard BCIs' role in public health objectives such as lowering the burden of neurological diseases.

However, the use of BCI will also increase and there is a need for frameworks that are proactive and involve interdisciplinary approaches that take into account inputs from neuroscience, legal and public health stakeholders (Williams et al., 2025). These include rules of computer safety, prolonged monitoring, fair sharing in worldwide. Without these frameworks changing alongside one another, it is possible that the transformative potential of BCIs might become hindered by concerns of compliance, conflicts over value, and inconsistencies. Policy reforms should be flexible, have a risk-based approach and should also be responsive to technology but also important respect human dignity and social good.

3.1 Privacy and Data Protection

Neural data is extremely sensitive and can divulge thoughts, intentions, emotions and cognitive states, making privacy and data protection one of the biggest and most dynamic legal questions in BCIs today. Neural signals bring new potential for intrusion into mental states, unauthorized monitoring or manipulation of the mind, compared with conventional biometric or health information.

Federal protection is available, but it is restricted in the USA. Neural data however, would remain largely unprotected – as neural data from consumer neuroscience would not be regulated by HIPAA. Addressing that deficit, pioneering state laws have started to come into place; Colorado (2024) and California (amendments becoming effective 2025) explicitly define 'neural data', information output generated by the monitoring of either the peripheral or central nervous system as a 'sensitive personal information' under their comprehensive privacy acts. Collection, processing and sharing data with consumers must be done by their express consent, and with increased protection under these laws. Comparable initiatives have been taking place in other states, and federal plans such as the MIND Act seek to place more emphasis on the FTC in terms of protection for neural data.

In many cases, the data of neural information is considered to be a special type of biometric or health data under the General Data Protection Regulation (GDPR) of the European Union, placing a high proportion of lawful basis requirements, rules of data minimization, purpose limitation, and rights to retrieval, rectification and erasure. But there are shortfalls, since GDPR fails to be responsive enough to the special inferential capacity or real time nature of BCI data. The EU AI Act follows suit, focusing on the high-risk availability of AI systems that process neurodata, where transparency and risk management are key. The neurorights movements are seeking new protection for cognitive liberty and mental integrity.

This includes the restoration of communication after locked-in syndrome or constrolling epilepsy: from the public health and neuroscience perspectives, well-designed privacy arrangements are essential to improve uptake and foster trust. However, there must remain some rules to keep data sharing down – it is important for the development of BCI algorithms. Various challenges present themselves including the static consent models (not applicable to adaptive/long term BCIs), aggregation of anonymous data that may be anonymized as a whole by an individual who then manages to dis-aggregate the elements to the individual level, cyber-security concerns (brain hacking), and access to brain signals for employers / insurance companies (Abdulrahman Satam & Szabolcsi, 2025).

User-centric approaches like data sovereignty, edge computing to process data at the edge, and user-privacy principles for device design offer opportunities. Privacy-enhancing tech and public/private partnerships can serve to establish ethical data repositories that use patent strategies. ICJ's precepts of international harmonization remain significant to prevent 'forum shopping' and uniformity of protection at the border.

Needing more flexible and specific laws to guarantee privacy and data security for BCIs recognising the uniqueness of neural data and the requirement for novel lawmaking ways. A 'changing standard', where voice of various stakeholders, such as regulators, developer, neuroscientists, public health authorities, cooperating, can serve to secure mental autonomy with the healthcare value of this transformative technology. As trials expand and consumer applications are created and vulnerable groups are being exposed, one would expect that these legal deficits will be ramped up as BCIs provide them with a "boost".

4. PUBLIC HEALTH IMPLICATIONS AND OPPORTUNITIES

Maintaining a natural rhythm and keeping them engaged in quality eye care and daily tasks is crucial, and public health implications of Brain-Computer Interfaces (BCIs) are profound, gesturing at this neurotechnology as a potential game-changer in tackling the global burden of neurological disorders, which, according to the World Health Organization, affects more than one in three people worldwide. The possibilities for directly controlling the motor function, communication and sensory function in stroke, spinal cord and amyotrophic lateral sclerosis (ALS) or epilepsy and neurodegenerative diseases with a BCI are promising. BCIs can help patients interact with their prosthetics, computers or exoskeletons in ways that are thought mediated, leading to increased independence, decreased reliance on other people, and an improvement in their quality of life, consequently easing the burden on their healthcare system and minimising the long term socio-economic cost of living with disability.

There are a great number of opportunities available in public health. In high-income countries, BCIs are incorporated into rehabilitation programs, allowing for tele-rehabilitation and monitoring at home and helping to ensure that the aging population is also catered for, as well as decrease hospital readmissions. Medical applications are expected to fuel the global BCI sector growth from the current $2 billion to over $3.4 billion by 2033, according to market projections. These minimally invasive or non-invasive methods of BCIs in low- and middle-income countries (LMICs) where more than three-quarters of care for neurological illnesses are still unmet, may offer a route to make assistive technologies more accessible and inclusive, ensuring dignity, inclusion and employment (Ogayemi et al., 2025). With innovations in technologies that significantly reduce surgical challenges such as endovascular stents (such as Synchron's Stentrode) that allow greater scalability or portable EEG systems, the technology can be easily deployed in resource-heavy environments.

BCIs enable precision medicine from a population health standpoint, by facilitating personalized interventions with real-time data on the brain's activity, seizure prediction, mental health tracking, care, and cognitive rehabilitation. The possibility of integration with AI and telemedicine has the potential to revolutionize chronic disease management and shift to proactive, not reactive, care. All public health systems benefit from both less burden on care and more productivity – and cost savings could exceed the billions of dollars per year for the cohorts of paralyzed and stroke patients alone. The global potential of BCIs applied to the field of health equity could be accomplished by bringing the technology to underserved areas via patent licensing or by public-private collaborations paying for access.

Implications, however, suggest that there could be an impact on health inequalities. Frequently, because of the high cost of benefits, specialized infrastructure and training needs, these benefits may be limited to the wealthier population segments, thus deepening the disparities between rich and poor countries, or urban and rural areas. Neural devices, due to their cybersecurity weaknesses, present public health risks including vulnerable patients having information breached. Effort should be made to harmonise requirements to ensure that safety and efficacy are met across borders (Zhang et al., 2025).

A variety of policies and policy opportunities exist; for example including BCIs in national health plans or investing in the training of the healthcare workforce and highlighting humanitarian licensing and capacity building in LMICs with collaborative models, such as WHO-led plans. The more patients enroll in trials, the more evidence will be available for insurers and public payers to make coverage decisions. Raising our number of patients enrolled in clinical trials will create more evidence to inform coverage, whether from insurers or the public payers. Brain-Computer is are an intersection between neuroscience and public health which will re-shape disability supports and preventive care. Deliberate efforts are needed to make sure that these opportunities are realized, bringing together innovation and technology with equitable health outcomes for different populations in the global community.

5. CHALLENGES, ETHICAL CONSIDERATIONS AND FUTURE DIRECTIONS

The challenges of development and deployment of Brain-Computer Interface (BCI) technology have many facets technical, clinical and societal ones. However, technical challenges, such as the attitude towards long-term biocompatibility, diminishing signal power over time, infections caused by implants, and the requirement for new materials, including flexible electrodes or graphene, to increase the durability of implants and decrease tissue damage, still exist. Neural decoding is algorithmically susceptible to providing variable quality for different parties and costs and surgical expertise, both of which restrict scalability (Vaseghi, 2025). Clinically, there is still a lot of confusion about the safety of utilizing them in the long-term, explanting them, and using them with other therapies that have already been developed, even in the face of trial success.

Ethical considerations have a major focus and are fundamental, based on principles of neuroethics, like cognitive liberty or mental privacy, autonomy of action, and identity. Potential privacy violations, unauthorized access, "brain hacking" and/or commercial exploitation of neural data, can compromise mental integrity. Patients with cognitive impairments have cognitive and communicative challenges to informed consent, and there are ethical problems raised when patients' decisions are affected by the BCI, and when BCI enhances the human-AI cognition. Enhancement/therapy debates raise questions about social inequalities given that wealthy individuals might have cognitive advantages, foreshortening inequalities. Beyond neural privacy issues with violation of the self-concept are wider problem, such as the impact of neural data on the notions of employer or insurance misuse of such information, and its use in military applications as an example of a dual-use scenario (Sharma et al., 2026).

6. CONCLUDING REMARKS

BCI may end up being merely an instrument of privilege, rather than a panacea. The acceptance is not certain and certain vulnerable groups may be co-opted or stigmatized. Across jurisdictions, there is regulatory fragmentation that makes it more difficult to have clear, principled regulation, and patent thickets have the potential of focusing on profitability over access. Suggestions for future directions are responsibly oriented innovation via interdisciplinary collaboration. New laws that reflect the developments of emerging neurorights instruments, which seek to define "mental privacy" and "cognitive freedom" should be drafted, and can be built on existing model laws such as California's regime of protections for neural data or the EU AI Act. Technological progress in how to control an electrode array with closed-loop BCIs, progress in how information can be transfer to and from the network without invasive contact, and the progress in how invasive devices can be used for mental health, pain management and everyday augmentation will increase the range of applications. Ethical guidelines, patent pooling with regard to humanitarian access and capacity building among LMICs may be promoted by the international standards organised by inter-agency organisations such as WHO (Barker et al., 2026).

The researcher priorities are about longitudinal outcomes studies, minimizing the bias users bring into the field of AI, and user design with a variety of other voices embedded. Public engagement will generate trust and transparent governance will build trust. Hybrid BCI systems as a fusion of VR/AR and robotic systems—may revolutionize the healthcare, educational and HCI sectors by 2030 and beyond. Policymakers have to work out a way to strike a balance between incentivising innovation and protecting humanity, using adaptive regulation, ethical review board, global funding etc.

But all these obstacles can only be surmounted through a proactive strategy, which starts with values (Guo et al., 2026). With careful use, BCI may promote humanflourishing and support the dignity, equity and autonomy of each person. Finally, the next ten years will be critical to determining if this technology will advance socially and inclusively, or heighten new inequalities. To guide the responsible trajectory of future directions, there is a need for ongoing dialogue between and among neuroscientists, ethicists, regulators, and communities.

REFERENCES

Abdulrahman Satam, I., & Szabolcsi, R. (2025). Ethical and Safety Challenges of Implantable Brain-Computer Interface. *Interdisciplinary Description of Complex Systems: INDECS, 23*(2), 82–94. DOI: 10.7906/indecs.23.2.1

Barker, K. K., Madden, E. F., Lowe, P. L., & Rickers, K. (2026). The Neuro-Fiction of Addiction Immunizations. *Social Science & Medicine, 394*, 119059. DOI: 10.1016/j.socscimed.2026.119059 PMID: 41671876

Cavanaugh, C. (2026). *Legal Ethics in AI Healthcare for Brain Computer Interfaces: A Policy Analysis* (Doctoral dissertation, University of Pittsburgh).

Guo, W., Wang, H., Bai, Y., & Tan, M. (2026). Global Patent Landscape of Marine Functional Foods: Technological Trends, Hotspots, and Future Challenges. *Trends in Food Science & Technology*, 105555.

Lavazza, A., Balconi, M., Ienca, M., Minerva, F., Pizzetti, F. G., Reichlin, M., Samorè, F., Sironi, V. A., Sosa Navarro, M., & Songhorian, S. (2025). Neuralink's brain-computer interfaces: Medical innovations and ethical challenges. *Frontiers in Human Dynamics, 7*, 1553905. DOI: 10.3389/fhumd.2025.1553905

Lewis, J. S. (2025). Brain–Computer Interface Integration in Mental Health: Clinician Perspectives on Diagnostic Efficacy and Ethical Implications.

Ng, J. Y. (2025). Exploring the intersection of brain-computer interfaces and traditional, complementary, and integrative medicine. *Integrative Medicine Research, 14*(2), 101142. DOI: 10.1016/j.imr.2025.101142 PMID: 40290410

Ogayemi, A., Oyasiji, O., Okesiji, A., Omosule, A., & Olafimihan, O. (2025). *When Thought Becomes Tradeable: Legislating Neuroprivacy Frameworks in the Brain-computer Interfaces (BCIs)*. Commercial Era.

Said, G. (2025). Brain-Computer Interface 5.0: Potential threats, computational law and protection of digital rights. *Legal Issues in the digital. The Age (Melbourne, Vic.)*, (2), 134–160.

Sanders, S. (2025). *Brain–Computer Interface Integration in Mental Health: Clinician Perspectives on Diagnostic Efficacy and Ethical Implications* (Doctoral dissertation, Walden University).

Sharma, K., Agrawal, D., & Gabrani, R. (2026). A Patent Review on Traumatic Brain Injuries (2020-2025). *International Journal of Neuroscience*, (just-accepted), 1-27.

Varughese, J. S., Arjun, M., Mishra, S., & Venkatesh, M. P. (2025). Brain-computer Interface on Medical Devices: A Promising Technology with Limitless Possibilities. *Applied Drug Research, Clinical Trials and Regulatory Affairs, 11*(1), E26673371314770. DOI: 10.2174/0126673371314770241020145227

Vaseghi, M. (2025). Comparative Study of Legal Protection of Human Brain Data in the Context of Neurotechnologies, with Emphasis on Brain-Computer Interfaces (BCI). *Majlis and Rahbord, 32*(122), 5–32.

Vasiliu-Feltes, I. (2025). Neurotech frontiers: Ethics, identity, and the evolution of brain–computer interfaces. In *Nanomedical Brain/Cloud Interface: Explorations and implications* (pp. 4–1). IOP Publishing. DOI: 10.1088/978-0-7503-2144-0ch4

Williams, C., Anik, F. I., Hasan, M. M., Rodriguez-Cardenas, J., Chowdhury, A., Tian, S., He, S., & Sakib, N. (2025). Advancing Brain-Computer Interface Closed-Loop Systems for Neurorehabilitation: Systematic Review of AI and Machine Learning Innovations in Biomedical Engineering. *JMIR Biomedical Engineering, 10*, e72218. DOI: 10.2196/72218 PMID: 41191851

Zhang, Q., Zhang, C., Ji, H., Chen, J., Wang, X., Zhang, T., Liu, P., Wang, Z., & Xu, Y. (2025). Ethical governance of clinical research on the brain–computer interface for mental disorders: A modified Delphi study. *General Psychiatry, 38*(4), e101755. DOI: 10.1136/gpsych-2024-101755 PMID: 40735361

Zhu, R., Zhao, Y., & Li, Y. (2025). Paradigm Shift in Global Governance of Medical Brain-Computer Interface: Addressing Practical Challenges Through Institutional Innovation. *Risk Management and Healthcare Policy, 18*, 3755–3768. DOI: 10.2147/RMHP.S555754 PMID: 41328405

Chapter 12
The Future of Communication Skills Training in Neuro-Digital Workplaces:
Brain-Computer Interface Challenges and Opportunities for Human Resource Development

Vartika Chaturvedi
http://orcid.org/0000-0001-8934-3592
IMS Noida, India

Anjali Khanna
Step by Step School, Noida, India

ABSTRACT

In the age of Digital Transformation and 'neuroscience' what digital transformation does to workplaces is a paradigm change that we now call the Neuro-digital Workplace. Not only will these spaces be defined by state-of-the-art technology, but the incorporation of neurotechnology as well, which will enable direct brain-computer interaction, thereby changing the ways by which a job worker can communicate, collaborate and pick up skills. BCIs are now beginning to be used for communication skills training, which is taking its place, as a neuro adaptive system based on techniques that involve workshop classes, role playing and feedback. BCIs can transmit brain signals to human-made machines or feedback, which might rectify physical handicaps, cognitive problems, and more they serve as additional

DOI: 10.4018/979-8-3373-9720-7.ch012

challenges for Human Resource Development (HRD) professionals. The present chapter addresses future landscape with a particular emphasis on training within neuro-digital environment based on BCI.

1. INTRODUCTION

This innovation in the field of workplaces (neuro-digital) the training of communication skills will be affected. Brain-Computer Interfaces (BCIs) offer unparalleled opportunities for direct thought-to-action communication, personalised neurofeedback and immersive training scenarios for developing interpersonal and professional skills for hybrid and AI-based work environments. But there are a number of technical, ethical, user training and equity issues that remain. This paper explores such dynamics and how BCI could change the HRD landscape by providing adaptive learning programs, cognitive augmentation and near real-time performance feedback. By understanding and conquering some of the barriers and opportunities, organizations can be able to design workplaces that will enhance the levels of inclusion, efficiency and innovation of their workforces, preparing them for the neuro-digital future.. BCIs are now beginning to be used for communication skills training, which is taking its place, as a neuro adaptive system based on techniques that involve workshop classes, role playing and feedback. BCIs can transmit brain signals to human-made machines or feedback, which might rectify physical handicaps, cognitive problems, and more they serve as additional challenges for Human Resource Development (HRD) professionals. The present chapter addresses future landscape with a particular emphasis on training within neuro-digital environment based on BCI. It highlights the state of critical issues/potentials and provides some understanding into HRD strategies that take into account the human aspects of innovation in addition to its nature. (Radu, 2025).

Neuro-digital workplaces combine neural monitoring, AI, VR/AR, and collaboration platforms for an EUREKA-inspired experience. Neuro-digital workplaces integrate all neural monitoring, AI, VR/AR and collaborative tools to provide a space that is responsive and cognition-informed. Neuro-digital workspaces are different from usual digital workplaces that focus on software such as Slack or MS Teams, and involve the use of real-time brain data in order to increase productivity, emotional intelligence training, and facilitate seamless interaction. Wearable BCIs for attention monitoring, neuro-feedback for stress management, and input and output via thought-controlled interfaces for inclusive communication are trends. In these environments, communication is not only limited to words on a page or voice to voice but can be "neural" as well, with potential for "brain-to-brain" collaboration and instant intent decoding. HRD needs to mainstream changes in training getting away from soft skills modules to strengthening neuro-cognitive skills (Terec-Vlad, L., & Rusu, A. (2026).

BCIs communicate directly between the brain and external devices, which extract data from the brain via the EEG or which employ invasive implants into the brain or hybrid approaches that combine the two methods. For workplace use there has been an expanding interest in non-invasive wearables that are more accessible and do not lead to fine wires into the brain like invasive ones such as Neuralink.

New features include speech decoding with high accuracy (the system has even achieved a 97% accuracy rate in some cases), operation of devices by thought, and signal processing improved with the aid of technologies handed over by generative AI. In communication training, the BCI can give real-time neurofeedback about empathy cues, intent clarity, or cognitive load, which can skyrocket learning speed (Kritika, 2026). BCIs can facilitate learning when training a superpower that's more essential to human interaction like communicating with empathy, clarity of intent, or reducing cognitive load at a much greater pace than traditional training methods.

Some barriers remain, although this promise is great. There are technical problems like, signal noise, inter-subject variability, and also essential users training problems (BCI 'illiteracy') that poses difficulties. At work, it's hard to stay accurate when during something active such as a meeting, it's the toughest to be accurate. Ethical and privacy concerns are also the standout ones: neural data is extremely delicate and could be utilized for such things as obtaining, bias in resourcing choices, or "mind reading" misuse. Equity issues occur when access leads to some groups being catered to at the expense of others, so as to widen workplace inequalities. The demands of constant monitoring and the mental pressure of having to adjust to the BCI-controlled communication also represent a risk. The cost of implementation, system integration, and regulatory access barriers are other factors that hinder adoption.

BCIs unlock transformative opportunities for HRD. Real-time brain data can be used to customise a training program, such as detecting anxiety during presentations and adaptive coaching. Say, you need to judge whether two people's cultures match, and there are high stakes involved in negotiations. When practice is necessary for a high-stakes negotiation or a cross-cultural interaction, you can do so safely every time, through immersive VR simulations and BCI control. The main applications of neuro-feedback are to improve emotional intelligence, attention and empathy training. BCIs can be used to provide alternative means of communication for employees or people who are neurodiverse or have a disability, thereby enhancing a workplace's approach to workplace inclusion. Combined (anonymised) data can be used to draw upon organisational insights in relation to team dynamics, further enhance the development of leadership and culture-building. Overall, it moves HR from being a service department, to enabling employees to be more productive and healthier through cognitive augmentation.

Strong frameworks are needed for responsible deployment. Some of these principles are informed consent, data minimisation, and "mental privacy" protection. Guidelines for HRD professionals to develop in cooperation with ethicists, neuroscientists and technologists. To keep the trust, transparency in the application of BCI, voluntary participation and bias audit are needed. Implementation strategies include pilot programs, gradual rollouts and extensive trainings for user and managers (Willianmson et al., 2026). The transfers will be achieved through interdisciplinary partnerships, resulting in human-friendly solutions that convey greater importance on man than on mere efficiency.

2. UNDERSTANDING NEURO-DIGITAL WORKPLACES

The neuro-digital workplace is the next generation in the evolution of the modern workplace where the digital workplace is enhanced with cognition-aware, responsive and adaptive neuro-techniques. Compared to traditional digital workplaces, which are digital platforms for collaboration tools, cloud services, knowledge bases, and communication systems, a neuro-digital workplace combines real-time brain monitoring, neural feedback, and brain-computer interface (BCI) with these technologies to engage employees at a deeper level through their cognitive and emotional responses.

These workplaces combine AI, VR/AR, wearable sensor data and Neuroergonomics to enhance human outcomes. Some of the core attributes are the ability to integrate the neural data seamlessly into productivity applications, from which there are several possible applications: real time mental workload assessment, emotion detection for understanding better team dynamics, and thought-augmented communication. For example, EEG-based wearables can help track the state of attention in virtual meetings, adapt the interface and propose breaks to avoid cognitive fatigue. Neurofeedback loops give real-time feedback on stress and concentration, helping to ensure that private well-being interventions are proactive.

Communication goes beyond verbal or textual expression in neuro-digital contexts. However, there are instances that workers can use the BCI directly to share their intentions, thus eliminating miscommunication among a hybrid team. This change will promote inclusion of neurodiverse individuals and will provide people with different cognitive profiles with alternative ways in which to interact (Mukherjee, 2025). In these workplaces, organizational strategy focuses on more than just the technology itself, it also focuses on cultural adaptation that is, building a neuro-literacy within the organization and dealing with issues related to surveillance.

Several reasons are driving the development of the neuro-digital workplace: the new normal of remote/hybrid working, rapid growth in wearable neurometric technologies with declining costs, and the need for improved productivity in the face of critical worker shortages. The market is expected to expand at a notable rate in the realm of work applications of neurotech, where it could be an addition to the HR practices revolving around performance, learning and wellness. To realize this potential requires assessing and managing both technical, ethical and social issues to enable these environments to participate in supporting, rather than policing, their employees' participation, ultimately to create truly inclusive and productive futures of work (Musole, 2026).

3. BRAIN-COMPUTER INTERFACES: FUNDAMENTALS AND EVOLUTION

BCIs enable direct communication between a human brain and external devices without the use of normal, neuromuscular communication. At the core, BCIs capture brain signals, analyse, interpret the signals with algorithms, and derive command or feed back of the Brain. Methods of signal acquisition include non-invasive (electro-encephalograph (EEG); could also be portable to check on patient privacy), semi-invasive and invasive (electrocorticograph (ECoG) provides even higher resolution; intracortical implants (such as Neuralink's threads) is used in the invasive approach).

These include signal acquisition, extraction of the features from the signals (to filter out noise), classification/translation into the outputs (what you're looking for, or to see whether signal acquired is equivalent, de-translation), and feedback mechanisms that close the loop for learning. BCIs were initially implemented for medical purposes, for example, for patient communication through spelling devices or cursor control for locked-in patients. The advance has been remarkable: basic experimental systems back in the '70s to systems today that are able to decode speech, movement intentions and even higher-order cognition.

Significant strides (2025-2026) have been made that are moving rapidly. Many companies, including Neuralink, Synchron, Paradromics, and more, have made progress with human trials, with some giving people a sight back in life, some a sense of movement and others digital interaction. Leading the way is the advancement of non-invasive wearables enhanced by improved clinical dry electrodes, multimodal sensing (synaptic electrodes, fNIRS, and/or eye-tracking) and the use of generative AI to strengthen signal quality and generate synthetic data to deal with inter-subject variability and noise.

BCIs for transformative applications in communication skills training. Visualization of brain patterns related to empathy or clarity of thought can be used to teach emotional intelligence in real-time neurofeedback training. VR-BCI can provide an immersive environment to both practice negotiations or public speaking with varying levels of difficulty according to the cognitive load. Thought-to-text or brain-to-brain collaboration prototypes suggest the future of 'Telepathic' team interactions, and dramatically transform remote workplaces.

This trend is supporting the market, which is set to experience high growth rates and a wide range of applications across the medical, consumer, and workplace markets. Challenges are still unresolved: signal stability, user training (BCI illiteracy affecting some users), ethical questions involving data privacy and agency, and level of access. Surgical invasive systems are better performing, and non-invasive systems are more safe and scalable (Arivunambi et al., 2025).

4. CHALLENGES OF BCI IN COMMUNICATION SKILLS TRAINING

Brain-Computer Interfaces (BCIs) are an emerging technology that has raised several tough challenges from technical, psychological, ethical, organizational, and social perspectives for use in communication skills training in a neuro-digital workplace. For the use of BCI as a tool for training, there are clear limitations that must be faced with practical use, such as difficulties in ensuring fair and effective use, difficulties in user adoption and assurance of efficacy due to persistent problems.

The major obstacle is the technical inability. Poor electrode contact, environmental interference and muscle artifacts are all sources of noise in non-invasive BCIs like EEG-based wearables, reducing the signal to noise ratio and making accurate decoding difficult in dynamic environments like in virtual meetings or negotiations at the workplace. The invasive systems are more reproducible, but come with risks associated with the surgery, stability concerns because of gliosis (brain tissue reaction to the implants), and biocompatibility concerns. However, the inter-subject variability is still large, with the users' performance being impacted by, among others, skull thickness, cognitive patterns, but also by the cognitive state of the brain during the day. This is a component of "BCI illiteracy" – the fact that a large proportion of people (in some studies 15-30%) are not see an upward trend in their control, making it impossible to scale in the program of corporate communication.

These problems are exacerbated by training and necessity issues. But due to the extensive user calibration and practice session needed to use BCI effectively, cognitive fatigue, frustration and lack of engagement in skill training are problem areas when using BCI (Vijayalakshmi et al., 2025). Whether in the context of communication, like predicting someone's intent, feeling, empathy, etc., or cursor control, or speech decoding, the mapping of brain signals to these attentions is much more complicated. Current systems can be prone to inaccuracy in multi-tasking applications, which can impact rather than improve training activities like role playing or public speaking tests, simulations, and the like. Furthermore, embedding BCIs into current VR/AR platforms or collaboration tools requires advanced multimodal fusion (such as integrating EEG with eye-tracking or fNIRS), a technology that is still in its developmental stages and uses complex computation.

Ethical and privacy issues are major and seem to be especially prominent when training individuals to communicate. Neural data exposes information related to thoughts, emotions, and cognition at a very high level of sensitivity, posing risks to the "mental privacy". With HR-led training, ongoing surveillance may result in unintentional surveillance, with enhanced monitoring of brain patterns associated with stress, disengagement or bias impacting on performance assessments or promotion outcomes. Issues regarding informed consent are complicated: employees might feel forced to use BCI because of career advancement which is to the detriment of their autonomy. Such unfairness in algorithms is a result of their training based on certain groups, for example, neurodiverse brains might perform poorly in some algorithms, and the same might be applicable for females of certain culture or minority groups. There is the possibility that's not a fair one, because some people who were trained on algorithms are from certain groups and that would make it unfair for someone who is neurodiverse, or for females, or for people from a certain cultural group or minority group to not perform well in that algorithm, thus increasing the inequities in the communication skill assessments.

They could make a positive contribution; however, they have to overcome the problems of organisational and implementation. The expenses associated with hardware, software, and dedicated training facilities to run BCI are hard to be restricted by the HR budget, particularly for the SMEs. To integrate with current HR systems and to safely store neural data for easy access or to manipulate plutonium IP, a significant investment is necessary, and these data need to be stored in a way that cannot be hacked. No direct physical damage from them is found, but rather, resistance is typically psychological that is employees are not 'accepting' the BCIs in the workplace and they have concerns about use of the BCIs as 'mind reading' instruments, legal issues of monitoring in the workplace (Balasundaram et al., 2026). There are still gaps in regulation few areas, such as California, have started to define "sensitive data" for neural data; standards surrounding using BCI in the workplace globally today are still not uniform.

Specific challenges include lack of use of interpersonal skills to replace communication technology, "deskilling" and the capacity to communicate thoughts from their brain in a meaningful and natural manner. Future research on brain plasticity, cognitive stress with extended feedback and team dynamics when employing BCI-enhanced communication is needed. This will require interdisciplinary innovation between neuroscientists, ethicists, HR professionals and engineers in order to bring about effective, user-centered solutions that are safe, equitable, and voluntary. These challenges, if not mitigated prior to BCI's implementation, can be detrimental to its mission to influence communication training in organizations that are neuro-digital, and can lead to disunity and distrust.

5. OPPORTUNITIES FOR HUMAN RESOURCE DEVELOPMENT

Brain-Computer Interfaces (BCIs) produce disruptive opening towards Human Resource Development (HRD), particularly in the communications skills training and overall capacities of employees of any neuro-digital workspace. BCIs enable direct access to human cognitive and emotional states thereby providing new HRD solutions not one size fits all, but highly individual, adaptive and effective, neuro-enhanced learning experiences. One of the terrific potential opportunities is real-time, data-driven personalization. The cognitive load, attention, emotional valence and engagement can be measured in training simulations and instantly reported to the trainee using the BCI.

The other is immersive trainings. Hyper-realistic trainings of high stakes/exchanging communication strategies such as negotiation, conflict situation or cross-cultural interaction can be achieved by integrating BCIs with VR/AR environments and use difficulty in training that depends on brain activity of the learner (Pandey et al., 2025). Thought-controlled interfaces help to easily interact and communicate within these environments deciding physical boundaries and assisting training of neurodiverse employees that might not have the ability to learn through conversation or motor. This is inclusive to all with disabilities and there are alternative modes of communication to enable them to participate in professional development. At the organizational level, neural HRD offers invaluable insights into team dynamics, leadership effectiveness, and organizational culture by aggregating and anonymizing neural data. HR professionals might pinpoint common areas of strength or areas of missed communication, and create specific plans to facilitate better collaboration and innovation. Enhanced accuracy in data driven talent management: BCIs can add that extra hunk of data as objective cognitive metrics to prevail in addition to the subjective ones pinpointing latent potential, optimal learning styles and their readiness for promotion or different roles.

There is much to be gained for cognitive augmentation and for initiatives promoting well-being. BCIs have the potential to promote neurofeedback techniques to improve focus, enhance creativity and protect against burnout, especially in demanding neuro-digital environments. This is the quicker acquiring of the skills, better retention, and transfer to real world skills in communication training. New uses include direct brain-to-brain collaboration prototypes for better team synergy and uses of AI thought-to-text for intent-sharing of multilingual, or exact, intent that decreases misunderstandings in global teams.

HRD professionals themselves acquire new roles as facilitators for introducing the programs of neuro-literacy in the organization, educating about ethics in technology usage, and using personal neural data information, and integrating BCI with human skills. This makes HR business partners of innovation and builds cultures that know and respect, continually learn and grow, and are resilient. Long-term, costs can also be better managed through cuts in training time, better return on development investments, and better employee retention using tailored development paths for employees.

There are additional opportunities, such as equity and accessibility. With smart design, BCIs can be used for a democratized access to high-level training for minority groups, allowing communication-intensive profession to become the same. Collaboration between HR, neurotechnology companies and academic institutions can move the process of developing low-cost, wearable solutions specifically designed for the workplace at an increased pace (Kies et al., 2025). Collaborating and cooperation is the key word between HR, neurotechnology companies and academia can help jump-start the development of lower-cost, more wearable technology that's optimized and designed specifically for the workplace. Ethical tools created during deployment such as trust and the focus on consent, transparency, and bias mitigation can foster trust and allow organisations to establish themselves as pioneers in responsible innovation.

6. ETHICAL, PRIVACY AND IMPLEMENTATION CONSIDERATIONS

The emergence of Brain-Computer Interfaces (BCIs) in the field of communication skills training at the smart workplace presents great ethical, privacy and implementation challenges that warrant serious consideration to support responsible innovation in the training of communication skills at the smart workplace. Finally, because they are integrated seamlessly into the neural system, BCIs are also relatively intrusive on the autonomy of the human system, the integrity of the human system and human rights in real-time feedback, personalized systems of AI-based coaching, and made intelligence "augmented" interactions. Human Resource Development (HRD) managers who have to roll out these technologies in an ethical and effective manner have to strike a balance between what can change and what needs protection.

Ethics issues are related to autonomy, consent and agency. Dealing with an informed consent process in the context of BCI applications in employment-related context is more complex due to disparities in power. Having to attend a training program to improve one's career can be regarded as an unplanned exercise and can be viewed as a commitment. Neural data may capture subconscious processes, emotions and intentions but could not be considered an informed consent because users might not be explicitly aware of what they sign up for when installing the device and starting its use. Furthermore, the compatibility of BCIs means that certain traumatic instances of its use in communication training might restructure individuals' expression of ideas or interpersonal interaction, causing them to become psychologically dependent upon the device, or exacerbate authentic interpersonal qualities.

Equity and fairness is another important ethical aspect of it. Going forward, there may be greater workplace inequities and inequalities as increasing access to advanced BCI systems increases the advantage for some over others who can use neural enhancements to communicate at a higher level. Additionally, the algorithms used to decode BCI signals are susceptible to biases in the data used for their training, typically limited to a specific subset of individuals or to one culture, which could disadvantage neurodiverse groups, cultural minorities, or women with different brain patterns and lead to skewed training results or to discriminatory evaluation or perception of their commas (Sheela et al., 2025). This could be reflected in unfair attribution of empathy or leadership potential in the context of communication skills. There are also greater social issues such as the potential that cognitive enhancement may introduce socioeconomic inequalities, thus generating neuro-enhanced hierarchies instead of the meritocratic concept.

Non-maleficence calls for careful assessment of the psychological and physical risks. Brain monitoring in training may lead to cognitive overload, anxiety and surveillance which reduces well-being. The invasive BCIs come with a surgical risk, and even non-invasive brain wearables can have its uncomfortable effects or even effects on brain plasticity and a class of problems we simply don't know about. The UNESCO 2025 Recommendation on the Ethics of Neurotechnology underscores the importance of mental integrity and avoiding mental manipulation, and calls for safeguarding human dignity, rather than efficiency. Neural signals provide unparalleled insight into what goes on inside a person's head their thoughts, unspoken intentions, and emotions—that could be deciphered for a communication training purpose. The potential for aggregated or individual neural information to be utilized in areas other than training or growth, such as performance measurement, team building or predictive analytics, also blurs the professional growth line in neuro-digital workplaces with that of invasive surveillance. Risks come down to leaked data, sharing with a third party (such as an insurer or a recruiter), or using the data improperly in some decision of consequence (promotion, for example).

Neural data is a type of sensitive information that is not adequately covered by current regulations, such as GDPR, which define neural data as such because of its unique characteristics and because it is not completely anonymizable. Probabilistic "mind reading" powers are a threat to freedom of thought, a basic human right. If everyone knows they might be monitored, they may be less likely to say out loud something that they would otherwise want to say privately (Kim, 2025). If it could be known that everyone is likely to be monitored, then there is a possibility of inhibiting genuine communication practice and creativity amongst employees. Entities such as the Neurorights Foundation suggest specific protections: mental privacy, access to neural data; to mental integrity, protection from harmful interference of neural data; and protection from algorithmic bias.

Accessibility thrusts further into complexity - practical considerations of implementation. In practice, there are technical challenges to seamlessly integrate BCIs into an existing HR system and into training platforms, and a need to protect that data from being hacked (cybersecurity) into the nervous system, as well as any solutions that need to be found for the signal to remain reliable in a dynamic workplace environment. Initial investment in hardware, calibration and maintenance are challenges, particularly for smaller businesses, and specialized skills in neurotechnology require considerable upskilling of HR, IT, and training.

Voluntary and opt-in participation in controlled environments such as VR-based communications simulations in a phasing process is recommended. Full user training in the operation of the BCI, in interpretation of the data and about their rights is essential to minimize frustration and to create trust in the BCI. It's essential to create strong governance structures across the board, convening a variety of committees comprised of ethicists, legal counsel, employee representatives, etc. and neuroscientists to monitor deployment. When data use is transparent, data is reviewed periodically for bias and effectiveness, and there are procedures for grievance redressal, accountability can be promoted.

There are new compliance opportunities and challenges. At present there are piecemeal international standards (such as the Recommendation of the UNESCO framework convention on art and asso-ciatively culture, ask for the Protection of Cultural Expressions from Plagiary and fraud 2026) and some national legislatures are introducing measures to protect neural data (as in Colorado and Minnesota). There are, as of 2026, splintered international standards (the Recommendation of the UNESCO framework convention on art and asso-ciately culture 2026) and beginning of national measures to protect neural data as in Colorado and Minnesota. HRD leaders need to promote and implement policies that are explicitly about opt-in consent, data minimization, purpose limitation and the "right to forget" or delete neural insights. Policies need to be clear in communication training to differentiate between therapeutic or skill groups, and possible enhancement groups, which may present different issues of fairness.

Efforts to implement need to be interdisciplinary. HRD's collaboration with developers at the interface of human beings and the digital device, academia, and policies can speed up the development of user-centered and ethical designs like privacy-by-design interaction and explainable AI for neural decoding. Important, too: cultural adaptation in organizations; educating about the benefits and risks reduces resistance and enables employees to engage in a knowledgeable and informed manner (Sudhani et al., 2025).

Long-term implications involve tracking the societal changes that may arise, including changes in norms at the workplace with respect to expectations of privacy, or the "normalization" of neural monitoring. Ethical implementation must prioritize: (1) reversibility, ensuring that use of the BCI does not leave users in an unhelpful position after termination and (2) equitable benefit-sharing allowing users of the BCI to add benefits to existing commerce and activity, without being economically disadvantaged. If training in communication skills specifically, safeguards are put in place to avoid technology dependency and insure continuity of interpersonal skills while retaining interpersonal aspects.

Considering these points in advance enables organizations to be leaders in responsible neuro-digital transformation. Incorporating ethical considerations, comprehensive privacy safeguards, and intentional implementation procedures, HRD has the potential to capitalise on BCI opportunities while addressing associated risks, fostering trust, inclusion, and sustainable innovation in the workplace (Bi et al., 2025). Not doing so, however, can destroy trust in employees, spark legal disputes, and frustrate the very human objectives these technologies attempt. The impact of BCIs on professional communication and organizational life hinges on the dialogue that occurs, adaptive governance, and human center values.

7. CONCLUSION AND FUTURE DIRECTIONS

AI may be embedded in the future, in all BCIs, and seamlessly communicate with them. These ideas will be hypothetical, such as direct wisdom sharing, instant multilingual thinking translation and collective wisdom platforms. HRD needs to invest in upskillings on Neuro-literacy, promote ethical values and build innovation eco-systems. carry out BCI readiness need assessments, create courses using mixed training methods, create cross-functional governance committees, and remain aware of what is happening in the world and make sure that BCI is used in a competitive way but with responsibility. When faced with these sounds, organizations can mount a challenge, assume a proactive stance and give members of their workforce a sense of resiliency and capability in the new neuro-digital era.

REFERENCES

Arivunambi, A., Naikwade, S. S., Sarkar, P., Lami, Z. F., Lourens, M., & Al-Tameemi, A. R. (2025). Optimizing HR Processes Using Brain-Computer Interface Technology. In *Concepts and Applications of Brain-Computer Interfaces* (pp. 287–300). IGI Global Scientific Publishing. DOI: 10.4018/979-8-3693-7427-6.ch017

Balasundaram, E., Aranganathan, P., Sujatha, S., Navalgund, N. R., & Gajendran, A. (2026). Transformative Potential of Neurotechnology and Brain–Computer Interfaces in Corporate Learning and Development.

Bi, Z., Gad, A., Younis, N., & Abu-Mulaweh, H. (2025). Critical Review on Brain–Computer Interfaces (BCIs) for Effective Human–Machine Interactions (HMIs). *Journal of Engineering*, *2025*(1), 6682954. DOI: 10.1155/je/6682954

Kies, A., De Keyser, A., Jaramillo, S., Li, J., Tang, Y., & Ud Din, I. (2025). Wired for work: Brain-computer interfaces' impact on frontline employees' well-being. *Journal of Service Management*, *36*(1), 1–26. DOI: 10.1108/JOSM-03-2024-0098

Kim, H. (2025). Transforming Individuals with Borderline Intellectual Functioning into Cognitively Augmented Workers: AI-Integrated Co-Adaptive, Closed-Loop Brain–Computer Interface. *MechEcology, 4*(2).

Kritika. (2026). The Future of Neuroscience-Driven Cybersecurity. In *Neuroscience Meets Cybersecurity: Applying Brain Science to Enhance Digital Protection* (pp. 403-436). Berkeley, CA: Apress.

Mukherjee, S. (2025). Neuro-Law and Brain–Machine Interfaces: Emerging Frontiers of Legal Responsibility, Rights, and Regulation. *AIJFR-Advanced International Journal for Research, 6*(5).

Musole, E. (2026). Governing Neural Data in the Global South: Toward a Neuro-Responsible Business Framework for Zambia. *International Journal of Advanced Business Studies*, *5*(1), 47–61. DOI: 10.59857/g3bvjx74

Pandey, B. K., George, A. S., Tiwari, S., Albermany, S. A., & Hung, H. S. (Eds.). (2025). *Brain-computer Interfaces and Applications in Business*. IGI Global. DOI: 10.4018/979-8-3373-5122-3

Radu, R. (2025). Cognitive frontiers: Neurotechnology and global internet governance. *Frontiers in Digital Health*, *7*, 1690489. DOI: 10.3389/fdgth.2025.1690489 PMID: 41459239

Sheela, S. C., Madanan, P., Sharma, R., Lami, Z. F., & Alanssari, A. I. (2025). Innovative Financial Services Enabled by Brain-Computer Interface Technology. In *Concepts and Applications of Brain-Computer Interfaces* (pp. 211–226). IGI Global Scientific Publishing. DOI: 10.4018/979-8-3693-7427-6.ch012

Sudhani, H. P., Vattikuti, P., & Rekha, D. (2025). Challenges and future directions in brain–computer interface research for exoskeletons usage. In *Artificial Intelligence Applications for Brain–Computer Interfaces* (pp. 295–316). Academic Press.

Terec-Vlad, L., & Rusu, A. (2026). Neuro-Cybersecurity and the Future of Cognitive Rights: Legal Foundations for the Protection of the Human Mind in the Digital Age. *Revista Romaneasca pentru Educatie Multidimensionala, 18*(1), 82-104.

Vijayalakshmi, R., Krishna, S. H., Sahu, A. K., Adel, A. H., Lourens, M. E., & Al-Tameemi, A. R. (2025). Transforming Human Resource Management With Brain-Computer Interface Innovations. In *Concepts and Applications of Brain-Computer Interfaces* (pp. 257–272). IGI Global Scientific Publishing. DOI: 10.4018/979-8-3693-7427-6.ch015

Chapter 13
The Impact of Neural Data Rights Awareness on Consumer Attitudes Toward Neurotechnology Products

Aastha Sawhney
Independent Researcher, India

Ankita Bajpai
Inderprastha Engineering College, Sahibabad, India

Amit Kumar Pandey
http://orcid.org/0000-0001-5767-6333
Institute of Management Studies (Business School), Ghaziabad, India

Shashank Chaudhary
Independent Researcher, India

Vartika Saxena
Institute of Professional Excellence and Management, Ghaziabad, India

ABSTRACT

Consumer-associated neurotechnology devices, like EEG systems and brain computer systems (BCIs), are proliferating quickly, touching controversial issues of neuroscientific knowledge, which may uncover deep psychological, emotional and cognitive variations that are shared with the wearer amongst a household's constituents or

DOI: 10.4018/979-8-3373-9720-7.ch013

with strangers. The aims of this chapter are to explore consumer attitudes towards the same products based on their knowledge of the rights of the neural data. Based on the surveys, policy analysis and industry reports it finds the following: low awareness is linked to increased privacy concerns and decreased usage; education about rights translates to increased trust and usage. But there is still a lot of work to be done in terms of transparency and regulations in companies.

1. INTRODUCTION

With the emergence of consumer neurotechnology, the way humans interact with machines has just entered into another dynamic, with potential benefits in areas like focus, meditation, sleep tracking, games, and even cognition. Wearable EEG headsets from companies like Muse, Emotiv or the new BCIs fit into our lives and don't hinder. However, with this innovation come unparalleled dangers to mental privacy, across the collection of neural data, or signals reflective of brain activity, are able to be inferred to determine the emotions, attention, intentions and even sub-conscious state of the brain as well. Consumer attitudes are significantly influenced by knowledge of "neural data rights": the rights of consumers to control, access, delete and consent to the use of these data. There is a correlation between consumer awareness and engagement, as well as belief that regulations are effective, with a tendency toward greater levels of positive engagement for consumers who are more aware.Greater levels of consumer engagement and a greater sense of the effectiveness of protection tend to be seen as more positive as levels of consumer awareness are higher, and less questionable and hesitant. It is all the more essential for the capacity to boost neural data rights awareness, as a way to strike a tradeoff between development and mental privacy, and help consumers make informed choices in a booming market that should expand significantly.

Neural data is different from traditional personal data because it is unique, personal and specific to individuals. Whereas fitness tracker information such as steps taken can be correlated to brain activity, the signals may be used to help map cognitive patterns, stress responses, emotional reactions, or even make predictions on behavior. The government report mentions the potential for profiling with targeted advertising, surveillance, or manipulation, particularly "in the context of sharing with third parties or processing by artificial intelligence". According to a broader 2024 audit by the Neurorights Foundation of 30 consumer neurol tech companies, however, a cursory look at policies shows many of them have serious deficiencies — with only a small minority making a clear statement about neural data privacy, for example, many kept wide rights to potentially share or transfer neural data, and very few offered strong encryption, breach communications, or meaningful users rights to control data. More than 60% of those who have anything stated nothing specific about how the data is handled by the neural system, leaving consumers in the dark.

This opacity is directly affecting attitudes. Brain data is considered very sensitive by public perception studies, more so than genetic data, or financial data. If any consumer is not aware of his/her rights (or even the possible risks), he/she takes the safe route. People are not eager about the use of technologies involving the brain, because of concerns that data can be misused, accessed without permission, or the technology could 'read their minds' (Di Salvo, 2025). Potential inferences on mental health/biases would present discrimination issues, for example, in the employment or insurance sector. If there is no rights schema the end user has doubts that he/she actually owns "her" outputs or if there exists the possibility that they could be used indefinitely by the company.

Rise in consciousness about neural data rights can work towards a positive change in attitude, on the other hand. The education on issues such as informed consent, principle of data minimisation, rights to deletion and rules for prohibiting the sharing of data without consent enhance users' power. Jurisdictions with protections already in place tended to see more trust as it became easier to see how data was used, as seen in jurisdictions where neural data is sensitive and falls under consumer privacy law that is now in effect, like Colorado and California. For those jurisdictions that created protections, like those that classify neural data as sensitive, under consumer privacy law in force, increased transparency was found to increase trust. California's law starts in phases applies to data related to the nervous system as well and allows for the explicit opt-in consent to some uses while imposing more protection over deletion rights and access rights, while Colorado's pioneering legislation explicitly extends protection to nervous system data. These are steps measures that communicate to consumers that they're being given 'mental privacy', and that could move the adoption of the product along with people who may be more privacy conscious.

1.1 Background on Neurotechnology Products

Neurorights movements have a similar impact on a global level. The consumers are more willing to buy and use the product when they can see definite policies, quality responsiveness and commitment to de-identification or encryption that are clearly communicating these rights. Raising awareness with successful cases, like lawsuits enforcing brain data privacy, further increase the confidence.

However, challenges persist. Many companies are neurotech companies working in a niche between health-care and marketing regulatory requirements; they are selling their devices as health and/or wellness tools avoiding strict medical oversight. Whereas privacy policies tend to be wordy and ambiguous, and claims to anonymisation of neural datasets are suspect in the face of re-identification threats with rich datasets. Even low level of awareness of consumers, depending on education, media coverage and Digital literacy (Chand et al., 2025). Although these risks have been expressed, the benefits of using lithium last-generation technology, such as improved concentration or highly immersive gaming, might be more important to a younger user or techies; meanwhile, certain vulnerable groups may feel more threatened by loss of autonomy.

1.2 Emergence of Neural Data Rights

The implications are far reaching and relate to market dynamics. Low rights awareness received can hinder growth as it can generate boycotts or bad reviews, which can have a negative impact on the brand's reputation. But, with incidents like schools using brain-monitoring headsets without parental permission nor informed consent, a backlash is well warranted. Conversely, businesses that make responsible investment choices informed consent, user-friendly controls and independent audits—can stand out in the crowd and gain customer and investor loyalty that accepts responsible innovation. This makes an ideal cycle wherein well-informed customers challenge industry to upgrade and better quality products put demand on customers.

Like with genetic information or biometrics, transparency helps reduce the "privacy paradox" whereby expressed privacy and confidentiality concerns do not necessarily reconcile with actual behavior. This can be overcome by using targeted education using the app interfaces, policy summaries or public campaigns. In neurotech this could be visuals on the data flow or an explanation of the rights on introduction to the machine. However, there is also evidence that perceived control (such as good data portability or ability to opt out) can also have a significant positive impact on attitudes and intentions to use.

Equity is facilitated when individuals are aware of it within entire societies. If not, then benefits can be subsequently enjoyed by those who are at ease in handling complicated terms, further widening divides. One of the tenets of ethical principles is cognitive liberty, a right to mental autonomy (Ajmal & Sudhakar, 2026). As the lines between medical and consumer uses get even bluer and blurrier, consistent standards should have been put in place to stop malicious use and to help progress with novel technologies such as restorative BCIs for the paralyzed.

Recommendations for policies in the U.S. include federal unified or harmonized legislation (e.g., in the form of the proposed MIND Act), mandating disclosures for neural data, and incentives for privacy-enhancing technologies such as on-device processing. There is a need for voluntary codes which are above the minimum requirement for industry and more studies be done on the longitudinal impact of awareness interventions on adoption.

2. NEURAL DATA RIGHTS: CONCEPTS AND FRAMEWORKS

Neural data rights are an application of human rights and data protection laws to the specific characteristics of neural data. Neural data are original or processed signals recorded from a human's central nervous system (brain) or peripheral nervous system (nerves, muscles), such as the information gathered from a headset when an individual is wearing it to measure their EEG activity, patterns detected with fMRI, or signals obtained from brain-computer interfaces (BCIs) (Muravieva, 2025). This data can be used to identify basic physiological conditions as well as very personal information such as mood, thoughts, intentions, attention, subconscious beliefs, mental illnesses, mental health indicators and behavioral predictions of personalized data.

Neural data are uniquely sensitive, unlike more traditional personal information (such as location, where you've been, etc.), but it is directly linked to the biological substrate of thought, identity and autonomy. Four fundamental neurorights are noted: mental privacy (the right not to have brain data entered without consent), cognitive liberty (freedom to control mental states), mental integrity (the right to be protected from harmful changes to the brain), psychological continuity (the right to maintain one's identity). These draw on precedent models such as those that the GDPR establishes, such as the binding that sensitive data cannot be stored; however, they exceed and put the emphasis on the brain as the final refuge of personal space (Song et al., 2025).

Conceptual frameworks are informed by bioethics, human rights law and neurophilosophy. Neurorights groups like the Neurorights Foundation advocate for greater protections over neural data as compared to genetic data, but additional protections because of its real time, dynamic, and potentially decodable quality. The main principles are the right to informed consent, where data is locked down instead of collected from point A to B, and to purpose limitation (data is used only for the purpose it was intended for).Informed consent (explicit, granular and revocable), data minimization (collect only what is necessary), purpose limitation (data is used for the purpose it was meant for) and transparent data processing (every way data gets used is visible to the user and documented) are the main principles, together with strong security protection, preventing unauthorized data breaches and re-identification. Anonymization is especially tricky due to the power of AI systems that are able to match anonymous neural data with an individual, and thus defeat the anonymization they have been subjected (Pathak & Bhardwaj, 2026).

More general principles, including UNESCO's Recommendation on the Ethics of Neurotechnology (adopted November 2025), emphasize that technologies must be governed in a human-centered manner: (a) Manipulating or exploiting the human response to technology, for example, neuromarketing during sleep, is proscribed, and (b) equity and access to technologies should be encouraged. They deal with the dual-use issue: uses in the healthcare sector such as unlocking communication for patients in "locked-in" states and the uses in a consumer sphere, specifically overall surveillance, discrimination or cognitive manipulation. This approach should involve implementing user-centric controls, such as allowing users to export or delete their data easily, as well as having privacy-by-design features and on-device processing.

In the changing discourse it is acknowledged that neural data pitfalls into both medical and wellness uses, making upkeep hard. With the advent of new consumer devices, ranging from a "charm bracelet" that focuses your attention to an immersive gaming bCI, balance is key. If regulations are not conceptually sound, you might end up just fixing the next thing you run into. In the end, neural data rights would help to validate that the mind is not simply another kind of data source but the essence of a person's dignity, and that there's a need to be protected actively and adaptively as technology changes.

2.1 Existing Regulations and Neurorights Initiatives

With the rise of neurotechnology, as a result of this, there have been accelerated developments in international and national neurorights initiatives. Chile was a global first for constitutional protection, as it published an amendment that better safeguards mental integrity and neural data in 2021. This had an impact on Latin American countries such as Mexico (with the proposal of a comprehensive General Law on Neurorights), Brazil and others. Examples of enforcement involve Chilean courts ordering the deletion of brain data improperly collected.

UNESCO took action on the Ethics of Neurotechnology at the global level in November 2025, the first comprehensive world-wide scale ethical framework. It lays a foundation for ethical development, deployment and use, placing a focus on human rights, mental privacy, freedom of thought, and bans on undue influence or manipulation. This recommendation prescribes policy-related steps forward and measures to prevent or disable features and protection of AI-recommender systems.

Whereas in the United States, there is an absence of comprehensive federal legislation and so regulation is driven more at the state level. The Colorado Privacy Act, as amended by HB 24-1058 (effective August 2024), is the state's PIA and categorizes biological and neural data as "sensitive" and thus subject to more stringent protections and consent requirements. Next, California passed SB 1223 (effective 1/2025), which redefines the concept of neural data as a sensitive personal information category, which includes information generated by measuring activity of the central or peripheral nervous system, but not inferred from non-neural data. This provides consumers access, deletion, amendment and opt-out from sharing and selling.

Montana passed SB 163 (enacts October 2025) that incorporates data creation resulting from neurotechnology into its Genetic information privacy act. Connecticut enacted new legislation as of July 2026 that also provides enhanced protections for neural data. A few other states are moving bills along, which is good but bad in providing momentum and a patchwork.

2.2 Gaps in Consumer Protections

While there's improvement, there are still significant weaknesses in consumer protections for neurotechnology. In its groundbreaking April 2024 report, “Safeguarding Brain Data,” the Neurorights Foundation assessed 30 consumer neurotech firms, and found that 29 of 30 (96.7%) seemed to offer unconstrained rights to access neural data at minimal or no restraints, and more than 60% offered little to no specific reporting regarding neural data handling, while 96.7% reserved rights to transfer it to third parties. Few of the companies identified reported on strong user controls, encryption or breach notifications.

To avoid tougher medical device regulations (such as FDA control), many companies regard products as wellness (or entertainment) devices, leaving broad privacy policies that are lacking in meaningful specificity for the pressing question: how do they treat what are often sensitive signals—a neural fingerprint? De-identification claims may be misplaced, with increasingly sophisticated AI systems being capable of re-identifying individuals from highly granular datasets. Claims of de-identification may be mistaken, given the advances in AI technology that can allow for re-identification from rich data sets. There are often poor granular consent rights when it comes to data sharing with third parties, such as for advertising or AI training.

At the federal level, the U.S. has no single data law to govern the nervous system. No, relying on FTC Section 5 is not sufficient or proactive in future rights of access and deletion. However, bills, such as the MIND Act, that are under draft are yet to go through, raising the spectre of hazard for consumers in a fast-growing market. National companies have to grapple with a compliance bubble that is produced by State laws which have different definitions, consent conditions and effective dates.

Harmonization to the international level is poor. The UNESCO 2025 Recommendation offers ethical principles, but these are not binding. While GDPR is highly general, it doesn't actually refer to neural inferences or real-time brain signals. A few jurisdictions have no specific rules governing neural data; it would fall under some general category of personal information rules when viewed as evidence of someone's “mental conditions” even after anonymization.

There are gaps as consumer awareness is low, many don't know their risks or rights. Children and elderly or cognitively challenged persons are at higher risk for being exploited. Prohibitions are weak for the ability to use secondary applications, such as for insurance and employment and for manipulative applications. Securing standards are frequently insufficient and minimal to provide dedicated CPU or quick warning if security is breached.

3. CONSUMER AWARENESS OF NEURAL DATA RIGHTS: LEVELS OF PUBLIC KNOWLEDGE AND PERCEPTIONS

The news coverage of data rights behind the brain isn't ubiquitous, but it is not particularly welcome. Results from a survey of brain data sensitivity conducted nationally throughout the United States in the year 2024 showed mixed data with respect to perceptions of the data underlying each brain signal being highly private, similar to or less sensitive than traditional private data types such as Social Security numbers. This disparity shows a disjointed perception of the risks, meaning there is only a partial understanding of how neural data can be used to make inferences about emotions, intentions, mental health or unconsciousness.

Among the general consumer population, there is little overall awareness of specific concepts of "neurorights", including mental privacy, cognitive liberty and rights to access, delete and control the neural data (Yang & Jiang, 2025). Wellness or entertainment marketing efforts account for most users' experience with neurotech products, with few users ever hearing explicit mention of data risks and protections. Research shows increased concerns of privacy are intuitive, but few consumers actually are looking to learn more about policies or new laws from the companies, such as the ones that were prominently publicized in California and Colorado. Greater awareness on young people, tech-savy, and educated, even then, limited.

Risk identification and emphasis frequently shift focus to the negative side of things – toward skepticism. Brain data is often considered to be unique intimacies data; the last frontier of intimacy; the "last frontier of Privacy", because it may be at risk of being used for cognition manipulation, it may be a basis of discrimination in employment, insurance or it may be a ground of cognitive profiling, the last frontier of surveillance. But, if they are unaware of the information, many select to express a concern then continue to use because they believe they will gain something from it, such as benefits in focus, or health benefits, etc. The ones that perceive either a lower level of awareness or lesser trust show less willingness to change, and their insights call for more protective measures (Praveen et al., 2025). Educating people on this knowledge gap is critical to enable consumers to become empowered and to drive the growth of markets responsibly.

3.1 Factors Influencing Awareness

Consumer awareness of neural data rights is influenced by a number of interrelated characteristics. Media attention and public debate have an important defining function: high-profile coverage of news regarding neurorights projects such as the Chilean constitution and its ban on altering the human brain of patients, or state legislation in the United States regarding scientific interventions on legal persons' brains pushes these projects up the agenda; but coverage is local and sporadic. Backgrounds in technology, law, or ethics are associated with higher levels of knowledge, lending weight to the educational levels and digital literacy as strong predictors of knowledge about concepts such as mental privacy and informed consent.

There are demographic factors at play, too: younger people and users from urban and higher-income backgrounds tend to be more exposed through app usage/facets and marketing, but it rarely correlates with a strong grasp of rights. On the other hand, older people or groups more accustomed to traditional methods and/or less comfortable with technology are more likely to be underreported on regarding their awareness and worry in respect to vulnerability. Trust in institutions and companies also plays a role when it comes to perceptions – when talking about neural data, skepticism about Big Tech increases privacy concerns.

Building awareness through reporting on policy actions, pushing on policy, and campaigns (e.g., UNESCO recommendations, U.S. MIND Act discussions, etc.) due to regulatory developments and advocacy work of organisations such as the Neurorights Foundation. Enforcement, however, is low and laws are weak and disjointed, causing confusion. Onboarding and product design experiences are powerful: Apps that provide clear data practices lead to more knowledge, and not-so-clear interfaces lead to less. The cultural attitude towards privacy high in Europe and low in other parts of the world is another possible tempering variable of engagement. So, people experiences can drastically raise awareness, as when the data is leaked or if they are directly educated through workshops. Specific campaigns, participatory design and inclusive education is needed to raise public awareness among various groups and population segments (Mouammine & Azdimousa, 2025).

3.2 Role of Transparency in Neurotech Companies

A foundational element in the development of consumer awareness and trust in neural data rights is transparency in the companies manufacturing neurotech products. Transparency in neurotech companies is a fundamental piece of the puzzle in raising awareness and trust amongst consumers regarding their rights to neural data. The audit of 30 consumer companies conducted by the Neurorights Foundation in 2024 showed that only 43% did explicitly refer to neural data in their policy while more than 60% did not provide any specific detail of the handling practices of their own data. Most companies did not limit access to and sharing of neural data with third parties at all. Very few were willing to adhere to encryption or breach notification or provide transparent user controls.

This opacity directly affects consumer awareness and awareness cannot be exercised if one is not aware of the existence of rights or its meaning. Beware of padded and fuzzy wellness salesmanship, as it does not contribute to informed consent or reduced doubt when you learn of the dangers. Conversely, the corporations that respond with best practices—including use of plain privacy notices at the point of collection, granular consent choices, data-flow visualizations, and proactive rights explanations—are great for boosting user information and positive attitudes. The laws in California and Colorado mandate that neural data be treated as sensitive information that must be disclosed, and are used as models.

There is informed decision making, reduction of the privacy paradox and differentiation between artful leaders in an competitive market because of transparency. It minimises the risks of reputational harm arising in the wake of backlashes and assists regulatory compliance. Examples of effective strategies include onboarding policies (written in plain language), regular updates with user notifications, independent audits, and a function of rights information in apps. In conclusion, corporate transparency connects the technological innovations and empowers consumers, making the leap from potential fear to confident use while maintaining mental privacy standards. As the market continues to grow, greater commitment from industry is essential.

4. IMPACT ON CONSUMER ATTITUDES TOWARD NEUROTECHNOLOGY

Consumer attitudes toward neurotechnology in 2026 reflect these various factors of excitement around what it can do and deeply-rooted concerns about mental privacy. EEG headbands for focus and meditation help sharpen mental clarity, improve stress management, and assist with sleep regulation, while sleep trackers provide valuable insights into our sleep patterns and behaviours, and new brain-computer interfaces offer intuitive user interaction, enhanced cognitive function, and even better mental health. The personal nature of the neural data, however the emotions, intentions, cognitive modus operandi and subconsciousness - leads to suspicions. People sometimes feel brain data is more delicate and fragile and therefore adopt a more guarded approach to sharing it with others.People think that brain data is more sensitive than information from their finances or their genes and therefore are more hesitant to share it.

The report on Neurorights Foundation 2024 was influential as it revealed most of the 30 companies audited had policies that lacked sufficient restrictions and controls for users and third-party sharing rights were significant. This opacity towards consumer privacy leads to the Privacy paradox: Consumers voice deep privacy concerns, but they might suspect that they can gain benefit by using these devices in some regard. California, Colorado, Montana, Connecticut and Vermont (along with new neurological rights in 2026) have regulations that represent progress by establishing that the neural data are sensitive, mandate improved consent and are confusing and not uniform.

Bigger populations are skeptical of AI, and in particular nervous about being monitored, discriminated against or manipulated by AI, whereas people that know about it and are tech-savvy are positive in general (Radu, 2025). The market is rapidly moving towards the tens of billions and attention on neurorights campaigns (such as the proposed federal MIND Act) is slowly linking the formerly negative feelings of fear and avoidance with a positive, conditional feeling of acceptance when there are ethical safeguards discernable. To bridge knowledge gaps, through education and corporate responsibility is an important part towards mainstreamed adoption.

4.1 Trust, Privacy Concerns, and Adoption Barriers

As privacy concerns linger at the end of mid-2026, so do barriers to adoption in using neurotechnology products. Other biometrics (such as body scans, image analysis, or gait recognition) may seem as private as neural data, as privacy and objectivity are paramount to its effectiveness.Other biometrics include body scans, image analysis, gait recognition—and these have a perceived greater level of privacy than neural data; which is highly valued in its effectiveness. The long-term effects of the audit by the Neurorights Foundation have served to damage the trust in the mechanism: 96,7% of companies admitted that they allow for broad access with almost no restrictions (free intention, the term is freely accessible), more than 60% of them did not have specific details on neural data, and consumers are frequently provided with third-party sharing rights.

Customers have concerns about unauthorised watching, breach of data, insurer/employer profiling and brain-worming. Marketing of benefits clearness and focus on wellness instead of sleep disorders, or the like strengthens the trust in the policy, opacity strengthens the doubt. There are many who are seeing the "privacy paradox" superficial use with limited data sharing. Risk is exacerbated for vulnerable groups (children, elderly, less tech-literate) because of inadequate consent, and because risks are downplayed, while benefits are upplaying the younger generations in the entertainment/wellness framing.

State laws are required to provide enhanced protection and disclosure (California SB 1223 is set to take effect 2025, Colorado, Montana, Connecticut, Vermont 2026 neurological rights bill but it is a regulatory patchwork). Barriers to adoption are slow buying and negative reviews, as well as non-neural alternatives. Much attention has been paid to the MIND Act and FTC investigation not only to increasing awareness of the laws and issues, but identifying areas in which they lag. To restore trust, businesses must provide transparent business practices, strong security measures, and user controls so users can learn to put their trust in them and engage with the business with confidence and open arms, which will then pave the way to greater market opportunities.

4.2 Positive Effects of Awareness on Informed Consent

Consumer neurotechnology informed consent processes are greatly enhanced by attention to data rights pertaining to neurons. Getting users familiar with mental privacy, cognitive liberty, access/deletion, and potential pitfalls such as re-identification or secondary use goes beyond taking a reactive stance on terms to choosing them for their values. If education really addresses the world, it also invites a more detailed consideration of policy—such as whether it has implications for mental health and/or feelings—in addition to seeking the answers of 'how' and 'why'.In addition to the questions of 'how' and 'why', asking education real-world questions also invites the questions of 'how' and 'why' of policy.

The privacy paradox is reduced by awareness, as they get closer to the behavior of the concern. Clear disclosures, diagrams around the flow of data and laws (such as opt-in consent requirements under California and Colorado law) help give the required user control and thereby provide satisfaction (Hussain, 2025). The activities of the Neurorights Foundation, UNESCO ethics guidelines and press reports about enforcement cases further boost knowledge.

Benefits are lower rate of regretting use, increased depth of engagement, prolonged usage, and user enthusiasm for using items ethically. When consumers are informed, pressure is placed on companies to promote a privacy by design, on-device processing or revocation of permissions. The increasing awareness leads to a shift from vulnerability and feelings that lack of control to agency, as state protections grow stronger, and federal initiatives such as the MIND Act catch on. Helps to establish a robust ecosystem with true consensus and inclusive innovation of respecting mental autonomy.

4.3 Potential for Market Growth Through Ethical Practices

Neurotechnology with a focus on ethical foundations, particularly those based on neural data rights awareness, has significant promise to stimulate sustainable market growth for neurotechnology in 2026 and beyond. Businesses that go proactively beyond compliance standards as they start to allow its users to control their data, provide clear policies, implement robust security measures, have proven policies that can be audited independently, and give users the ability to delete their information easily, differentiate themselves and foster loyalty in a context of trusting relationships.This includes user-centric controls, such as easy deletion; independent auditing of proven policies; strong security measures; transparent user policies; and the ability to easily delete user data, as businesses move beyond compliance requirements to differentiate and build loyalty in a trust-sensitive world. The 2024 Neurorights Foundation report highlights the negative repercussions of deficiencies on reputation; executives that choose to move to higher levels draw privacy-conscious consumer in essence.

As the sector is expected to expand significantly (and even "surpass $50 billion" in the next decade or so), ethical differentiation offers a premium positioning, positive word-of-mouth and backlash/rescussion. State laws and new-federal interest set expectations; companies that meet expectations by taking proactive steps, such as on-device processing, enjoy a competitive edge and partnerships are made easier.

Ethical solutions also provide for wider applications, wellness to restorative technology and fair access and community acceptance. They establish a virtuous cycle whereby people knowledgeable about the products value the responsible innovation, thus fostering uptake into mainstream use and investment. With anticipating risks, potential risks are highlights of opportunities for responsible growth, not threats towards the loss of viability if handled responsibly by addressing gaps and focusing on mental privacy along with benefits (Sattler et al., 2025).

5. CONCLUSION AND FUTURE RESEARCH DIRECTIONS

Neural data rights become a key factor in 2026 shaping consumer attitudes towards neurotechnology products. The close connection of the brain to these kind of bioinformation pieces – which can include indicators of mindsets, cognitive habits, feelings, and intentions – need greater safeguards, especially as sleeper tracking and home-use EEG headsets and brain–computer interface devices continue to proliferate. This study draws on findings that indicate a low level of awareness impacts on issues of trust erosion, increased privacy concerns, barriers to adoption, and a continued privacy paradox. Deeper understanding of mental privacy, cognitive liberty, informed consent, access, deletion and opt-out, on the other hand, promotes positive attitudes as well as a sense of control and eagerness to experience moral products. In Chile, for example, existing laws, including the landmark protections contained in the Constitution, represent an important step in the classification of neural data as sensitive, as do UNESCO's Ethics Recommendation (2025) and state laws in California, Colorado, Montana, Connecticut and Vermont in the United States. But key gaps identified in the 2024 Neurorights Foundation audit remain to be causes for concern and inhibit mainstream uptake, including lack of third-party protection and ambiguities in policies.

A way forward is in ethical corporate actions and regulation. By making information more transparent, privacy by design, subject to on-device processing and strong user controls, the risks are reduced and significant market growth potential created in an industry that is expected to continue growing rapidly. Empowering consumers to make informed decisions can improve how they manage their digital relationship, while neural data rights awareness can readily balance the technological benefits and gains on cognitive enhancement and insights into mental health with the societal implications of surveillance, discrimination, and the diminishing mental autonomy associated with the use of human competitors. This awareness reflects on a basic level the dignity of a person, respecting and enhancing rather than diminishing the final frontier of privacy: the human mind. The results show how important it is to act responsibly and how necessary a collaborative approach is between the various stakeholders, such as the policy, business, advocacy and consumer sectors, in order to ensure compliance standards are harmonised, gaps in compliance are filled and mental integrity is focused on alongside technological progress.

5.1 Future Research Directions

These are the additional lines of inquiry that can help to further the understanding and inform practice at a deeper level. Changes in consumer attitudes and behaviours as a result of awareness-raising campaigns or regulatory changes and their effects over time (for instance the effects of California's SB 1223 and the proposed federal MIND Act) should be measured in a longitudinal manner. Although a comparison of informed and uninformed consumer groups is difficult to achieve in the real world, the setup of these experiments could incorporate either educational content or clear policies, or simulate the available information based on different scenarios, to generate causal evidence of attitude change and quality of consent.

Ways to understand them are by cross cultural analysis as well as demographic analysis taking into account differences in perception between areas that have privacy norms different from the others, in which the regulatory maturity is different, and in which the level of penetration of neurotechnology is different. Addressing inequities, children, elderly users and those who have cognitive differences must be given special focus. The effectiveness of certain transparency tools, such as data flow visualizations, plain-language notices and independent audits, could also be assessed in the development of trust.

The technological and ethical aspects should be looked at, such as privacy-preserving technologies such as federated learning, homomorphic encryption, or fully-on-device neural processing, and how they are developed and adopted by users. Uniting disciplines such as neuroscience, behavioral economics, and law, finally, could come together to evaluate long-term consequences of the societal implications, such as those on cognitive freedom or the potential for manipulation in immersive use of these technologies. Continued empirical monitoring is essential to make sure that neurotechnology is aligned with human values and neurotechnology benefits all. The market is changing – and continued empirical monitoring will play a key role in making sure that neurotechnology is aligned with human values and inclusive benefits.

REFERENCES

Ajmal, M. K., & Sudhakar, B. D. (2026). Consumer awareness and perception of neuromarketing tools: Insights from a technology acceptance model (TAM) perspective in South India. *SN Business & Economics*, *6*(3), 66. DOI: 10.1007/s43546-026-01066-z

Chand, T., Nair, V. S., Srinivasu, P. N., & Kumar, V. J. (2025). Prospects and challenges in decoding consumer behavior using neurotechnology. *Artificial Intelligence Applications for Brain–Computer Interfaces*, 161-182.

Di Salvo, M. (2025). The protection of neural rights in the age of neurotechnologies and AI. The ethical challenge for law and neuroscience. *Russian Journal of Economics and Law*, *19*(1), 202–233. DOI: 10.21202/2782-2923.2025.1.202-233

Hussain, S. (2025). The ethical frontier: AI-enabled neuromarketing and conscious consumerism. [DSSR]. *Dialogue Social Science Review*, *3*(01), 1040–1048.

Mouammine, Y., & Azdimousa, H. (2025). A Qualitative Analysis of Global Expert Opinions on Neuromarketing and the Role of Feel Data in Consumer's Behaviour. African Journal of Human Resources, Marketing & Organisational Studies (AJHR-MOS), 2(1).

Muravieva, L. (2025). Regulating Neurotechnologies and AI-driven neural implants in the European Union: Legal and ethical challenges.

Pathak, A., & Bhardwaj, S. (2026). A systematic literature review on the fusion of face recognition and neuro-marketing. *SN Business & Economics*, *6*(5), 129. DOI: 10.1007/s43546-026-01131-7

Praveen, R. V. S., Peri, S. S. R. G., Labde, V. V., Gudimella, A., Hundekari, S., & Shrivastava, A.RVS Praveen. (2025). Neuromarketing in the Digital Age: Understanding Consumer Behavior Through Brain-Computer Interfaces. *Journal of Informatics Education and Research*, *5*(2), 2112–2132. DOI: 10.52783/jier.v5i2.2667

Radu, R. (2025). Cognitive frontiers: Neurotechnology and global internet governance. *Frontiers in Digital Health*, *7*, 1690489. DOI: 10.3389/fdgth.2025.1690489 PMID: 41459239

Sattler, S., Mehlkop, G., Neuhaus, A., Wexler, A., & Reiner, P. B. (2025). Exploring disparities in self-reported knowledge about neurotechnology. *Scientific Reports*, *15*(1), 18488. DOI: 10.1038/s41598-025-00460-1 PMID: 40425633

Song, G., Gazi, M. A. I., Waaje, A., Roshid, M. M., Karim, R., Rahaman, M. A., Min, Z., & Senathirajah, A. R. B. S. (2025). The neuromarketing: Bridging neuroscience and marketing for enhanced consumer engagement. *IEEE Access : Practical Innovations, Open Solutions, 13*, 40331–40353. DOI: 10.1109/ACCESS.2025.3545742

Yang, H., & Jiang, L. (2025). Regulating neural data processing in the age of BCIs: Ethical concerns and legal approaches. *Digital Health, 11*, 20552076251326123. DOI: 10.1177/20552076251326123 PMID: 40162168

Chapter 14
Toward International Standards, Neurorights Legislation, and Responsible Innovation in the Brain-Data Era

Mohd Faiz Khan
School of Legal Studies, CGC University, Mohali, India

Saurabh Chandra
http://orcid.org/0000-0003-4172-9968
Symbiosis Law School, Symbiosis International (Deemed to be) University, Pune, India

ABSTRACT

The current brain-data era requires strong worldwide frameworks, such as regulations and guidelines for appropriate and responsible innovation that will safeguard human dignity and stimulate potential areas of therapeutic and cognitive research. The unique amendments to the Chilean Constitution inspired constitutional initiatives in the region as well as soft-law instruments by UNESCO, OECD and the Inter-American Juridical Committee. The constitutional amendments in Chile created a benchmark for similar initiatives in other nations and for soft-law instruments by UNESCO, OECD, and the Inter-American Juridical Committee. The piece explores how national-level responses have not been uniform but rather a mix of protective measures at the state level in the United States, and the evolution toward harmonized governance to help address concerns regarding cognitive liberty, and ensuring access to mental data and privacy.

DOI: 10.4018/979-8-3373-9720-7.ch014

1. INTRODUCTION

In the era of the brain-data, from wearable non-invasive EEG devices to brain-computer interfaces or sophisticated neuroimaging and neural decoders using AI technology, neuroscience has entered a new age of intimate mental information, that can be measured, shared, and manipulated. It requires a collective shift towards international benchmarks and specific legislations on neurorights as well as accountable innovation practices to avoid dystopian considerations and to reap societal advantages in health, education and human enhancement. Conventional approaches to human rights protections that were developed before what is now called the 'neurotech era' are inadequate for addressing first-hand access to, or modification of, brain activity, thus justifying the creation of specific protections (Zhu et al., 2025). It asks for a diversity of stakeholders to work together, design notions to be ethical rather than coercive, and regulations to be adaptive and flexible, finding a balance between innovation and protection against misuse to ensure the technology can be used for the benefit of humanity without compromising our mental autonomy and without intensifying inequalities.

In the year 2021, with provisions of laws 21383, Chile became the first country in the world to explicitly protect "brain activity" and "the information derived from it" in its constitution – all with concepts of mental privacy, identity, free will, and mental integrity. It is even a fundamental reform, sparked by the Neurorights foundation and neuroscientist Rafael Yuste, and needing scientific and technological progress to comply with physical and psychic integrity (DI Salvo, 2025). A related bill (still working its way through chambers as of 2026) aims for adoption of these rights by drafting a statute on how neurotechnologies are to be used, including within kids, and to regulate their use by consumers, placing them in the category of medical devices. Judicial teeth on the other hand, have been exercised in Chile though: the Supreme Court has ruled that brain data collected by an American company on a consumer headset must be deleted. There were also signs in other parts of the Global South, with other countries in the region such as Mexico, Brazil, Colombia, Argentina, and Uruguay taking steps to start debates on the issue.

Soft law instruments, when it comes to the international level, offer a basic guidance, not as treaty. OECD followed by a dozen countries, the 2019 Principles of Responsible Innovation in Neurotechnology include nine fundamental principles that underscore the need for safety, inclusiveness, data protection, responsible stewardship and the awareness of potential misuse. The toolkit that accompanies it helps policymakers move forward with the process of implementation, emphasizing protection of individual brain data and public discussion and engagement (Mia, 2025). There has been particular activity under the auspices of UNESCO, with reports by the International Bioethics Committee, and the 2025 Recommendation on the Ethics of Neurotechnology providing ethical foundations based on human dignity, freedom of thought, mental privacy and autonomy. These call for action of member states to legally combat coercive application, surveillance or manipulation and to ensure equal access. In 2023, the Inter-American Juridical Committee issued its declaration, which sets out ten principles for the Americas, with some views emphasising the need to interpret a right rather than create new ones (Radu, 2025).

Progress is more segmented in the USA and Europe. Several U.S. States (CCPA amendments in 2024-2025 to define neural data as sensitive, Colorado, Montana and Connecticut) have extended consumer privacy laws, providing consumers the right to access, delete, opt-out and limit sharing of neural data. Part one separates raw neural signals from information gleaned from them, while part two is beginning to create a sense of the need for enhanced protection from general biometrics or health data for information acquired from the brain. On the federal level, initiatives such as the MIND Act (2025) spearheaded studies on neural data governance and advocates are working towards more widespread laws. The EU uses indirect access by its AI Act, GDPR, and Medical Device Regulation, while it remains to be seen whether there is a need for any AI-specific regulations or for adapting the existing ones to incorporate neurorights. The Digital Rights Charter of Spain 2021 mentions mental agency and neurotech rights.The Spanish Digital Rights Charter (SRP) of 2021 mentions the rights of mental agency and neurotech.

At the heart of these efforts is responsible innovation, which goes beyond compliance to the ethical integration of innovation throughout the R&D process. The frameworks are based on Responsible Research and Innovation (RRI) principles for neurotech namely anticipation, reflexivity, inclusion, and responsiveness. These involve: thorough safety and risk considerations, informed consent processes invented, which take into account the special sensitivity of the neural data, interdisciplinary cooperation between neuroscientists, ethicists, legal experts, and users, and public engagement to establish societal norms, and stewardship and accountability mechanisms in the private sector. A code of conduct, conduct impact assessments, and reducing data collection are encouraged, as are avoiding algorithmic bias in neural decoding systems. Cautious deployment is guided by epistemic humility: recognising limits of current understanding of consciousness and long-term compound effects (Ding, 2026).

2. UNDERSTANDING NEURORIGHTS WITH COGNITIVE LIBERTY, MENTAL PRIVACY, MENTAL INTEGRITY AND PSYCHOLOGICAL CONTINUITY

Neurorights are the ethical, legal, social or natural rights and entitlements of freedom or protection of the collective brain and mind, in the context of new technologies that modify and alter the human brain and mind, such as brain-computer interfaces (BCIs), neuro-imaging, neuro-stimulation and using AI tools for neural data decoding in clinical, consumer, military and judicial applications (Sosa Navarro, 2026). Such rights arise from the fact that existing human rights doctrines are foundational but do not necessarily provide relief in situations involving techno-capabilities that can directly record, decode or modulate neural activities, thereby gaining access to or having a direct impact on the human subject's very personal and highly vulnerable inner sanctuaries of thought, emotion, identity, and agency. By building on earlier concepts of cognitive liberty from Boire and Sententia in the early 2000s, and embraced by neuroscientific friends like Rafael Yuste, pioneering work by Marcello Ienca and Roberto Andorno in 2017 led to a set of four core neurorights principles; cognitive liberty, mental privacy, mental integrity, and psychological continuity.

Cognitive liberty, regarded as the root of the Neuroright, is the creature of freedom for the individual to manipulate their own consciousness, thoughts, and application of neurotechnology without pressure and outside interference. Both positive and negative aspects: The right to use, manipulate or augment mental processes rather than failing to do so with the aid of a BCI (enhancement and/or protection) and banning governments, corporations or anyone else from doing so (forge and/or manipulate). Cognitive liberty allows that the mind is the final frontier of one's individual sovereignty, and is therefore essential to other freedoms, such as thought and expression, in a world where individuals' neural states were in some instances subject to decisionmaking or neural monitoring in the workplace (Lee, 2026). It originates in some preexisting ideas of freedom of conscience, but expands its coverage to suspicious brain manipulations and subliminal neural marketing being used in security situations.

The mental privacy concern is hugely the need to ensure that the information extracted from brain activity, whether raw or interpreted, is not accessed, collected, stored, shared, or monetized without the person's consent. Neural data, unlike traditional data, provides insights into intimate thoughts, feelings, memories, and even subconscious tendencies, without the conscious gatekeepers or privacy protections that conventional information is filtered through. Consumer EEG headsets, wearable neurotech and cutting-edge BCIs such as those being developed by Neuralink come in with a number of risks: data dumps from user headsets could reveal banking details and personal secrets through “mind reading” algorithms, consumer pervasiveness could be seen as a form of neuromarketing, and police use of brain scans for lie detection or pre-crime profiling is a possibility. Mental privacy requires explicit and informed consent, and that neural information is particularly sensitive and, when compared to genetic or biometric information, often more so, and needs to be strongly regulated, deleted upon demand, not used in secondary applications that might threaten autonomy. Chile's early legislative attempts at implementing this right, such as eliminating brain data collected by consumer devices, illustrate its application on the legislative front.

Mental integrity extends existing protections against harm or unwanted physical or functional interference to brain processes to include threats to brain processes using neurotech – an extension of the concept of right to mental health to be included in Article 3 of EU Charter of Fundamental Rights. Protection against malicious neurohacking, unwanted deep brain stimulation, forced or harmful erasure or insertion of memory, and targeted or harmful psychological manipulation through neuromodulative activity that affects a person's cognitive ability, distress or personality (Bariffi, 2026). In non-therapeutic or "adversarial" applications, like enhancing performance in the military or controlling behavior to avoid the violation of physical (and psychological) inviolability, it requires very strong regulation of the body instead; while in field (therapeutic) use its application for such purposes is dubious and must be closely monitored. Mental integrity points to the fact that the brain is not just an organ but is the organ of the person, that its unjustified modification is an unbearable attack upon human dignity.

Psychological continuity, which may be associated with personal identity, helps maintain the continuity of an individual's mentality, memory of his biography and life in general against a change in personal characteristics that might break or misrepresent his personality, interests, values, or personal experiences, without expressing his consent. Final scenarios might turn into a man altering his memory in a way that the memories appear entirely different as the archive uploads and forces a reconstruction of identity._memory_removal', tagged with AI-assisted disclosure via personality profiles or devices that can eventually become integrated with the brain could result in a revival of identity rather than its elimination.Tagging with memory removal, AI-assisted disclosure through personality profiles or seamless brain-device integration could lead to the experience of a revival of identity, rather than its removal. That right encompasses harmful modifications, as well as more subtle ones such as neuromarketing that changes the desire without knowledge, or improvements that, while intended for a purpose, end up sapping authenticity. It maps into philosophical issues of personal identity, with a focus on the continuity of consciousness being crucial in shaping moral agency and legal liability (Terec-Vlad & Rusu, 2026).

These neurorights collectively constitute an integrated and comprehensive set of rules for managing neurotechnology in a way that encourages good innovation while avoiding negative consequences. They supplement or, as in the case of established rights like privacy, freedom of thought, or bodily integrity, they demand their re-thought under official documents and instruments such as the Universal Declaration of Human Rights. There has been a growing policy momentum from several fronts: constitutional protections for brain-related activities and information for the first time have been developed in Chile, international policies recognized by UNESCO and the Neurorights Foundation seek to establish common standards appropriate to mental privacy, free will, personal identity and equitable access, and rights that protect bias, and academic networks work towards ethical guidelines for research and deployment (Possa, 2025). There are challenges to be sure such as definitional precision to not over/under protect, balance individual rights and social values (such as justice or benefits to public health), equity in access to enhancements, and enforcement across borders in the fragmented tech realm, where inferred data is often preferable to raw neural data. Some worry about the need for new rights, others emphasize the qualitative difference of intimacy and potency in the use of neurotech.

Relying on cognitive liberty, mental privacy, mental integrity, and psychological continuity within the inner citadel of the mind is about protecting what is human about us, in the presence of instruments capable of looking into and shaping our minds. With the rise of neurotechnology, there will be a need for proactive ethical/legal frameworks, and their nature will decide whether they will free the human spirit or undermine the principles of liberty they seek to improve. This requires continuous dialogue between different disciplines, dialogical approaches within the public sphere, firm governance and a consciousness of human dignity, which ensures that the sanctuary of the brain is not opened to the chaos of digital and neural revolution to come (Li, 2026).

3. BRAIN DATA AS SENSITIVE PERSONAL INFORMATION

Brain data as the information gathered from the measurement of neural activity in central and peripheral systems, are increasingly acknowledged to be a physically highly sensitive type of personal information, requiring a greater level of protection than other types of personal information. In contrast to traditional information like browsing history or biometric so-to-say personal information, neural data may also safeguard not only the physical states but also significant sensual information about cognition, feelings, intentions, subconscious tastes or even probable future behavior. It places it more directly into our brain than genetic or health data, and is more revealing in many contexts than those other data in that direct connection to our biological substrate of thought, identity, and agency.

To protect neural data, legislators around the world are reacting by defining it as sensitive. Politically, there have been explicit mentions of neural data in such definitions as either "sensitive personal information" (via SB 1223 in California, amending the CCPA) or "sensitive data," in states such as Colorado, Montana and Connecticut where consumers have rights around access, deletion, refusal of sharing and opt-out options. These laws are generally monochotomous laws that differentiate the raw or directly measured neural signals from inferences from non-neural sources. Chile's constitutional amendments of 2021 has provisions dedicated to protecting brain activity and information derived from it, where previously, a precedent-setting court ruling to delete brain activity data from consumer neurotechs is in effect. Internationally organisations and institutions such as the UNESCO indicate its sensitivity when recommending its correct treatment to be equivalent to special category data within regulations such as GDPR, but with a lack of details regarding non-medical consumer applications (Johnson, 2026).

This is not a classification that deals only with transactions but means that brain data can be considered as existentials. It may make mental privacy problematic, allow discrimination on the basis of mental type or lead to manipulation. Regardless of the neurotechnologies available – ranging from consumer EEG products, to sensors with increased levels of sophistication and precision claiming brain data is 'extra sensitive' lays the groundwork for data minimization, purpose limitation, stringent security protocols, and explicit consent.

3.1 Unique risks of neural data

In particular, because neural data is directly connected to the human mind and could be used to gain unprecedented insight and interfere with that mind, there are many risks that neural data presents not shared with other types of personal or biometric data. Neural patterns are not easily replaceable, unlike passwords and credit card numbers and more so than credit card details that can be changed. If they are broken, they cannot be fixed and will be an intensely personal event (Yang & Jiang, 2025). With AI as the power behind the algorithms, advanced decoding technologies can probe the brain to reveal thoughts, emotions, memories, mental health, political stance, or even even intentions and do it without engaging the conscious mind or important privacy filters.

The major challenges are as follows: unauthorized "mind reading" occurs when the brain-tapping or decoding of brain signals by an entity outside the BCIs owner is possible; privacy concerns are especially relevant in wireless BCI devices susceptible to cybersecurity vulnerabilities such as the ability to alter signals as they are being transmitted or received. Storing data could reveal internal biases or vulnerabilities that could result in the posting, targeted manipulation, or the use of discriminatory practices by governments, insurers and employers engaging in blackmail. For this reason, neuromarketing might have applications in consumer marketing that alter preferences in an imperceptible fashion and might lead to pre-crime profiling or behavioral control in a security or military application. A long-term integration with AI has the potential to result in personality changes or fragmentation of identity unless these changes remain small and gradual.The subconscious and psychological impact of long-term integration with an AI might lead to slight changes in one's personality or a sense of 'fractured self' if there are significant changes.

Other issues include accuracy of inferences, algorithmic biased versions, and the-filter-vs-the-information. Non-invasive wearables not only decrease barriers to mass collection but also increase the risks of surveillance, which people are unaware of. Increased inequality occurs when improvement takes place in society for some people but not for others; when some people have access to life supporting technologies and not others. These are unaccounted for in existing laws as those are made for less intimate data types (BUIATTI, 2025). Neurorights frameworks try to address this by placing greater emphasis on mental integrity and privacy, but they are hard to enforce and remains out of pace with the technological possibilities.

3.2 Consent and data ownership

Two key principles that govern brain data are consent and the ownership of its information, but they present significant challenges given the intimate and dynamic nature of brain data. Traditional notice-and-consent frameworks are not necessarily enough to be effective: people may not adequately understand the meaning of the neural data or what information might be gleaned about their personal attributes by a person via AI in the long run. Consent should be explicit, informed, granular, revocable and renewed for new uses and third-party sharing—prescribed by new laws such as Colorado's opt-in requirements and the recommendations of UNESCO.

Data ownership still remains an issue. The individual (the person who has the neural data) should have the major control over their data, such as rights to using it, correcting it, deletion and portability, but often companies secure the licenses in the user agreement. This is the one that was brought to light with the Emotiv case in Chile, where courts ruled in favor of giving people the right to have their data removed, and in favor of users' rights over commercial data retention without due and solid consent. Concern remains about whether or not sensors being equipped by buyers of wireless devices actually own the raw signals they record. For AI training and processed inferences, what about aggregated datasets or processed inferences? Rights-based control over neural information is also problematic in light of the non-rivalrous, persistent nature of neural information, resulting in a preference by many experts to controls that encompass rights.

Dynamic consent methods (such as per-session notifications), data minimization, purpose limitation and conditions that prohibit tying it to data disclosure that is not needed for services to be provided are best practices. Exceptions and inferences, and Special Rules apply to these groups. Immediate deletion on all systems should occur on revocation of access with some sort of audit trail for retrieving who did what. Issues range from power imbalance between users and tech giants, cross-border enforcement to the fact of how informed consent may be in a complex neuroscience world (Souza, 2025).

3.3 Commercial and state use of brain data

Both commercial and non-commercial applications have enormous potential in terms of the uses to which brain data can be put, but also enormous risks in terms of stalking and exploitation. Commercial sphere: Companies in the field of consumer neurotech gather large volumes of neural data for human wellness, gaming, concentration boost, etc., and neuromarketing. Many companies so keep broad rights to sell or profit from such information, with little protection for users, and allow for ad-targeting that taps into subconscious desires or stalking to check employees' productivity. The reports indicate that the privacy policies of most consumer neurotech products provide inadequate protections, and that they are used for secondary use without consumer knowledge, or for perspectives profiling.

These are exacerbated if they are used on the state level. It is possible for governments to use neural data to identify whether someone is lying, to screen individuals for security, to monitor individuals' mental health or even to predict who might be likely to turn violent in the future, raising concerns about infringement of mental privacy and cognitive liberty. In authoritarian situations, it might be able to implement thought verification or control. Dual-use technologies will have a tendency to merge or overlap between therapeutic and surveillance uses, and the military's focus upon superior performance or neural weapons introduces existential risks.

The reactions are different in different countries: the U.S. state legislation constitutes consent and usage limits as primarily directed towards private subjects, while the Chilean framework constitution defines limits as constitutional ones for commercial and public activity (Hertz, 2025). The principles of UNESCO and OECD emphasise the needs for openness, accountability and against coercive applications. Protecting while at the same time promoting innovation need clear limits that is prohibiting non-consensual manipulation, conducting impact assessments, and setting up independent oversight bodies.

4. TOWARD INTERNATIONAL STANDARDS: NEED FOR GLOBAL HARMONIZATION AND ETHICAL PRINCIPLES FOR NEUROTECHNOLOGY

The rapid rise of the integration of neuroscience, artificial intelligence, and digital technologies has made it imperative to develop international standards and global harmonisation in the field of neurotechnology governance. Leave solutions to the brain-data era uncoordinated, and the era of forum-shopping by corporations, rapidly contradicting regulations for individuals, and poorly enforced in uncoordinated jurisdictions could quickly follow. Unilateral measures are not enough to cross borders and overcome natural, national borders in the areas of sales chains, data flows, research partnerships, or consumer markets with respect to neurotechnologies. Global harmonization aims at creating minimum standards for the protection of mental privacy, cognitives freedom and mental dignity and also for responsible innovation, fair access and cross-border interoperability.

Raised by OECD in 2019 this is the first international standard in the field adopted by dozens of countries, the OECD Recommendation on Responsible Innovation in Neurotechnology is the first on the subject to be developed at the international level. It provides nine guidelines referring to overall security evaluation, representation, scientific cooperation, public discussion, brain data responsibilities, and expectations of possible misuse. A 2025 guidebook uploads to this website provide practical guidance to policymakers for implementation. On this basis, UNESCO in November 2025 made a groundbreaking step by introducing the Recommendation on the Ethics of Neurotechnology, the first pan-Industrial normative document devoting itself to these issues. It comes into force on 12 November 2025 and establishes the concept of sensitive category of neural data; it highlights the human rights principles for the protection of neural data; mental privacy; freedom of thought; informed consent; transparency and protection for vulnerable subjects, such as children (Johnson et al., 2025). It recognises and takes into account the entire process of neurotechnology, from design, to deployment, and calls for the states to avoid coercive uses, subliminal manipulation and surveillance in the workplace, and to foster inclusivity and equitable access to these technologies.

Ethical Principles that appear in several of these documents are: respect for mental integrity and human dignity; proportionality and necessity for interventions; privacy-by-design; accountability, redress; non-discrimination and bias in neural algorithms; public engagement. Other tenets highlight the need for epistemic humility about the long-term implications of consciousness and identity research; dual use risk management, particularly in the military context; and stewardship that must take account of individual freedom alongside societal benefits in medical, educational and rehabilitative applications. These principles are based on existing human rights instruments like the ICCPR on freedom of thought and extend this to new possibilities of neurotechnology such as real-time brain decoding and memory modulation.

There are a number of practical reasons for the need for harmonization. Conflicting national laws might prevent cooperation in research; might raise trade barriers; might actually provide varying levels of protection to users in different jurisdictions. Even in advanced legislation, such as Chile's, there is room for debate about whether the data inferred from the neural devices is processed (insights, rather than neural signals) or not. These standards enable global recognition, technical interoperability (e.g., for secure brain-data communications protocols) and capacity-building for developing countries. They also serve as a counteraction to "neuro-colonialism," whereby high income countries or corporations access data from the Global South without receiving commensurate benefits (Alomaka et al., 2025). The non-binding recommendations and gaps in enforcement, fast technological changes, and conflicting objectives between recommendation for innovation and precautionary measures are all the challenges that come up. Some critics are concerned that too viele rules will make it impossible for progress to happen, and some proponents argue that the intimate experience is significantly better with such rules than with previous technologies.

Strengthened harmonization can be achieved through multi-stakeholder platforms (governments, industry, civil society and academia, potentially future treaties, UN General Comments, technical standards by ISO etc.). Regional convergence can contribute to global convergence and implement the principles of the Inter-American Juridical Committee. Finally, successful international standards will not be only about risk alleviation, but about channeling neurotechnology towards bringing about human flourishing; the preservation of the mind, humanity's final frontiers of freedom in an interdependent world.

5. NEURORIGHTS LEGISLATION ACROSS JURISDICTIONS

The coverage of neurorights legislation has developed in a piecemeal manner and is subject to varying degrees of progress in different jurisdictions, partially due to the differences in their legal backgrounds, technological capabilities, and policy concerns. Chile is still the leader in the world in this regard, has incorporated mental privacy, personal identity, free will and mental integrity into the 2021 Constitution (Law No. 21.383) which provides for the protection of brain activity and derived information. This constitutional principle, further strengthened by a ruling from the Supreme Court in 2023 that compelled a U.S. business (Emotiv) to eliminate the brain data of consumers, has left a strong impression. These rights remain to be carried out through follow-up legislation, giving special attention to neurotechnologies as if they were medical devices and moving in consumer applications. The experience of Chile has been a factor of influence for other Latin American countries such as Mexico, Brazil, Colombia, Argentina and Uruguay that have introduced bills, and for the Latin American Parliament (Parlatino) that proposed a Model Law on Neuro-rights in five key areas.

Progress in the states of the United States is state-driven – with a focus on data protection, not sweeping constitutional neurorights. Consumer privacy laws in California, Colorado, Montana, and Connecticut have been updated to include neural data as sensitive personal information, allowing for consumers to have access to, erase, opt out of, and restrict the processing of their neural data. Such laws tend to distinguish between the raw signals and inferences, but focus more on consent and limitation of purpose, especially in the context of non-medical devices. Meanwhile, Federal discourse on neural data governance, including proposed measures such as congressional hearings on the topic, are lagging, with a disconnect that leaves consumer neurotech working under different degrees of protections (Botes & Naidoo, 2026).

A more indirect solution is applied in Europe with the GDPR, Medical Device Regulation and AI Act which provide avenues for the regulation of neurotechnology. The GDPR classifies neural data as special category (sensitive) data and puts it in a class with data that needs specific consent and special protections. Mental agency is mentioned in the Spanish Digital Rights Charter and in the policies and legislation of digital rights at the regional level (for instance, in Cantabria, there is a policy on consumer neurotechnology). Ministers from several EU nations signed several treaties that affirm their approach to regulation should be a humanistic one in the 2023 León Declaration. Ethical guidelines continue with the European Charter for the Responsible Development of Neurotechnologies, which further emphasizes proper ethics, but where explicit integration of neurorights is still left to be desired. Conformity assessments and high impact prohibitions are preferred by the EU over risk-based regulation for high-risk BCIs.

In other regions there are already some beginnings or supplementary concerns. UNESCO's 2025 Recommendation asks all member states to connect national policies and programmes with internationally agreed-upon moral frameworks, as a soft-law link. The Recommendation of 2019 has a global appetite - it continues to shape policy in Asia and beyond. There are countries that consider that the freedom of thought, privacy and respect for the human body is enough, saying that there is no need for new rights but to be flexible in defining them within current rights. Enforcement issues in cross-border situations, scope (raw data vs. inferring data), balancing between innovation and protection and equity (who benefits from augmentation and who does not), are examples of challenges.

They vary due to factors such as the level of constitutional protection (entrenchment in Latin America, statutory in the U.S.), cultural differences regarding privacy and economic motivations for the neurotech sector (Stahl, 2025). The patchwork strengths are experimentation, and tailoring; weaknesses are protection gaps, regulatory arbitrage. Future enrichment can happen using mutual recognition, skills development training and embedding of international standards in national law.

6. CONCLUSION AND FUTURE DIRECTIONS

The line becomes blurry when it comes to definitions as to what constitutes "neural data" versus inferred insights derived from behavior and other biometrics. How to give incentives to innovators while keeping sufficient protection in place to prevent therapeutic breakthroughs for Parkinson's, Epilepsy, Depression, and Paralysis from turning to something potentially harmful, to others or to patients? Equity issues are enormous will "pro-cognitive" improvements contribute to the growing worldwide disparity between tech-savvy BCI users and abк users? But the cross-border movement of data makes enforcement more difficult, as there are "dual use" risks with security and advertising. Some object to the new rights, claiming that they are pushed for either inflation or duplication; in this regard they prefer the interpretation of other instruments, such as the Universal Declaration of Human Rights (freedom of thought) or ICCPR Article 17 (privacy). Enthusiasts insist that it is time to explicitly acknowledge this qualitative shift in intimacy with the brain that neurotech affords, in order to narrow gaps in protection of this organ.

Possible avenues forward are multi-level governance (constitutional principles and laws in Chile, harmonization at the regional level, e.g., via OAS, EU, and soft law convergence at the international level, towards a potential UNESCO declaration, or UN General Comment on neuro-technology and human rights). Technical norms can be set by international standards organizations for secure protocols on the transmission of brain data, compatibility with privacy by design, and certification of responsible neurotechnology. Public-private partnerships, in keeping with successful biomedical ethics framework, and independent oversight bodies would engender trust. Continuous monitoring, through horizon scanning, and adaptive regulation ensures the frameworks stay current with technological advancements such as future seamless brain-cloud interfaces or memory-editing. Raising international standards, neurorights laws, and responsible innovation in the brain-data era is not just a housekeeping task, it's an imperative of the civilizational process. Whether neurotechnology is a liberating revolution at the service of the handicapped, can advance humanity into new frontiers of knowledge, and can restore agency for those who have lost it or expand the inequality that humanity does not require will depend on how it is used.

REFERENCES

Bariffi, F. (2026). Mind, machine, and the law: Reimagining neurotechnology governance through disability rights. *Journal of Law and the Biosciences, 13*(1), lsag011. DOI: 10.1093/jlb/lsag011 PMID: 42147125

Botes, W. M., & Naidoo, T. (2026). Before the mind is touched: What Chile's neurorights mean for South Africa's legal and ethical framework. *South African Journal of Bioethics and Law, 19*(1), 25–32. DOI: 10.7196/SAJBL.2026.v19i1.4772

BUIATTI, F. (2025). Brain Computer Interfaces In The Medical Field: Legal And Ethical Considerations Surrounding The Global Protection Of Human Rights. *L'Europe Unie*, (23), 33–55.

Di Salvo, M. (2025). The protection of neural rights in the age of neurotechnologies and AI. The ethical challenge for law and neuroscience. *Russ. J. Econ. & L., 19*(1), 202–233. DOI: 10.21202/2782-2923.2025.1.202-233

Ding, Y. (2026). From Ethics to Governance: Why Neurotechnology Requires Institutionally Actionable Concepts. *Neurotechnology. Society & Governance, 1*(1), 93–119.

Hertz, N. (2025). Workplace brain surveillance: The need for new approaches to protect mental privacy and neural data? *International Data Privacy Law, 15*(2), 123–137. DOI: 10.1093/idpl/ipaf014

Johnson, W. G. (2026). Rights experimentalism under uncertainty: Transnational law and human rights for neurotechnologies. *Human Rights Law Review, 26*(1), ngaf038. DOI: 10.1093/hrlr/ngaf038

Johnson, W. G., Tournas, L. M., & Magistro Nadler, R. (2025). Implementing Neurorights: Legal and Regulatory Considerations. *Neuroethics, 18*(1), 5. DOI: 10.1007/s12152-024-09576-z

Lee, A. (2026). Neurorights as Constitutional Rights: Enforcement Gaps in Chile and Lessons for Comparative Neurodata Governance. *Neurotechnology. Society & Governance, 1*(1), 21–39.

Li, C. (2026). Governing Brain-Computer Interfaces: The Categorical Gap Hypothesis and a Five-Dimensional Global Typology of Neurotechnology Governance (2010-2026). *Neurotechnology. Society & Governance, 1*(1), 1–20.

Mia, A. P. (2025). From Brain Evidence to Neurorights: Rethinking Criminal Responsibility in the Age of Neurotechnology. *Available at SSRN* 5588370. DOI: 10.2139/ssrn.5588370

Possa, A. A. (2025). Neurorights. In *Neurorights and the Era of Neurotechnologies: An Analysis of the Brazilian Constitutional Law and the Need for New Fundamental Rights* (pp. 17–39). Springer Nature Switzerland. DOI: 10.1007/978-3-031-92002-8_3

Radu, R. (2025). Cognitive frontiers: Neurotechnology and global internet governance. *Frontiers in Digital Health*, *7*, 1690489. DOI: 10.3389/fdgth.2025.1690489 PMID: 41459239

Sosa Navarro, M. (2026). Workplace Neurosurveillance: Is the Employee's Mental Privacy Protected Under International Law?. *BIOLAW JOURNAL*, (Special Issue 1/2026), 93-113.

Souza, J. D. N. (2025). Exploring New Frontiers in Personalized Criminal Responsibility through Neurotechnologies: Ethical Dilemmas and the Neuro-Rights Framework. *BioLaw Journal-Rivista di BioDiritto*, (4), 211–228.

Stahl, B. C. (2025). The Ethics of Data and Its Governance: A Discourse Theoretical Approach. *Information (Basel)*, *16*(6), 497. DOI: 10.3390/info16060497

Terec-Vlad, L., & Rusu, A. (2026). Neuro-Cybersecurity and the Future of Cognitive Rights: Legal Foundations for the Protection of the Human Mind in the Digital Age. *Revista Romaneasca pentru Educatie Multidimensionala, 18*(1), 82-104.

Yang, H., & Jiang, L. (2025). Regulating neural data processing in the age of BCIs: Ethical concerns and legal approaches. *Digital Health*, *11*, 20552076251326123. DOI: 10.1177/20552076251326123 PMID: 40162168

Zhu, R., Zhao, Y., & Li, Y. (2025). Paradigm Shift in Global Governance of Medical Brain-Computer Interface: Addressing Practical Challenges Through Institutional Innovation. *Risk Management and Healthcare Policy*, *18*, 3755–3768. DOI: 10.2147/RMHP.S555754 PMID: 41328405

Chapter 15
Understanding Emotional Well-Being in Indian Policing Through a Cognitive and Neuroethical Lens

Priyamvada Singh
http://orcid.org/0009-0003-6145-0603
Jagran Lakecity University, Bhopal, India

Priyanka Nema
Jagran Lakecity University, Bhopal, India

ABSTRACT

Emotional well-being amongst Indian police personnel has been inadequately studied in the context of significant work related stressors such as long hours of work, exposure to trauma, scarcity of resources, sociocultural stressors and more. In this paper, the challenge is explored from a cognitive and neuroethical point of view, drawing upon the field of neuroscience on emotional regulation processes such as amygdala/prefrontal cortex interactions and cognitive reappraisal as well as some ethical aspects of the moral injury concept, the right to decision making and institutional responsibility. It looks into how cognitive tools and neuroethical perspectives can contribute towards building resilience. Recommendations include culturally-informed training, organizational support and ethical guidelines to improve officers' health, efficiency and effectiveness and build community trust.

DOI: 10.4018/979-8-3373-9720-7.ch015

1. INTRODUCTION

Police Emotional Wellness is the ability of a police officer or any law enforcement individual to process an experience of trauma, handle stress, maintain a balance of emotions and respond in an ethical manner when facing stressful situations. Police in the Indian scenario work in a very peculiar environment as they face high outdoor temperatures and threats of violence, long working hours of upto 16 hours and scrutiny of the people and separation from their families especially for the paramedial units like the CRPF where personnel are separated from their families in parched conditions. Research has shown that a high percentage of them had poor mental state (up to 73% in one sample from Rajasthan), a situation characterized by symptoms of anxiety, depression, burned out, and/or signs of post-traumatic stress disorder or increased risk of suicide. Employees with lower ranks, like sub-inspectors and constables often have higher distress than officers, mainly because of operational exposure and lack of resources.

Established cognitive models in neuroscience/psychology are used as a basis for a cognitive lens. Recent developments in the Theory of Constructed Emotion and dual-process models underscore the need to conceptualize emotional experiences as constructed by the interplay of the amygdala (which is activated when detecting threat and responding fearfully) and prefrontal cortex (PFC, which is responsible for the reappraisal and regulation of emotion) (Bhattacharya, 2025). The sustained activation of the sympathetic nervous system and hypothalamic-pituitary-adrenal (HPA) axis can contribute to increased cortisol levels that can impact function of PFC, resulting in hyper-vigilant or exhausting responses, or impulsive reactions, in high stress policing situations. Cognitive reappraisal – reshaping a situation to change how it affects us – seems to be an effective way to reduce the activation of the amygdala whilst still keeping cognitive resources for more effective decision making. Other moderators of the risk of burnout are the components of emotional intelligence (EI): self-awareness, self-regulation, empathy, and social skills. EI training really improves people's capacity to tolerate stress and control their impulses, which are important skills for de-escalating and interacting with other community members.

In addition, neuroethic considerations are added to deepen the understanding of the moral and philosophical aspects of these cognitive behaviors in law enforcement. Neuroethics asks the question of what happens to autonomy, responsibility and justice when there are interventions to the brain? Officers do not just get a blow to the head when shooting people; they may suffer from "moral injury" due to actions or inactions that go against their values, like when someone is forced to shoot in an uncertain situation or sees a failure within the system. This can even result in feelings of not being well or cynicism and depersonalization. There are some neuro-ethical considerations, therefore, that could be surfaced and discussed in relation to the methods of improving emotional regulation, such as biofeedback, mindfulness activities, or neurofeedback that do not encourage officer agency, nor foster a false sense of performance enhancement that is either coerced or mandated. Questions of whether there is equity enter the picture: Are certain ranks or demographics benefitted more by these cognitive interventions? Mental health-related stereotypes and stigma, which often stems from a societal concern about perceived weakness, pose a barrier to receiving mental health care in India's layered and fragmented policing system (Logan et al., 2026).

The police experience multiple stressors in reality, as observed from the Indian experience. The demands of its operation are crowd control, counter insurgency and routine police work under extreme resource constraints. There are also aspects to the job that depend on the organization itself, such as awkward work prioritization, insufficient training and unclear work-life balances. Familiar stresses including nuclear vs joint-family relationship or financial issues are linked to mental health, while better salary, rank is linked to better psychological health. Challenges faced by women officers are greater in environments where there are more men, such as greater anxiety. The findings are similar to the worldwide pattern of higher rates of PTSD among first responders (which could be up to 1/3 of the population), with the added difficulty in India that there is limited specialized mental health services for those who have been exposed to repeated trauma.

1.1 Contextual Challenges in Indian Law Enforcement

There are innovative approaches in cognitive interventions. There are approaches that appear to be effective in decreasing perceived stress and enhancing regulation: Mindfulness Based Stress Reduction (MBSR) skills training, Dialectical Behavior Therapy (DBT) skills training (emotion labeling and distress tolerance), and cognitive-behavioral skills. Encounters with biofeedback products that monitor autonomic responses allow for real-time awareness and biofeedback self-modulation. Programs that focus on resiliency, peer support and emotional survival training (including emotional numbing and hypervigilance) wouldn't have much problem if they were based on a neuroplasticity philosophy, i.e. ultimate rewiring through repetition. The acceptability of adaptations should involve the cultural features, aspects of yoga or community based ethics in the Indian context.

Neuroethically, the first of these two principles should be beneficence and the second is non-maleficence. It is important that training does not diminish or pathologize normal reactions to unusual circumstances, or undercut officers' moral reasoning. Addressing the root causes, rather than the symptoms, involves institutional reforms, including confidential counseling, decreasing the stigma through modeling and reasonable policy changes and leave. Ethical approaches promote "trauma-informed" policing to be actively engaged in the well-being of cops and "community," while minimizing the adversarial dynamic (Kritika, 2026).

1.2 Overview of Cognitive and Neuroethical Perspectives

There is still little research on policing mental health in Indian context and most information is at the level of specific small studies and/or regional studies. Programs that have come from the Western world need to be proven to be scalable. Future directions encompass longitudinal studies incorporating (where possible) neuro-imaging data and qualitative data obtained from lived experience, culturally sensitive EI curricula development, and incorporation of neuroethics into Police Academies. Organizational metrics should be used to measure well-being as well as performance, since healthy officers help provide improved public safety and reduce officer turnover.

So, emotional health in the policing in the Indian scenario needs to be understood in an interdisciplinary framework. The effective application of cognitive neuroscience-inspired practical regulatory strategies and a neuroethical approach to responsible implementation can lead stakeholders to work towards system change (Mia, 2025). This would not only reduce the personal pain of officers but also enhance the moral standards of the police, contribute to a stronger force, and make it more compassionate and efficient to meet the societal demands of India. These lenses will be given priority because it is a pledge of humanistic policing with scientific and moral standards.

2. COGNITIVE FOUNDATIONS OF EMOTIONAL REGULATION

An important framework to understand cognitive processes of emotional regulation is important for Police Officers who work in high stress environments to process and regulate their emotions in a way that keeps them effective and healthy. Emotional regulation involves strategies to help people affect what emotions they have, when they have them and how they feel (and later how they express them). In policing, this includes regulating the responses to the acute threat, chronic stressors and interpersonal conflict that are common to police work. It is an interaction between automatic emotional reactivity and deliberate cognitive control and an area cross-cutting neuroscience and psychology (Logan et al., 2025). Emotion regulatory models such as James Gross's process model of emotion regulation emphasize the use of antecedent-focused (rather than response-focused) strategies (e.g., situation selection, modification, attentional deployment, and/or cognitive change). For officers, effective regulation helps to prevent burnout, make better choices when presented with a crisis, and have compassion when interacting with the community. Chronic dysregulation, on the other hand, is associated with hypervigilance, emotional exhaustion, maladaptive behaviour and the rest. The principles upon which these are based are rooted in neuroplasticity: Repeated practice of these regulatory techniques can develop neural pathways, making us more resilient. A culturally relevant practice within Blue Origin, such as mindfulness or yoga, or a combination of physical and cognitive-based techniques could be adopted in the Indian policing context, where understanding the socio-cultural and operational stressors faced by both officers and the communities they serve is crucial. In sum, such foundations move past a negative focus on negative emotional reactions, and towards a positive understanding that there are emotionally driven skills that can be trained which are necessary for good ethical, effective policing.

2.1 Neural Mechanisms of Stress and Emotion in High-Pressure Environments

Neural systems involved in stress and the emotional response to pressure involve the reciprocal interactions between subcortical "limbic" and cortical "regulatory" circuits. The amygdala is a fast reacting threat detection system that coordinates responses to fear and arousal through the hypothalamic-pituitary-adrenal (HPA) axis, resulting in an increase in circulating cortisol levels and activation of the sympathetic nervous system (Nasyi'ah et al., 2025). This affects the body in the context of police interactions, including when it comes to how alert someone is and how much stress they experience in their entire body—when dealing with people in crowds, fighting, or extended police shifts. Chronic activation leads in which chronic elevated cortisol levels lead to reduced function in the hippocampus (affecting memory and contextual processing) and prefrontal cortex (PFC) loss of efficiency suboptimally functioning in PFC dorsolateral prefrontal cortex and anterior cingulate cortex (ACC) – both critically involved in executive control and conflict monitoring.

Acute stress increases amygdala/PFC connectivity for adaptive reactions, but chronic stress decreases amygdala/PFC connectivity, causing emotional dysfunction, decreased gray matter in the amygdala regulatory regions and changes in e/i balance (lower glutamate in dorsal ACC associated with burnout). Other mental demands appear to be placed on resources determined by parieto-occipital areas, which result in hyperarousal or hypoarousal. HRV measures suggest that autonomic dysfunction, characterized by weaker levels of the parasympathetic system, slower recovery from stressors. The mechanisms are not unique to India but more pronounced because of other factors such as lack of staffing, trauma exposure, etc., in the Indian police force. PFC-Amical coupling can be restored by decreasing PFC&amygdala coupling through biofeedback or coherence-building interventions which establish parasympathetic dominance. It helps to recognize these processes and subsequently offer specific resources to lessen the biological burden of policing and redeem the development of psychopathology (Taimur, 2026).

2.2 Cognitive Reappraisal and Emotional Intelligence in Policing

Police officers have the potential for powerful tools for emotional regulation within the cognitive foundations: it is cognitive reappraisal and emotional intelligence (EI). Reappraisal is a process of reinterpreting the meaning of a stressor and changing its affect, for example, for a stressful event that is an angry encounter, reinterpreting it as one of anxiety and not personal threat. In the brain, reappraisal activates prefrontal and parietal control areas to inhibit amygdala activity and spare cognitive resources to keep room for more rational processing and de-escalation. This approach is particularly effective in policing, to reduce the risk of hasty responses, lessen distress or guilt, and maintain ongoing effectiveness in dealing with uncertainty.

The skills of perceiving, using, understanding, and managing emotions in oneself as well as others (as outlined by Mayer & Salovey in their ability model) are complementary to reappraisal. Higher EFIs in officers are associated with higher self-awareness, better emotion regulation, empathy and social skills, which helps them more effectively handle conflict, establish trust in the community and are less susceptible to burnout. In law enforcement, there are indications that increased EI can be related to reduced stress levels within the organization as well as improved decision making and job satisfaction. EI competencies like: noticing emotions, using emotions to support thinking, or working with emotions of others, are enhanced through training programs, which help build the child's resilience. EI resists depersonalization in high demands, by counteracting demands for using emotional labor (Radroff, 2025). In Indian policing, where there may be hierarchical ambiguity, including cultural stigma associated with mental health issues, it may be necessary to develop EI based on culturally modified curricula (culturally embedded within practicums localized practices and norms, which will address rank specific vulnerabilities, with Indian constables being at the highest risk. When reappraisal and EI work together, they promote adaptive coping, ethical behavior and sound operational strategies and thereby help transform potential vulnerabilities into assets to help officers functioning in tricky socio-emotional terrain.

3. NEUROETHICAL DIMENSIONS OF POLICE EMOTIONAL HEALTH

Neuroethics is a field that considers the moral, legal and philosophical issues arising from neuroscience's impact on human behaviours, especially in professions that are high stakes such as policing. The issue of emotional health and happiness of an officer while dealing with matters of policing is not just a psychological or medical problem, it is also a very deep and immergent neuroethical problem where autonomy, dignity, responsibility and justice of the society are involved. Common decisions made by police officers involve the challenges of being called on to engage in morally complex situations that involve either their emotional or their cognitive neural circuits, asking very real questions about how to apply brain-based knowledge of emotional and cognitive stress and regulation to institutional practices. Neuroethics point out the two-fold problem of neuroenhancing resilience using tools that could end up involving cognitive enhancement for an officer's mental state in order to make him more efficient for the organisation; there's a lack of mechanisms to ensure he retains agency in his personal use. Equity problems occur in the hierarchical police structures and resource limited police system of India – if interventions take place, they often create disparities in favor of those living in urban areas or those with more experience in the profession, deepening existing inequities. Stigma related to mental health, as well as expectations of masculinity and duty, deeply rooted in traditional gender roles, also shape how one is expected to engaging ethically with neuroscientific knowledge.Stigmatization of mental health and the normalised expectation of stoicism further complicate the challenge of ethical deployment of neuroscientific insights.

Furthermore, the study and analysis of the role and impact of emotional dysregulation in moral thought and public responsibility is a prerequisite for neuroethics. Avoidable situations may be affected if brain function is impacted by chronic stress, which could negatively affect the ability to control impulses or accept and demonstrate empathy with others in use of force situations or in community relations scenarios (Tanson, 2025). Ethical duty is held for institutions: where the officers' emotional issues are ignored, it is a type of systemic neglect which will have a direct impact on human rights issues for both officers and the public they serve. The narrow theme is balancing beneficence (promoting well-being) versus non-maleficence (avoided harm through over-medicalisation and coercion). The guidelines of Indian policing shall accommodate the concept of justice creating culturally sensitive, voluntary and transparent approach for the future. Highlighting these dimensions will enable stakeholders to create policies that acknowledge the role of officers as moral actors and take advantage of neuroscience to create healthier, more ethical policing.

3.1 Ethical Implications of Cognitive Interventions

The ethical considerations of cognitive interventions in police emotional self-regulation (e.g., mindfulness-based practices, cognitive behavioral therapy [CBT], neurofeedback, and emotional intelligence programs are critical and must be approached with great care. This creates issues of autonomy and informed consent from a neuroethics perspective. In Indian police forces where training is compulsory, and command positionalities are hierarchical, there can be subtle pressures for officers to engage in the training which can impact on volunteer participation and personal agency. The danger of enhancement versus therapy is also present: is this program actually therapeutic to trauma-exposed officers or are these programs designed to make officers more "operationally ready" with a focus on performance optimization and not health?

Perspectives on equity are well represented. However, socioeconomic and geographic factors might determine access to treatments such as biofeedback or program with neuroimaging, and elite or metropolitan units may have more access to treatments than rural or lower-ranked personnel or whether there will be access for them to advanced interventions due to higher stress levels. Another ethical principle is cultural appropriateness—adjustment of elements such as yoga or mindfulness to fit Indian context or use techniques that have been influenced by Western practice but are rooted in traditional Indian philosophies to avoid claims of cultural imperialism and higher levels of acceptability.

There are other privacy and data security issues to address. Brain data and other kinds of physiological data that might be collected in interventions might be sensitive data, with potential stumbling blocks of misuse for selection, promotion or stigmatization. Institutions should have strong ethical monitoring mechanisms and clear data policies and set up independent review committees. Moreover, over-dependence on cognitive interventions can involve the localization of systemic issues, including understaffing, insufficient equipment and low quality of work life, and compel more specific interventions to intervene without addressing the wider issues of organizations needing to reform.

Evidence-based implementation and careful assessment of effectiveness is a prerequisite for beneficence, but non-maleficence obligates the need for side-effects to be monitored and may imply increased self-surveillance or downplaying the truth of moral distress by suppressing emotions. In conclusion, ethical cognition intervention in police work in India ought to strengthen — and not take the place of — structural change and enable — and not overlook or impose on— Filipino officers' dignity while nonetheless empowering them to be heroes to promote justice.

3.2 Moral Injury, Decision-Making, and Neuroethical Responsibility

Moral injury is a severe psychological injury that occurs when a person commits acts of aggression, observes aggression, or fails to stop other people committing aggressive acts that their values of right and wrong consider unlivable. Indian Police often find themselves in situations of Excessive Use of Force on protesters, Corruption and overwhelmed by systemic constraints where they suffer from a moral injury. This can be expressed as guilt, shame, betrayal and lack of trust; these feelings are unique, but usually can accompany PTSD. Moral injuries alter neural pathways within brain regions that play a key role in emotional regulation and the making of ethical choices – the ventromedial prefrontal cortex (vmPFC), anterior cingulate cortex, and amygdala.

These injuries have an impact on officers' ability to provide good judgment, and that is considered neuroethical responsibility. Ongoing process of moral distress can diminish one's ability to be cognitively flexible; they can become cynical or depersonalized, and this can also impact de-escalation attempts as well as the trust that others place in them. With less control from the pre-frontal region of the brain, people make decisions under moral ambiguity and may end up committing impulsive or questionable acts. The issues such as the political intervention, scarcity of resources, and expectations of society make the scenario worse in the Indian context, especially for the frontline constables (Blume, 2026).

Institutional collective responsibility to reduce moral injury is expressed in taking proactive steps to prevent it, including training on aspects of trauma, peer support groups, restorative practices, and ethical reflection forums. Leaders need to show vulnerability and try to create a "psychological safe" environment. Reducing holistic moral harm should be addressed in accountability frameworks as well as contributing factors at the individual and a systemic level. The questions of justice do come—that is, how to assign justly the moral duty of maintaining the order of public life in a multi-ethnic democracy? Interventions need to have a sense of agency as a moral being, yet not pathologize the officers.

Integrated cognitive-neuroethical approaches can help heal moral injury and bring about post-traumatic growth and a return to moral integrity in decision making. This involves developing moral repair through narrative therapy, affirming values and cultivating organizational cultures and values to create the space for ethical bravery. Adopting a sense of responsibility with regards to neuroethics implies that moral harm can become less frequent and more useful to more bountiful, thoughtful, and effective policing in India.

4. INSIGHTS AND CHALLENGES SPECIFIC TO INDIAN CONTEXT

The unique socio-cultural, operational and structural milieu of Indian policing creates a complex set of emotional stresses that are most pronounced when working with crime victims.Emotional stress in the Indian context emerges from a unique web and interplay of socio-cultural, operational and structural issues that are particularly relevant during interactions with crime victims. The low ratio of police to population is often less than 150 or 200 officers per 100,000 population, resulting in officers having long working hours, which is often just 12-18 hours per week, with no off days or typically not decent rest. This results in widespread stress and fatigue, lack of sleep and burnout, especially among the lower ranks, such as constables, who are the backbone of day-to-day law enforcement. Evidence based on reports such as the Status of Policing in India indicate that as much as 70-80% of the police officers have complained of a worsening of their physical and mental well-being resulting from the workload.

Exposure to traumatic events is common such as violent offences, crowd control at protest events, counter-insurgency operations (particularly in conflict areas) and responding to accidents or deaths. These are exacerbated by organizational stressors such as bureaucratic pressures, politics, lack of resources and infrastructure. At a much deeper level, socio-culturally, Indian police face a paradox, as help-seeking is despised by society and the media, and they are expected to uphold strict code of masculinity. The irregular timings, posting away from our home, financial constraints and all the social pressures and obligations in a joint family system makes family strains acute. Females officers have a number of gender issues to deal with, such as harassment and the dual burden of domestic responsibilities.

These factors all increase anxiety and depression, as well as symptoms of PTSD, drug and alcohol abuse and suicide risk. Kerala, Rajasthan, and Maharashtra have shown that officers suffer from high levels of stress (65-83%), and factors such as physical inactivity, alcohol or tobacco use, and comorbidities (hypertension, diabetes) contribute to their stress levels (Agarwal & Kumar, 2025). However, mental well-being is still not being addressed sufficiently, as there is limited funding for such care, a huge cultural taboo attached to mental health, and a dedication toward fitness instead of mental strength. Hierarchy makes vulnerability more difficult to the point of being impossible and rural deployment aggravates isolation.

From a neuroethical and cognitive perspective, the problems affect the prefrontal regulation system, increasing reactivity to the amygdala working system, which disturbs decision-making and moral behavior. Within the Indian context, there is a need for culturally-sensitive strategies that can be combined with family support systems and embracing elements of Yoga. These can only be resolved by systemic change, such as more staff, setting reasonable duty hours, enacting policies that take trauma into account, and modeling well-being from leadership. If there are no appropriate measures taken, then the issue of emotional dysregulation will continue to play havoc in India's diverse democratic structure, with regards to operational effectiveness, public trust and officer retention.

4.1 Stressors: Workload, Trauma Exposure and Socio-Cultural Factors

A major stressor in Indian policing is workload, which is compounded with vast shortage of manpower and the growing responsibilities. Insufficient support has been provided for officers to handle their law enforcement, V.I.P. security and disaster response and administrative duties. On the national level survey figures show an average workday of 14 hours, 80% of which is spent on duty, while many workers don't get any weekly offs. In states such as Kerala, shifts result in a drastic change (between 11-18 hours), causing chronic fatigue, affecting sleep patterns and in turn, causing burnout. It all falls heavily on the floor staff and extra work and paperwork adds to the pressure. Too much and not enough work-life balance will prevent your families from spending time together and from recovering.

The impact of trauma adds to the strain of workload. Officials deal with violent situations, road traffic accidents, murders, mob fights and insurgencies in particular in the places like Naxal affected areas, or in Jammu & Kashmir. Frequent exposures trigger chronic levels of stress, which increase the likelihood of PTSD symptoms being reported (with a substantial proportion) and hypervigilance and emotional numbing. Critical incidents (protest or scenes of suffering) have long-lasting psychological effects and if not debriefed immediately, are not necessarily processed.

These stress factors are uniquely affected by socio-cultural factors. Officers face challenges in a collectivist society where public expectations around authority and impartiality are high and the media are increasingly focused on them. Many people are reluctant to discuss mental health issues because of the stigma attached to it, fear of work and career consequences. Strain is worsened by other family factors such as financial considerations, childcare and keeping social standing in nuclear or separate households. Gender dynamics can be complicated: officers are exposed to bias and/or double emotional workload in male-dominated marginalised environments. routine interruptions or events such as festivals, rituals, lead to feelings of guilt and isolation.

Organisational culture, hierarchy, politics, poor preparation for resilience also impacts resilience. In a diverse and populous nation there are various situations which may be emotionally charged and need to be deescalated publically in a way that respects human rights. These cumulative stresses interfere with cognitive-emotional systems making people risky, hyper-mobile, cynical, and vulnerable to harm from moral injury. Researchers have associated them with increased use of drugs, alcohol and higher blood pressure, among other factors, and a diminished quality of life (Cheng & Cheng, 2025).

Multifaceted strategies are needed for mitigation: Rationalizing workload: recruitment; Trauma informed work processes; Socio-culturally sensitive supports: peer network; Family-inclusive supports. Understanding the thrust of these all interlinked stressors is of crucial importance to ensure that officers, who will serve the state in a sensitive social, political, and academic environment with India, can become responsible, competent, and benign officers.

4.2 Current Mental Health Landscape and Interventions

However, the mental health system in Indian Police is severely distressed with the highly inconsistent nature of interventions. Prevalence studies report high prevalence levels of occupational stress (65–75%+) across a variety of samples, anxiety, depression and other symptoms of burnout, as well as PTSD symptoms (occasionally higher than in the general population). The study in Kerala revealed that 65.6% of workers had organizational stress, 75.5% were in an active state and that these were linked with inactivity, substance use and health problems. Items of concern include rates of suicide and exhaustion, but the data from a systematic approach to research and reporting of national data is limited. Stigma, fear of confidentiality issues and the worry of affecting their careers discourage officers from seeking help; many officers espouse shame when they feel distress and make it a weakness.

Interventions are to the start and fragmented. In-house psychologists or tie-ups with hospitals have been made for providing some state forced or central forces (like CRPF) wellbeing programs, yoga/meditation classes and simple counseling services. Some awareness is being promoted by the Bureau of Police Research and Development (BPR&D) and Police Foundation, but the coverage is lacking. Peer support programs and resilience training are implemented inconsistently, and by combining strategies from around the world to create local examples, mindfulness/stress management workshops are offered. But most centers are only concerned with physical conditioning – not all-embracing psychological help. There is very limited Critical Incident Stress Debriefing and few special units that provide specific trauma care for young people out of the major city centres.

However, current challenges remain: First, resource limitations; secondly, social/cultural differences between the sharing of cognitive-neuroethical principles within forces; and thirdly, integration between cognitive-neuroethical principles and practice. Utilization is undermined by hierarchical culture, and by rural postings. Programs lacking in gender sensitivity and/or rank are inadequate. Assessment of current interventions is very limited, making it difficult to scale evidence-based interventions.

New initiatives include putting in place more CIT-type officer support programs, implementing mental health check-in technology, offering annual screenings (with protections in place), and initiating on-going destigmatization programs. Interventions that are culturally resonant, such as yoga, spiritual interventions and family counseling demonstrate potential (Parker et al., 2025). There are potential areas of collaboration for strengthening capacity with NGO's, Medical Colleges, etc. like NIMHANS. These neuroethical issues require a program that is voluntary, not coercive, and more than just treating with individual coping, but rather tackling its systems-level causes.

5. CONCLUSION AND PATHWAYS FORWARD

An indepth understanding of emotionality from the perspective of cognitive and neuro-ethics over the Indian policing scenario indicates high levels of susceptibility and immense potentials of improvement in addressing the psychological needs of officers in the Indian police. Indian policemen face a heavy workload due to understaffing, fretting about working for a long time, dealing with stressful scenarios, from time to time, political pressures and others' expectation of stoicism, all of which significantly increase their exposure to shock, burnout, moral injury, anxiety and depression. The roles of the sustained activation of the amygdala-HPA axis and of the normalization of impaired prefrontal regulation in emotional equilibrium and decision making about what defines moral behavior are shed light upon by cognitive neuroscience. Neuroethics, on the other hand, highlights the roles of institutions, to safeguard the autonomy, dignity and moral agency of the officers, whilst responsibly use interventions based on neuroscience and restructured professional identities. These views come together to push for a change of tongue from an individual pathological to systemic and humanistic reform with the understanding that healthier officers are vital to better, empathetic and just policing in a diverse Indian democracy.

Pathways to the future require multi-level approaches, combined cognitive tools and neuroethical protections and organizational change. As the technique is adapted with Indian practices like yoga and meditation, it can support strengthening cognitive reappraisal and emotional intelligence (EI), which is achieved through enhancing the neuroplasticity and autonomic balance. These extensive resilience courses need to be mandatory but non-coercive with an emphasis on emotional labeling, using biofeedback and scenario-based ethical self-reflection as components to reduce moral hurts. Similarly, organizational change is key: having adequate numbers of staff, having reasonable shift limits, ensuring appropriate rest, providing adequate infrastructure, and setting up confidential peer support networks and staff mental health workers. Leadership needs to demonstrate vulnerability to remove the stigma and interventions need to be gender-sensitive and tailored to rank to address different burdens of constables and female police officers.

Policy-wise, the Ministry of Home Affairs and Bureau of Police Research and Development (BPR&D) will have to add well-being indicators to the performance ones so that the well-being of a police officer is taken into account in the process of institutionalizing the department. This will involve creating national standards for trauma-informed policing, embedding trauma-informed policing principles into police training academies and building partnerships with other institutions such as NIMHANS for evidence-based trauma-informed policing programming. Funding for the infrastructure of mental health services for forces employees needs to be made a priority and legislative measures of the UK and the UK military need to ensure that seeking services for mental health does not compromise employment. It can be a vicious circle, with a reduction in the amount of conflict experienced by the public leading to greater officer stress, which in turn drives up the amount of adversarial interaction. good community oriented initiatives can help restore citizen trust and thus increase officer trust and reduce officer stress.

Future research can help answer the questions listed below: Longitudinal studies across multiple domains of neuroimaging (if possible), validated Indian scales, and author-created lived-experience story told, combining them, to map culturally specific stressors, intervention outcomes, etc., should be explored. Comparisons of hybrid (cog+eth neural) programs will improve the evidence-base. In the end, it's time for emotional investment, not an indulgence. Indian policing can move towards a more resilient policing body and be placed on "ethics" with this "cognitive-neuroethic" approach. This metamorphosis is capable of alleviating the suffering and attrition of the officers as well as improving public safety, ethical governance and peaceful living. Now it's time for bold, teamwork steps that are rooted in science, ethics and compassion to create a police that embodies the mission to serve and protect, and protects itself.

REFERENCES

Agarwal, S., & Kumar, N. (2025). Normal'vs' Abnormal': A Socio-Cultural Perspective of Neurodivergence in Sitaare Zameen Par.

Bhattacharya, M. (2025). Occupational Stress: A Review of Police Narrative. *Rethinking the Police for a Better Future: Navigating Policing Challenges with Accountability and Trust*, 191-202.

Blume, A. W. (2026). *Advancing Health Equity and Psychological Wellness in the Shadows of Colonialism: Reflections from Indigenous Psychology*. Bloomsbury Publishing USA. DOI: 10.5040/9798765129418

Cheng, S., & Cheng, Z. (2025). Public Policy Approaches to Addressing Neurojurisprudential Challenges and Enhancing Legislative Systems. *Lex Localis*, *23*(4), 1–25. DOI: 10.52152/2879

Kritika. (2026). Ethical and Policy Considerations in Neuro-Integrated Security. In *Neuroscience Meets Cybersecurity: Applying Brain Science to Enhance Digital Protection* (pp. 311-354). Berkeley, CA: Apress.

Logan, A. C., Berryessa, C. M., Callender, J. S., Caruso, G. D., Hagenbeek, F. A., Mishra, P., & Prescott, S. L. (2025). The Land That Time Forgot? Planetary Health and the Criminal Justice System. *Challenges*, *16*(2), 29. DOI: 10.3390/challe16020029

Logan, A. C., Mishra, P., Berryessa, C. M., Caruso, G. D., Hagenbeek, F. A., Denson, T. F., Robinson, J. M., & Prescott, S. L. (2026). Challenging the prescientific frameworks of criminal justice: Neurobiology and criminolytic interventions in the legalome era. *Frontiers in Psychology*, *17*, 1791262. DOI: 10.3389/fpsyg.2026.1791262 PMID: 42077290

Mia, A. P. (2025). From Brain Evidence to Neurorights: Rethinking Criminal Responsibility in the Age of Neurotechnology. *Available at SSRN* 5588370. DOI: 10.2139/ssrn.5588370

Nasyi'ah, I., Saifullah, S., Hidayah, K., Roibin, R., & Adityo, R. D. (2025). Penal sanctions for psychological domestic violence under utilitarianism theory: A new sentencing paradigm in the 2023 Indonesian criminal code. *El-Usrah: Jurnal Hukum Keluarga*, *8*(1), 593–617.

Parker, A. G., Vardoulakis, L. M., Alla, J., & Harrington, C. N. (2025, April). Participatory AI considerations for advancing racial health equity. In *Proceedings of the 2025 CHI Conference on Human Factors in Computing Systems* (pp. 1-24). DOI: 10.1145/3706598.3713165

Taimur, A. (2026). Neurorights in the age of AI: Universalism, cognitive vulnerability, and the limits of legal translation. *Rivista Di Diritti Comparati, 2026*(Special Issue VIII), 125-155.

Tanson, E. (2025). The Human Rights+ Framework: Understanding Harm Attribution Gaps and Invisible Harm in the Digital Age. *Available at SSRN* 5934074.

Compilation of References

Abdulrahman Satam, I., & Szabolcsi, R. (2025). Ethical and Safety Challenges of Implantable Brain-Computer Interface. *Interdisciplinary Description of Complex Systems: INDECS*, *23*(2), 82–94. DOI: 10.7906/indecs.23.2.1

Adinda, F. A., Rahmawati, E., Suparman, E., Arifin, R., & Ezzerouali, S. (2025). The challenge of admitting electronic evidence in civil procedure law. *Jurnal IUS Kajian Hukum dan Keadilan, 13*(3), 656-680.

Agarwal, S., & Kumar, N. (2025). Normal'vs' Abnormal': A Socio-Cultural Perspective of Neurodivergence in Sitaare Zameen Par.

Agarwal, A. (2022). Information technology vis-a-vis human rights: An analytical and legal approach. *Issue 2 Int'l JL Mgmt. &. Human.*, *5*, 106.

Aggarwal, N. K., & Jain, A. (2024). Neuroethics and neurolaw in forensic neuropsychiatry: A guide for clinicians. *Behavioral Sciences & the Law*, *42*(1), 11–19. DOI: 10.1002/bsl.2638 PMID: 37983666

Aguilar-Herrera, A. J., Hernández-Aguado, C. O., Monarres-Sokolovskaya, J. A., Pacheco-Ramírez, M. A., Khaleghian, B., Grassi, E., . . . Contreras Vidal, J. L. (2026, January). An Artistic BCI–GenAI System Enabling Real-Time Co-creation in Balinese Performance. In *International Workshop on Creative AI for Live Interactive Performances* (pp. 25-41). Cham: Springer Nature Switzerland. DOI: 10.1007/978-3-032-16893-1_2

Ajmal, M. K., & Sudhakar, B. D. (2026). Consumer awareness and perception of neuromarketing tools: Insights from a technology acceptance model (TAM) perspective in South India. *SN Business & Economics*, *6*(3), 66. DOI: 10.1007/s43546-026-01066-z

Alanazi, A. S., Salah Alanazi, A., & Benlaria, H. (2025, July). Enhancing healthcare for people with disabilities through artificial intelligence: Evidence from Saudi Arabia. [). MDPI.]. *Health Care*, *13*(13), 1616. PMID: 40648640

Albright, T. D., Baltimore, D., Mazza, A. M., Mnookin, J. L., & Tatel, D. S. (2023). Science, evidence, law, and justice. *Proceedings of the National Academy of Sciences of the United States of America*, *120*(41), e2312529120. DOI: 10.1073/pnas.2312529120 PMID: 37782804

AllahRakha, N. (2024). Demystifying the Network and Cloud Forensics' Legal, Ethical, and Practical Considerations. *Pakistan Journal of Criminology*, *16*(2).

Alonso, L. E. E. (2021). From Neuroethics to Neo-romanticism. Aldous Huxley in response to current proposals for ethical and legal regulation of neuroscience. *Scio*, (21), 113–148. DOI: 10.46583/scio_2021.21.783

Alzoubi, H. M., Shameem, B., Mushtaq, S., Al Kurdi, B., Joghee, S., & Hamadneh, S. (2025). Unveiling the role of artificial intelligence: Navigating personalized content marketing, customer engagement, and commitment with data transparency and security. *International Review of Management and Marketing*, *15*(2), 343–355. DOI: 10.32479/irmm.18499

Arivunambi, A., Naikwade, S. S., Sarkar, P., Lami, Z. F., Lourens, M., & Al-Tameemi, A. R. (2025). Optimizing HR Processes Using Brain-Computer Interface Technology. In *Concepts and Applications of Brain-Computer Interfaces* (pp. 287–300). IGI Global Scientific Publishing. DOI: 10.4018/979-8-3693-7427-6.ch017

Atlam, H. F., Ekuri, N., Azad, M. A., & Lallie, H. S. (2024). Blockchain forensics: A systematic literature review of techniques, applications, challenges, and future directions. *Electronics (Basel)*, *13*(17), 3568. DOI: 10.3390/electronics13173568

Atreyapurapu, L. D. (2025). AI-Enhanced Customer Loyalty Systems: A Collaborative Framework. *Journal of Computer Science and Technology Studies*, *7*(11), 284–290.

Bakhtiar, H. S. (2023). The role and nature of evidence: Forensic insight. *Human Rights (Chicago, Ill.)*, *8*(1), 81–100. DOI: 10.35586/jyur.v10i2.7072

Bakhtiary, H., Eslamitabar, S., Shiarzian, S., & Lame, E. (2026). Challenges of the Application of Emerging Neuroscience Technologies in Courts. *Avicenna Journal of Medical Biotechnology*, *18*(1), 32. DOI: 10.18502/ajmb.v18i1.21043 PMID: 42080114

Balasundaram, E., Aranganathan, P., Sujatha, S., Navalgund, N. R., & Gajendran, A. (2026). Transformative Potential of Neurotechnology and Brain–Computer Interfaces in Corporate Learning and Development.

Bariffi, F. (2026). Mind, machine, and the law: Reimagining neurotechnology governance through disability rights. *Journal of Law and the Biosciences*, *13*(1), lsag011. DOI: 10.1093/jlb/lsag011 PMID: 42147125

Barker, K. K., Madden, E. F., Lowe, P. L., & Rickers, K. (2026). The Neuro-Fiction of Addiction Immunizations. *Social Science & Medicine, 394*, 119059. DOI: 10.1016/j.socscimed.2026.119059 PMID: 41671876

Bhattacharjee, A., Pilkington, J., & Farahany, N. (2025). Fiduciary AI for the Future of Brain-Technology Interactions. *arXiv preprint arXiv:2507.14339.*

Bhattacharya, M. (2025). Occupational Stress: A Review of Police Narrative. *Rethinking the Police for a Better Future: Navigating Policing Challenges with Accountability and Trust*, 191-202.

Bi, Z., Gad, A., Younis, N., & Abu-Mulaweh, H. (2025). Critical Review on Brain–Computer Interfaces (BCIs) for Effective Human–Machine Interactions (HMIs). *Journal of Engineering, 2025*(1), 6682954. DOI: 10.1155/je/6682954

Blitz, M. J. (2026). Cognitive Liberty and Rights to (and Against) Cultural and Chemical Transformations of the Mind. In *The Law and Ethics of Freedom of Thought, Volume 2: Cognitive Liberty, Mental Privacy, and International Law* (pp. 151-189). Cham: Springer Nature Switzerland.

Blume, A. W. (2026). *Advancing Health Equity and Psychological Wellness in the Shadows of Colonialism: Reflections from Indigenous Psychology*. Bloomsbury Publishing USA. DOI: 10.5040/9798765129418

Bolarinwa, O., Mohammed, A., Igharo, V., & Shongwe, S. (2025). Leveraging artificial intelligence for inclusive maternity care: Enhancing access for mothers with disabilities in Africa. *Women's Health (London, England), 21*, 17455057251326675. DOI: 10.1177/17455057251326675 PMID: 40089873

Botes, W. M., & Naidoo, T. (2026). Before the mind is touched: What Chile's neurorights mean for South Africa's legal and ethical framework. *South African Journal of Bioethics and Law, 19*(1), 25–32. DOI: 10.7196/SAJBL.2026.v19i1.4772

Bruce, A., & Williams, L. A. (2025). Access and citizenship for those with disabilities: digitally enabled education and AI as a bridge to innovative inclusion. In *Digital Citizenship and the Future of AI Engagement, Ethics, and Privacy* (pp. 31-78). IGI Global Scientific Publishing. DOI: 10.4018/979-8-3693-9015-3.ch002

Bublitz, J. C., & Blitz, M. J. (Eds.). (2026). The Law and Ethics of Freedom of Thought: Vol. 2. *Cognitive Liberty, Mental Privacy, and International Law*. Springer Nature.

BUIATTI, F. (2025). Brain Computer Interfaces In The Medical Field: Legal And Ethical Considerations Surrounding The Global Protection Of Human Rights. *L'Europe Unie*, (23), 33–55.

Cabrera, L. Y., Evereteze, N., Shank, E. G., Wagner, J. K., Mekel, M., McCormick, J. B., & Wright, M. S. (2026). Neurotechnology Governance in the United States: Gaps and Opportunities. *Bioethics*, *40*(2), 225–235. DOI: 10.1111/bioe.70062 PMID: 41311287

Call, A. A., Wilson, L., & Wingrove, T. (2025). Neuroscience Evidence and Legal Decision-Making. In *Decision-Making in Life and Work: Foundations, Strategies, and Current Neuroscience* (pp. 209–256). Springer Nature Switzerland. DOI: 10.1007/978-3-031-88415-3_10

Cavanaugh, C. (2026). *Legal Ethics in AI Healthcare for Brain Computer Interfaces: A Policy Analysis* (Doctoral dissertation, University of Pittsburgh).

Chand, T., Nair, V. S., Srinivasu, P. N., & Kumar, V. J. (2025). Prospects and challenges in decoding consumer behavior using neurotechnology. *Artificial Intelligence Applications for Brain–Computer Interfaces*, 161-182.

Cheng, S., & Cheng, Z. (2025). Public Policy Approaches to Addressing Neuro-jurisprudential Challenges and Enhancing Legislative Systems. *Lex Localis*, *23*(4), 1–25. DOI: 10.52152/2879

Cornejo-Plaza, I., & Cippitani, R. (2025). Principles of Research with Neurotechnologies and Artificial Intelligence: A Comparative Analysis of Latin American and European Laws. In *Contextualizing Neuroprotection: Latin American Perspectives on the Impact of Neurotechnological Development in Life and Society* (pp. 205–220). Springer Nature Switzerland. DOI: 10.1007/978-3-031-96055-0_14

Cuk, M., & Batarelo Kokic, I. (2026). Techno-optimism or Thoughtful Scepticism? Demographic and Academic Differences in Student Views on Human Enhancement Technologies. *Nova prisutnost: časopis za intelektualna i duhovna pitanja*, *24*(1), 89-110.

Damani, D. N. (2026). Social Media, Algorithms and Children's Human Rights: Institutional Accountability in the Digital Age. *Algorithms and Children's Human Rights: Institutional Accountability in the Digital Age (January 18, 2026).*

Darby, R. R., Considine, C., Weinstock, R., & Darby, W. C. (2024). Forensic neurology: A distinct subspecialty at the intersection of neurology, neuroscience and law. *Nature Reviews. Neurology*, *20*(3), 183–193. DOI: 10.1038/s41582-023-00920-0 PMID: 38228905

Darby, W. C., MacIntyre, M., Cockerill, R. G., Stephens, D. B., Weinstock, R., & Darby, R. R. (2023). In the courts: Ethical and legal implications of emerging neuroscience technologies used for forensic purposes. In *Ethics and Clinical Neuroinnovation: Fundamentals, Stakeholders, Case Studies, and Emerging Issues* (pp. 173–193). Springer International Publishing. DOI: 10.1007/978-3-031-14339-7_10

Darmawan, D. (2025). Customer Confidence as a Business Asset: The Role of Transparency and Data Ethics in Loyalty and Reputational Resilience. *International Journal of Service Science, Management, Engineering, and Technology*, *7*(3), 35–44.

DeMatteo, D., & Olver, M. E. (2022). Use of the Psychopathy Checklist-Revised in legal contexts: Validity, reliability, admissibility, and evidentiary issues. *Journal of Personality Assessment*, *104*(2), 234–251. DOI: 10.1080/00223891.2021.1955693 PMID: 34357807

Demirezici, A. S. (2025). The cybercriminal risks and threats of body-hacking crimes under the legal framework of Budapest Convention. *Bioethica*, *11*(2), 8–26. DOI: 10.12681/bioeth.42841

Di Ieva, A., Tavallaii, A., Somerville, M. A., Suero Molina, E., DeGaetano, A., McCay, A., ... & Rosenfeld, J. (2026). The Declaration of Sydney: Ethical, Legal, and Professional Foundations of Computational Neurosurgery. *Legal, and Professional Foundations of Computational Neurosurgery (February 08, 2026).*

Di Salvo, M. (2025). The protection of neural rights in the age of neurotechnologies and AI. The ethical challenge for law and neuroscience. *Russ. J. Econ. & L.*, *19*(1), 202–233. DOI: 10.21202/2782-2923.2025.1.202-233

Ding, Y. (2026). From Ethics to Governance: Why Neurotechnology Requires Institutionally Actionable Concepts. *Neurotechnology. Society & Governance*, *1*(1), 93–119.

Dixon, J., Bark, H., Fang, C., Laing, J., & Patsios, D. (2026). The use of mental capacity and mental health laws in the care of people living with dementia in residential and hospital settings: A systematic review of the literature. *Dementia (London)*, *25*(3), 654–673. DOI: 10.1177/14713012251367810 PMID: 40816887

Echeverría Munoz, D. E. (2025). *Legal impact of Artificial Intelligence (AI) hallucinations* (Master's thesis, Quito, EC: Universidad Andina Simón Bolívar, Sede Ecuador).

Erbas, R. (2021, December). Evidentiary challenges to an effective criminal investigation for domestic violence: an introduction. The 10th Anniversary of The Istanbul Convention: Italian–Turkish Conference, ed. by Valentina Bonini & Rahime Erbaş, Pisa University Press.

Fabian, J. M. (2026). Forensic Neuroscience and the Law: The Brain on Trial. *Forensic Neuroscience and Violence*, 678-696.

Fabiano, N. (2025). *Artificial Intelligence, Neural Networks and Privacy: Striking a Balance between Innovation, Knowledge, and Ethics in the Digital Age*. goWare.

Faqir, R. S. (2023). Digital criminal investigations in the era of artificial intelligence: A comprehensive overview. *International Journal of Cyber Criminology, 17*(2), 77–94.

Farahany, N. A. (2023). *The battle for your brain: defending the right to think freely in the age of neurotechnology*. St. Martin's Press.

Findlay, M., & Grix, J. (2003). Challenging forensic evidence? Observations on the use of DNA in certain criminal trials. *Current Issues in Criminal Justice, 14*(3), 269–282. DOI: 10.1080/10345329.2003.12036267

Foley, A., & Melese, F. (2025). Disabling AI: Power, exclusion, and disability. *British Journal of Sociology of Education*, •••, 1–22. DOI: 10.1080/01425692.2025.2519482

Fry, E. (2014). The nature of international crimes and evidentiary challenges: Preserving quality while managing quantity. *Pluralism in International Criminal Law, Elies van Sliedregt and Sergey Vasiliev, eds (Oxford University Press, 2014).*

Gabelaia, I. (2025). AI and Consumer Engagement: Leveraging the Attention Economy for Enhanced Brand Loyalty.

George, A. S. (2024). Protecting Brain Privacy in the Age of Neurotechnology: Policy Responses and Remaining Challenges. *Partners Universal Innovative Research Publication*, 2(5), 18–33.

Goncalves, M., & Dangelo, D. (2025). Regulating the Mind: Neuromarketing, Neural Data and Stakeholder Trust Under California's CCPA. *Administrative Sciences, 15*(10), 386. DOI: 10.3390/admsci15100386

Goswami, D., & Khan, M. N. I. (2025). Cybercrime and Contractual Liability: A Systematic Review of Legal Precedents and Risk Mitigation Frameworks. *Journal of Sustainable Development and Policy*, *1*(01), 10–63125.

Gridin, E. (2026). Digital Jurisprudence by Design: The Digital Warrant, Neuro-Symbolic Compliance Architecture, and Evidentiary Non-Repudiation in Transnational AI-Assisted Legal Practice. *Neuro-Symbolic Compliance Architecture, and Evidentiary Non-Repudiation in Transnational AI-Assisted Legal Practice (March 23, 2026).*

Grimm, P. W. (2017). Challenges facing judges regarding expert evidence in criminal cases. *Fordham Law Review*, *86*, 1601.

Guo, W., Wang, H., Bai, Y., & Tan, M. (2026). Global Patent Landscape of Marine Functional Foods: Technological Trends, Hotspots, and Future Challenges. *Trends in Food Science & Technology*, 105555.

Guterres, A., Martins, L. T., & de Carvalho, S. Q. (2026). Legal and Ethical Policies for Human Brain-Computer Interfaces Storage in The Cloud Era: Privacy Rights Protection and Neurological Data Treatment. *Indonesian Cyber Law Review*, *3*(1), 1–16. DOI: 10.59261/iclr.v3i1.37

Hammer, A., Ohlig, M., Geus, J., & Freiling, F. (2023). A Functional Classification of Forensic Access to Storage and its Legal Implications. *Digital Threats : Research and Practice*, *4*(3), 1–14. DOI: 10.1145/3609231

Harrison, A., & Horsfield, N. (2025). The Role and Use of Artificial Intelligence (AI) in Disability Inclusion.

Hefetz, I. (2025). Integrating AI systems in criminal justice: The forensic expert as a corridor between algorithms and courtroom evidence. *Forensic Science*, *5*(4), 53. DOI: 10.3390/forensicsci5040053

Helbing, D., & Mahajan, S. (2025). Repairing, Reviving, and Upgrading Democracies in the Age of AI. *ResearchGate preprint.* https://www. researchgate. net/publication/394105855. *Accessed, 18.*

Hertz, N. (2025). Workplace brain surveillance: The need for new approaches to protect mental privacy and neural data? *International Data Privacy Law*, *15*(2), 123–137. DOI: 10.1093/idpl/ipaf014

Hussain, N. (2025). The Role of Forensic Evidence in Criminal Trials: Legal Reliability and Challenges. *Journal for Current Sign*, *3*(4), 329–340.

Hussain, S. (2025). The ethical frontier: AI-enabled neuromarketing and conscious consumerism. [DSSR]. *Dialogue Social Science Review*, *3*(01), 1040–1048.

Ibrahim, T. M. F. H. T., Muhamad, N. H. N., & Baharuddin, A. S. (2025). Maqasid Al-Shariʿah and Digital Forensics: Towards a Fiqh-Based Evidentiary Model in Syariah Criminal Justice. *Al-'Adalah, 22*(2).

Ilhan, M. A. (2025). *Predictive Artificial Intelligence Tools in the US Criminal Trial: Reflections on Technology and Justice* (Doctoral dissertation, Université Côte d'Azur).

Istace, T. (2025). Exploring the Essence of the Freedom of Thought–A Normative Framework for Identifying Undue Mind Interventions. *Neuroethics*, *18*(1), 10. DOI: 10.1007/s12152-025-09582-9

Jalava, J., Griffiths, S., & Larsen, R. R. (2023). How to keep unreproducible neuro-imaging evidence out of court: A case study in fMRI and psychopathy. *Psychology, Public Policy, and Law*, *29*(1), 1–18. DOI: 10.1037/law0000383

Jbara, H., El Nemar, S., Bakhit, W., Vrontis, D., & Thrassou, A. (2026). Impacting Brand Awareness and Emotions in Retail Consumer Decision-Making Within a Digital Context. *Analytics*, *5*(2), 16. DOI: 10.3390/analytics5020016

Johnson, W. G. (2026). Rights experimentalism under uncertainty: Transnational law and human rights for neurotechnologies. *Human Rights Law Review*, *26*(1), ngaf038. DOI: 10.1093/hrlr/ngaf038

Johnson, W. G., Tournas, L. M., & Magistro Nadler, R. (2025). Implementing Neurorights: Legal and Regulatory Considerations. *Neuroethics*, *18*(1), 5. DOI: 10.1007/s12152-024-09576-z

Kadir, Z. K., & Mappaselleng, N. F. (2026). Neurocriminology and evidentiary standards in Indonesian courts. *Priviet Social Sciences Journal*, *6*(1), 579–588. DOI: 10.55942/pssj.v6i1.786

KAN, C. H. (2025). The examination of neuroscientific evidence in the criminal trial process: The importance of collaboration between criminal law and neuroscience. *International Journal of Eurasia Social Sciences/Uluslararasi Avrasya Sosyal Bilimler Dergisi, 16*(59).

Kapoor, A. (2022). Assessment Of Intrusion Monitoring Methods Using Digital Forensics In A Cloud Infrastructure. *Available at SSRN* 4267941. DOI: 10.2139/ssrn.4267941

Kazaure, A. A., Yusoff, M. N., & Jantan, A. (2023). Digital Forensics Investigation Approaches in Mitigating Cybercrimes: A Review. [JIStaP]. *Journal of Information Science Theory and Practice*, *11*(4), 14.

Kchaou, M., Munusamy, Y., Alharthi, K. A., & Al-Mahmodi, A. F. (2025). Industry 5.0 adaptation for disability-inclusive healthcare: A review of emergent and AI technologies for assistive digital health. *Digital Health, 11*, 20552076251395558. DOI: 10.1177/20552076251395558 PMID: 41229932

Khanam, T., Siuly, S., Ahmad, K., & Wang, H. (2025). A novel channel reduction concept to enhance the classification of motor imagery tasks in brain-computer interface systems. *PLoS One, 20*(10), e0335511. DOI: 10.1371/journal.pone.0335511 PMID: 41171945

Kies, A., De Keyser, A., Jaramillo, S., Li, J., Tang, Y., & Ud Din, I. (2025). Wired for work: Brain-computer interfaces' impact on frontline employees' well-being. *Journal of Service Management, 36*(1), 1–26. DOI: 10.1108/JOSM-03-2024-0098

Kim, H. (2025). Transforming Individuals with Borderline Intellectual Functioning into Cognitively Augmented Workers: AI-Integrated Co-Adaptive, Closed-Loop Brain–Computer Interface. *MechEcology, 4*(2).

Koecke, D. (2025). Merging man and machine: A legal assessment of brain–computer interfaces in armed conflict. *International Review of the Red Cross, 107*(928), 176–199. DOI: 10.1017/S1816383125000098

Kopsaj, V. (2025). The future of social inclusion in the digital age: Challenges and opportunities of AI and digitisation. *Sociology and Social Work Review, 9*(1), 170–181. DOI: 10.58179/SSWR9112

Krishnapriya, P. (2025). Contemporary Judicial Perspectives on E-Contracts. *Alliance Journal of Corporate and Commercial Law*, 49-58.

Kritika. (2026). Ethical and Policy Considerations in Neuro-Integrated Security. In *Neuroscience Meets Cybersecurity: Applying Brain Science to Enhance Digital Protection* (pp. 311-354). Berkeley, CA: Apress.

Kritika. (2026). The Future of Neuroscience-Driven Cybersecurity. In *Neuroscience Meets Cybersecurity: Applying Brain Science to Enhance Digital Protection* (pp. 403-436). Berkeley, CA: Apress.

Kritika, M. (2026). Ethical and legal dimensions of integrating neurotechnology with cybersecurity, a critical reflection for information and communication technology (ICT) policy and practice. *International Cybersecurity Law Review, 7*(1), 1–61. DOI: 10.1365/s43439-026-00168-6

Kumar, A. B., & Sanjaya, K. (2025). Ethics, algorithms, and the rules of evidence: new era of ai-driven forensics. In *Forensic Intelligence and Deep Learning Solutions in Crime Investigation* (pp. 103–124). IGI Global Scientific Publishing. DOI: 10.4018/979-8-3693-9405-2.ch006

Lai, M. (2023). Transcribing and translating forensic speech evidence containing foreign languages—An Australian perspective. *Frontiers in Communication, 8*, 1096639. DOI: 10.3389/fcomm.2023.1096639

Lavazza, A., Balconi, M., Ienca, M., Minerva, F., Pizzetti, F. G., Reichlin, M., Samorè, F., Sironi, V. A., Sosa Navarro, M., & Songhorian, S. (2025). Neuralink's brain-computer interfaces: Medical innovations and ethical challenges. *Frontiers in Human Dynamics, 7*, 1553905. DOI: 10.3389/fhumd.2025.1553905

Lee, A. (2026). Neurorights as Constitutional Rights: Enforcement Gaps in Chile and Lessons for Comparative Neurodata Governance. *Neurotechnology. Society & Governance, 1*(1), 21–39.

Lewis, J. S. (2025). Brain–Computer Interface Integration in Mental Health: Clinician Perspectives on Diagnostic Efficacy and Ethical Implications.

Li, C. (2026). Governing Brain-Computer Interfaces: The Categorical Gap Hypothesis and a Five-Dimensional Global Typology of Neurotechnology Governance (2010-2026). *Neurotechnology. Society & Governance, 1*(1), 1–20.

Li, W., Gao, C., Li, Z., Diao, Y., Li, J., Zhou, J., Zhou, J., Peng, Y., Chen, G., Wu, X., & Wu, K. (2025). BrainFusion: A Low-Code, Reproducible, and Deployable Software Framework for Multimodal Brain–Computer Interface and Brain–Body Interaction Research. *Advancement of Science, 12*(32), e17408. DOI: 10.1002/advs.202417408 PMID: 40470749

Logan, A. C., Berryessa, C. M., Callender, J. S., Caruso, G. D., Hagenbeek, F. A., Mishra, P., & Prescott, S. L. (2025). The Land That Time Forgot? Planetary Health and the Criminal Justice System. *Challenges, 16*(2), 29. DOI: 10.3390/challe16020029

Logan, A. C., Mishra, P., Berryessa, C. M., Caruso, G. D., Hagenbeek, F. A., Denson, T. F., Robinson, J. M., & Prescott, S. L. (2026). Challenging the prescientific frameworks of criminal justice: Neurobiology and criminolytic interventions in the legalome era. *Frontiers in Psychology, 17*, 1791262. DOI: 10.3389/fpsyg.2026.1791262 PMID: 42077290

Lopes, A. M. D. A. (2026). *Challenges for the regulation of neurotechnology companies*. Livraria do Advogado.

Malviya, R., & Rajput, S. (2025). *Advances and insights into AI-created disability supports*. Springer Nature. DOI: 10.1007/978-981-96-6069-8

Marchant, G. E. (2026). Applications of Forensic Neuroscience and the Law. *Forensic Neuroscience and Violence*, 643-654.

Mathur, S., & Singh, A. (2026). Cybersecurity and Forensics for Multimedia Investigation. In *Cyber Security, Forensics and National Security* (pp. 244-281). CRC Press.

Mia, A. P. (2025). From Brain Evidence to Neurorights: Rethinking Criminal Responsibility in the Age of Neurotechnology. *Available at SSRN* 5588370. DOI: 10.2139/ssrn.5588370

Mohammed, U. M., Omolara, A. E., Abiodun, O. I., Rasheed, J., Osman, O., Lar, P. M., Adeyinka, P. O., & Olugbenga, A. G. (2025). Cyber threat in drone systems: Bridging real-time security, legal admissibility, and digital forensic solution readiness. *Frontiers in Communications and Networks*, *6*, 1661928. DOI: 10.3389/frcmn.2025.1661928

Mouammine, Y., & Azdimousa, H. (2025). A Qualitative Analysis of Global Expert Opinions on Neuromarketing and the Role of Feel Data in Consumer's Behaviour. African Journal of Human Resources, Marketing & Organisational Studies (AJHRMOS), 2(1).

Mouazen, B., & El Bouyed, Z. (2025). Toward Ethical and Transparent Brain-Computer Interfaces: Challenges and Perspectives in EEG-Based AI.

Moulin, T. (2022). 'I Will Control Your Mind': The International Regulation of Brain-Hacking. *San Diego Int'l LJ*, *24*, 65.

Mukherjee, S. (2025). Neuro-Law and Brain–Machine Interfaces: Emerging Frontiers of Legal Responsibility, Rights, and Regulation. *AIJFR-Advanced International Journal for Research*, *6*(5).

Muravieva, L. (2025). Regulating Neurotechnologies and AI-driven neural implants in the European Union: Legal and ethical challenges.

Musa, B. B., Jamal, F., & Yakasai, H. S. (2025). The role of cyber forensics in enhancing police investigation. *Матеріали IV Міжнародної конференції молодих учених та здобувачів вищої освіти „Філософські виміри техніки "*, 65-72.

Musole, E. (2026, April). Cognitive Extraction and the Neuro-Chilimba Framework: An Indigenous ROSCA-Based Governance Architecture for Neural Data in Zambia. In *International Journal of Applied Research in Business and Management*.

Musole, E. (2026). Governing Neural Data in the Global South: Toward a Neuro-Responsible Business Framework for Zambia. *International Journal of Advanced Business Studies*, *5*(1), 47–61. DOI: 10.59857/g3bvjx74

Nasyi'ah, I., Saifullah, S., Hidayah, K., Roibin, R., & Adityo, R. D. (2025). Penal sanctions for psychological domestic violence under utilitarianism theory: A new sentencing paradigm in the 2023 Indonesian criminal code. *El-Usrah: Jurnal Hukum Keluarga*, *8*(1), 593–617.

Ng, J. Y. (2025). Exploring the intersection of brain-computer interfaces and traditional, complementary, and integrative medicine. *Integrative Medicine Research*, *14*(2), 101142. DOI: 10.1016/j.imr.2025.101142 PMID: 40290410

Nguyen, K. H., Trinh, A. T., Tran, M. D., & Duong, T. T. T. (2025). Uncovering the evolution of brand transparency in corporate social responsibility: A holistic perspective. *Corporate Social Responsibility and Environmental Management*, *32*(6), 7671–7696. DOI: 10.1002/csr.70099

O'Callaghan, P., & Shiner, B. (2026). Privacy 6.0: Privacy as Mental Integrity. In *The Law and Ethics of Freedom of Thought, Volume 2: Cognitive Liberty, Mental Privacy, and International Law* (pp. 93-115). Cham: Springer Nature Switzerland.

Ogayemi, A., Oyasiji, O., Okesiji, A., Omosule, A., & Olafimihan, O. (2025). *When Thought Becomes Tradeable: Legislating Neuroprivacy Frameworks in the Brain-computer Interfaces (BCIs)*. Commercial Era.

Olawade, D. B., Bolarinwa, O. A., Adebisi, Y. A., & Shongwe, S. (2025). The role of artificial intelligence in enhancing healthcare for people with disabilities. *Social Science & Medicine*, *364*, 117560. DOI: 10.1016/j.socscimed.2024.117560 PMID: 39612748

Omokhabi, U. S., Erumi, B. S. U., Omilani, M. A., & Omokhabi, A. A. (2025). Empowering women with disabilities: Ai-driven reproductive health solutions. *ShodhAI: Journal of Artificial Intelligence*, *2*(1), 40–48. DOI: 10.29121/shodhai.v2.i1.2025.30

Omri, A., Slimani, S., & Afi, H. (2025). The Role of Artificial Intelligence and Digital Solutions in Transforming Educational and Employment Access for Individuals With Disabilities. *The British Journal of Sociology*, *76*(4), 873–897. DOI: 10.1111/1468-4446.13225 PMID: 40344422

Owusu-Berko, L. (2025). Harnessing big data, machine learning, and sentiment analysis to optimize customer engagement, loyalty, and market positioning. *Int. J. Comput. Appl. Technol. Res*, *14*, 1–16.

Pandey, B. K., George, A. S., Tiwari, S., Albermany, S. A., & Hung, H. S. (Eds.). (2025). *Brain-computer Interfaces and Applications in Business*. IGI Global. DOI: 10.4018/979-8-3373-5122-3

Parker, A. G., Vardoulakis, L. M., Alla, J., & Harrington, C. N. (2025, April). Participatory AI considerations for advancing racial health equity. In *Proceedings of the 2025 CHI Conference on Human Factors in Computing Systems* (pp. 1-24). DOI: 10.1145/3706598.3713165

Pathak, A., & Bhardwaj, S. (2026). A systematic literature review on the fusion of face recognition and neuro-marketing. *SN Business & Economics*, *6*(5), 129. DOI: 10.1007/s43546-026-01131-7

Perez-Sales, P. (2026). Coercion without contact: New technologies and the boundaries of torture. *Torture Journal, 36*(1).

Perlin, M., Ellis Cucolo, H., & Kulesza, J. (2025). Artificial Intelligence, Algorithmic Bias, and Mental Disability Law: Ethical Challenges and Regulatory Solutions. *Algorithmic Bias, and Mental Disability Law: Ethical Challenges and Regulatory Solutions (December 15, 2025).*

Possa, A. A. (2025). Neurorights. In *Neurorights and the Era of Neurotechnologies: An Analysis of the Brazilian Constitutional Law and the Need for New Fundamental Rights* (pp. 17–39). Springer Nature Switzerland. DOI: 10.1007/978-3-031-92002-8_3

Praveen, R. V. S., Peri, S. S. R. G., Labde, V. V., Gudimella, A., Hundekari, S., & Shrivastava, A.RVS Praveen. (2025). Neuromarketing in the Digital Age: Understanding Consumer Behavior Through Brain-Computer Interfaces. *Journal of Informatics Education and Research*, *5*(2), 2112–2132. DOI: 10.52783/jier.v5i2.2667

Radu, R. (2025). Cognitive frontiers: Neurotechnology and global internet governance. *Frontiers in Digital Health*, *7*, 1690489. DOI: 10.3389/fdgth.2025.1690489 PMID: 41459239

Reddy, K. J. (2025). Neuroscientific Evidence in Legal Proceedings. In *Foundations of Criminal Forensic Neuropsychology: Bridging Mind, Law, and Criminal Justice* (pp. 213–238). Springer Nature Switzerland. DOI: 10.1007/978-3-031-83771-5_9

Reji, S. K., Moulya, B., & Rajeswari, P. S. (2025, April). The Role of Ethical Marketing in Building Consumer Trust and Loyalty: A Review. In *2025 12th International Conference on Computing for Sustainable Global Development (INDIACom)* (pp. 1-5). IEEE. DOI: 10.23919/INDIACom66777.2025.11115671

Rituraj, A. (2026, March). Achieving child-friendly justice through the integration of artificial intelligence in healthcare systems for victims of child sexual abuse. In. AIP Conference Proceedings: Vol. 3386. *No. 1* (p. 020084). AIP Publishing LLC. DOI: 10.1063/5.0322628

Robertson, L. J., Higgins, N. L., Maier, M. J., Carter, A., & Gardner, J. G. (2025). Ethical Governance Strategies for the Responsible Innovation of Neurotechnologies: A Scoping Review. *Journal of Bioethical Inquiry*, *22*(4), 1–18. DOI: 10.1007/s11673-025-10440-9 PMID: 41217705

Roberts, P. (2018). The forensic challenge. *Frontiers L. China*, *13*, 43.

Rudroff, T. (2025). A Framework for Responsible Innovation. In *AI for the Healthy Brain and Neurological Disorders: Neuroscience Innovation in an Anti-Science Era* (pp. 405–420). Springer Nature Switzerland. DOI: 10.1007/978-3-032-11596-6_18

Rustamov, N., Souders, L., Sheehan, L., Carter, A., & Leuthardt, E. C. (2025). IpsiHand Brain–Computer Interface Therapy Induces Broad Upper Extremity Motor Rehabilitation in Chronic Stroke. *Neurorehabilitation and Neural Repair*, *39*(1), 74–86. DOI: 10.1177/15459683241287731 PMID: 39345118

Rys, M., & Gorska, A. M. (2026). Inclusive innovation: Balancing gender equality and gender neutrality in hackathons. *Equality, Diversity and Inclusion*, *45*(2), 292–309. DOI: 10.1108/EDI-08-2024-0344

Said, G. (2025). Brain-Computer Interface 5.0: Potential threats, computational law and protection of digital rights. *Legal Issues in the digital. The Age (Melbourne, Vic.)*, (2), 134–160.

Sanders, S. (2025). *Brain–Computer Interface Integration in Mental Health: Clinician Perspectives on Diagnostic Efficacy and Ethical Implications* (Doctoral dissertation, Walden University).

Sanni, B. (2025, January). *Leveraging artificial intelligence in women's leadership training: Personalized learning paths for skill enhancement.*

Santillan-Lima, J. C., Díaz, J. F., Piccirilli, D., Haro-Tufiño, K. A., Urgirles-Rodríguez, B., & Molina-Granja, F. T. (2025, October). Admissibility of digital evidence: integration of technical and legal standards in forensic and judicial contexts. In *International Conference on Advanced Research in Technologies, Information, Innovation and Sustainability* (pp. 252-266). Cham: Springer Nature Switzerland.

Sarkar, R. (2026). Policy Regression, Mental Health, and the Lived Experience of LGBTQ+ Students in Anti-DEI Times: Queer Futures Denied. In *Impacts of Anti-DEI Initiatives on Educational Institutions and Policy* (pp. 119-146). IGI Global Scientific Publishing.

Sattler, S., Mehlkop, G., Neuhaus, A., Wexler, A., & Reiner, P. B. (2025). Exploring disparities in self-reported knowledge about neurotechnology. *Scientific Reports*, *15*(1), 18488. DOI: 10.1038/s41598-025-00460-1 PMID: 40425633

Shafik, W. (2025). The intersection of technology and inclusion for people with disabilities and marginalized communities. In *Global Sustainable Transition with Inclusion: A Focus on the People with Disabilities and the Marginalized* (pp. 185–212). Springer Nature Singapore. DOI: 10.1007/978-981-96-6557-0_7

Sharma, K., Agrawal, D., & Gabrani, R. (2026). A Patent Review on Traumatic Brain Injuries (2020-2025). *International Journal of Neuroscience*, (just-accepted), 1-27.

Sharp, D. N. (2025). Comparative frameworks for a human rights-based approach to psychedelics. *Human Rights Quarterly*, *47*(1), 63–86. DOI: 10.1353/hrq.2025.a951572

Shen, Z., Li, H., & Zhang, Y. (2025). The mediating role of brand equity in corporate social responsibility and customer purchase intention based on text-CNN model. *Scientific Reports*, *15*(1), 44391. DOI: 10.1038/s41598-025-28118-y PMID: 41436517

Shukla, A., Soni, M. P., & Rawat, T. (2025). Consumer Loyalty to Digital Brands: The Power of Transparency and Ethical Marketing. *Journal of Marketing & Social Research*, *2*, 315–321.

Singh, P., Kumar, S., Singh, S. K., & Singh, H. (2026). Privacy in mental healthcare by data protection: Exploring AI-powered psychological assessment and identity crisis intervention with legal provisions. In *Imposter syndrome and AI: Navigating human identity in the age of intelligent machines* (pp. 327–346). IGI Global Scientific Publishing.

Soldatic, K., Lee, M., Tunggal, E., Liao, A., & Magee, L. (2025). Rethinking digital and AI inclusion: Participatory and intersectionality-informed methods for disability and migrant justice. *Frontiers in Sociology*, *10*, 1593330. DOI: 10.3389/fsoc.2025.1593330 PMID: 40799256

Sommaggio, P. (2024). Protecting my mind: Cognitive liberty, commons, and neurorights. In *The Discourse of Biorights: European Perspectives* (pp. 133–145). Springer International Publishing. DOI: 10.1007/978-3-031-66804-3_9

Song, G., Gazi, M. A. I., Waaje, A., Roshid, M. M., Karim, R., Rahaman, M. A., Min, Z., & Senathirajah, A. R. B. S. (2025). The neuromarketing: Bridging neuroscience and marketing for enhanced consumer engagement. *IEEE Access : Practical Innovations, Open Solutions*, *13*, 40331–40353. DOI: 10.1109/ACCESS.2025.3545742

Sosa Navarro, M. (2026). Workplace Neurosurveillance: Is the Employee's Mental Privacy Protected Under International Law?. *BIOLAW JOURNAL*, (Special Issue 1/2026), 93-113.

Souza, J. D. N. (2025). Exploring New Frontiers in Personalized Criminal Responsibility through Neurotechnologies: Ethical Dilemmas and the Neuro-Rights Framework. *BioLaw Journal-Rivista di BioDiritto*, (4), 211–228.

Spinello, R. A. (2026). *Cyberethics: Morality and law in cyberspace*. Jones & Bartlett Learning.

Splichal, S. (2022). *Datafication of public opinion and the public sphere: How extraction replaced expression of opinion*. Anthem Press. DOI: 10.2307/j.ctv2s2pp3n

Stahl, B. C. (2025). The Ethics of Data and Its Governance: A Discourse Theoretical Approach. *Information (Basel)*, *16*(6), 497. DOI: 10.3390/info16060497

Sudhani, H. P., Vattikuti, P., & Rekha, D. (2025). Challenges and future directions in brain–computer interface research for exoskeletons usage. In *Artificial Intelligence Applications for Brain–Computer Interfaces* (pp. 295–316). Academic Press.

Taimur, A. (2026). Neurorights in the age of AI: Universalism, cognitive vulnerability, and the limits of legal translation. *Rivista Di Diritti Comparati, 2026*(Special Issue VIII), 125-155.

Tanson, E. (2025). The Human Rights+ Framework: Understanding Harm Attribution Gaps and Invisible Harm in the Digital Age. *Available at SSRN* 5934074.

Terec-Vlad, L., & Rusu, A. (2026). Neuro-Cybersecurity and the Future of Cognitive Rights: Legal Foundations for the Protection of the Human Mind in the Digital Age. *Revista Romaneasca pentru Educatie Multidimensionala, 18*(1), 82-104.

Thamma, S. R., Prajwala, N. B., Pushpa, N. B., & Patra, A. (2025). Neuroimaging: A Computational Lens on the Brain. In *Visualization in Neuroanatomical Sciences* (pp. 53–68). Springer Nature Switzerland.

Tiwari, V., Dasari, V. S. R., & Wang, J. (2026, May). The Future of Artificial Intelligence in Forensics: Advancements, Challenges. In *Proceedings of IEMTRONICS 2025: International IoT, Electronics and Mechatronics Conference,* Volume 1 (Vol. 1, p. 351). Springer Nature. DOI: 10.1007/978-981-95-0429-9_24

Tkachova, Y. (2025). Integrating neuromarketing into brand trust building strategies in the digital environment. *Актуальні питання економічних наук*, (14).

Trinh, A. T., Duong, T. T. T., Nguyen, P. T., & Le, N. H. Q. (2026). Examining brand transparency as a driver of customer referral engagement in fashion context. *Journal of Global Fashion Marketing*, *17*(1), 94–112. DOI: 10.1080/20932685.2025.2548545

Turner, S., Yadav, P., Morrin, H., & Bhat, A. (2026). The future of psychiatry: Clinical practice, diagnosis, and treatment. *International Review of Psychiatry (Abingdon, England)*, *38*(1-3), 314–335. DOI: 10.1080/09540261.2025.2594523 PMID: 41295901

Urbaite, G. (2025). Advancements in Neural Implants: A Systematic Review of Neuralink-Enabled Brain-Machine Communication. *Luminis Applied Science and Engineering*, *2*(3), 46–65.

van Kolfschooten, H. (2025). Towards an EU charter of digital patients' rights in the age of artificial intelligence. *Digital Society : Ethics, Socio-Legal and Governance of Digital Technology*, *4*(1), 6. DOI: 10.1007/s44206-025-00159-w

Varsha, A., Kumar, N. A., Bichanga, S. N., & Chakraborty, P. (2025). Future Direction in Digital Forensics and Cyber Security. *Emerging Threats and Countermeasures in Cybersecurity*, 467-493.

Varughese, J. S., Arjun, M., Mishra, S., & Venkatesh, M. P. (2025). Brain-computer Interface on Medical Devices: A Promising Technology with Limitless Possibilities. *Applied Drug Research, Clinical Trials and Regulatory Affairs*, *11*(1), E26673371314770. DOI: 10.2174/0126673371314770241020145227

Vaseghi, M. (2025). Comparative Study of Legal Protection of Human Brain Data in the Context of Neurotechnologies, with Emphasis on Brain-Computer Interfaces (BCI). *Majlis and Rahbord*, *32*(122), 5–32.

Vasiliu-Feltes, I. (2025). Neurotech frontiers: Ethics, identity, and the evolution of brain–computer interfaces. In *Nanomedical Brain/Cloud Interface: Explorations and implications* (pp. 4–1). IOP Publishing. DOI: 10.1088/978-0-7503-2144-0ch4

Wakili, S. A., Obisesan, O. O., Ekpenisi, C., Antai, G. O., & Umo, M. E. (2025). Legal framework and challenges concerning forensic evidence in Nigeria. *Trunojoyo Law Review*, *7*(1), 33–64. DOI: 10.21107/tlr.v7i1.28599

Wallana, T., Banitsas, K., & Balachandran, W. (2025). Reviewing Breakthroughs and Limitations of Implantable and External Medical Device Treatments for Spinal Cord Injury. *Applied Sciences (Basel, Switzerland)*, *15*(15), 8488. DOI: 10.3390/app15158488

Williams, C., Anik, F. I., Hasan, M. M., Rodriguez-Cardenas, J., Chowdhury, A., Tian, S., He, S., & Sakib, N. (2025). Advancing Brain-Computer Interface Closed-Loop Systems for Neurorehabilitation: Systematic Review of AI and Machine Learning Innovations in Biomedical Engineering. *JMIR Biomedical Engineering*, *10*, e72218. DOI: 10.2196/72218 PMID: 41191851

Yang, H., & Jiang, L. (2025). Regulating neural data processing in the age of BCIs: Ethical concerns and legal approaches. *Digital Health*, *11*, 20552076251326123. DOI: 10.1177/20552076251326123 PMID: 40162168

Yuste, R., De La Quadra-Salcedo, T., & Fernández, M. G. (2023). Neuro-rights and new charts of digital rights: A dialogue beyond the limits of the law. *Indiana Journal of Global Legal Studies*, *30*(1), 15–37. DOI: 10.2979/gls.2023.a886161

Yuste, R., Genser, J., & Herrmann, S. (2021). It's time for neuro-rights. *Horizons*, *18*, 154–164.

Zhang, L., & Liu, W. (2025, October). Integrating Algorithmic Precision and Emotive AI Design: Two Pathways to Consumer Behavior and Brand Loyalty in Automotive Marketing. In *Proceedings of the 2025 2nd International Conference on Digital Economy and Computer Science* (pp. 1283-1289). DOI: 10.1145/3785706.3785909

Zhang, Q., Zhang, C., Ji, H., Chen, J., Wang, X., Zhang, T., Liu, P., Wang, Z., & Xu, Y. (2025). Ethical governance of clinical research on the brain–computer interface for mental disorders: A modified Delphi study. *General Psychiatry*, *38*(4), e101755. DOI: 10.1136/gpsych-2024-101755 PMID: 40735361

Zheng, D., Considine, C. M., Weinstock, R., Darby, W. C., & Darby, R. R. (2024). Forensic neurology: Practice considerations and training opportunities. *Neurology*, *103*(1), e209560. DOI: 10.1212/WNL.0000000000209560 PMID: 38833660

Zhu, R., Zhao, Y., & Li, Y. (2025). Paradigm Shift in Global Governance of Medical Brain-Computer Interface: Addressing Practical Challenges Through Institutional Innovation. *Risk Management and Healthcare Policy*, *18*, 3755–3768. DOI: 10.2147/RMHP.S555754 PMID: 41328405

About the Contributors

Róbert Szuchy is Vice-Rector for Educational Affairs and Full Professor at Károli Gáspár University in Hungary. His academic work focuses on energy law, commercial law, and European regulatory frameworks. He is actively involved in teaching, research, and academic leadership and he is the Director of the Law Program at the Faculty of Law. He is also the founder and director of the LLM programme in Energy and Natural Resources Law, offered in both Hungarian and English. Professor Szuchy is the author of several books and numerous scholarly articles, and a frequent speaker at international academic conferences, particularly in the fields of renewable energy and energy efficiency. Beyond the university, he is the Hungarian observing member of the European Federation of Energy Law Associations, President of the International Committee of the Hungarian Lawyers' Association, and Vice-Chair of the Civil Law Subcommittee of the Legal Committee of the Hungarian Academy of Sciences. His professional contributions have been recognised with the Hungarian Order of Merit (Knight's Cross).

Swarnima Gorani is an academician and legal scholar with specialisation in both the Criminal and Corporate arenas. She is actively engaged in teaching & research while pursuing her PhD from Himachal Pradesh National Law University, Shimla, in the domain of Forensic Psychology. She has a strong academic background, having earned a dual degree in Commerce and Law, as well as a postgraduate degree in Law (specialising in Criminal Laws) and a degree in Company Secretaryship. She has participated and presented at various international conferences and faculty development programmes with a major focus on Forensics and Artificial Intelligence, and contributed to book chapters and journal publications. Her accolades include holding an All India Rank of 13 (Company Secretary) and a Gold Medal in her Law Degree.

Laeeq Razzak Janjua has a Phd (Political Economy), from CAMS-USA, on PGD-COMPLIANCE. He is affiliated to COMPLIANCE OFFICE - TMF GROUP -

POLAND, and he is also a lecturer at WSB University Poland. Dr. Laeeq Razzak Janjua is a finance professional working in compliance, and academia, whose journey is characterized by dedication, expertise, and a commitment to excellence. Mr. Janjua's academic prowess is reflected in his extensive body of work, which includes the publication of a book on corporate social responsibility as co-author and over 40 academic research papers. These contributions have solidified his reputation as a thought leader and a respected authority in his field, earning him recognition and acclaim from peers and scholars alike. Currently serving as a Compliance Officer at TMF Group, Mr. Janjua brings a wealth of experience and expertise to his role, where he navigates the complex landscape of regulatory requirements with precision and proficiency. In addition to his role at TMF Group, Mr. Janjua also serves as a lecturer at WSB University in Poland, where he imparts his knowledge and insights to the next generation of professionals. Prior to his current roles, Mr. Janjua amassed over 10 years of invaluable experience in the financial industry, having worked with esteemed institutions such as Citi Bank, MoneyGram Payment International, and BNP Paribas. Driven by a passion for excellence and a dedication to making a positive impact, Mr. Janjua continues to be a guiding force in the fields of compliance and academia. His unwavering commitment to integrity, coupled with his extensive knowledge and experience, positions him as a leader and a trailblazer in his field, shaping the future of compliance and corporate social responsibility.

***

Ankita Bajpai is an Assistant Professor in Management with a Ph.D. in Entrepreneurship. Her doctoral research focused on measuring entrepreneurial competency in the emergence of small and medium-scale enterprises (SMEs). She has expertise in research methodologies and data analytics, with proficiency in statistical software such as SPSS and NVivo. Her research interests include entrepreneurship, innovation, small business development, and management education.

Binita Behera is Assistant Professor in School of Law of KIIT DU. She has fifteen years of experience in the development sector, both government and non government. She also has academic experience. Some of the notable organizations where she has worked are UNICEF, ActionAid, State Commission for Protection of Child Rights. She has a Ph.D in Sociology from Jawaharlal Nehru University, New Delhi. Her doctoral thesis is on the role of schooling system in the construction of gender identities. She has twenty publications to her credit. Her interest areas include gender, religion, education, ethnicity, environment and law.

Saurabh Chandra is an accomplished legal scholar with almost two decades of teaching experience. With a robust academic foundation, he earned his Bachelor of Arts and Bachelor of Laws (B.A. LL.B.) from the prestigious Aligarh Muslim University (A.M.U.). He further specialized in Business Laws, completing his Master of Laws (LL.M.) at the renowned National Law School of India University (NLSIU), Bangalore. Dr. Chandra's academic journey culminated in a Doctorate in Law (Ph.D.) from the esteemed National Law University (NLU) Delhi. His expertise is complemented by a robust portfolio of scholarly publications. Dr. Chandra brings a wealth of experience in Academic Administration, having successfully held various key administrative positions.

Shashank Chaudhary having more than 23 Years of distinguished experience in higher professional education with expertise in Academic Administration, Curriculum Development & Implementation, Teaching, Training and Research . Has been instrumental in steering Institutions towards Academic Excellence and embracing academic Industry interfere enabling holistic growth & development with workplace Harmony & Ethics .

Saurabh Kumar is an accomplished legal academic and practitioner with over 14 years of combined experience in legal practice and education. Supreme Court advocate turned Assistant Professor with a distinguished track record in human rights law, gender justice, and international law. Core Expertise: - Artificial Intelligence & Law - International Law & Criminal Law - Constitutional & Public Law - Space Law Academic Excellence: He is currently advancing his scholarly journey as a Ph.D. researcher at Chanakya National Law University. He holds advanced qualifications including an LL.M. from MUIT in Criminal Law, LL.B. (Hons.) from Banaras Hindu University. Dual NET qualified (2019 & 2025) with specialized training from The Hague Academy of International Law. Published researcher with peer-reviewed articles in leading law journals, focusing on women's rights and prison reform. Active participant in international legal discourse with certifications from prestigious institutions including WIPO, UNITAR, and the World Bank. Professional Distinction: - 7 years of Supreme Court practice (2012-2019) providing robust litigation experience - 5 years as Assistant Professor at GNSU

Priyanka Nema has completed her Ph.D. from Barkatullah University, Bhopal in 2015. She is currently an assistant professor of HR and OB area at Jagran lake city university, Bhopal, her area of interest includes Human resource management and Organizational Behaviour. She had a rich corporate experience of working with the Samsung group in Seoul South Korea. She had presented and attended various conferences including CERE and Academy of international business India Chapter in IIM Indore.

Pragya Singh is a distinguished legal academic and scholar currently serving as an Assistant Professor of Law at The Neotia University in Kolkata, West Bengal. With a comprehensive educational background spanning prestigious Indian institutions and over seven years of teaching experience across multiple universities, Dr. Singh has established herself as a dedicated educator and researcher in the field of law. Her academic journey reflects a deep commitment to legal education, research excellence, and the advancement of legal scholarship in contemporary India. Educational Background and Academic Credentials Dr. Singh's academic foundation is built upon a rigorous educational trajectory at some of India's most esteemed institutions. She completed her doctoral studies in Law at the University of Allahabad in 2025, marking the culmination of years of intensive research and scholarly inquiry. Prior to this, she earned her Master of Laws degree from Banaras Hindu University, Varanasi, in 2015, followed by her Bachelor of Laws degree from the same institution between 2009 and 2012. Her Undergraduate education includes a Bachelor of Arts with Honor's from Banaras Hindu University.

Abhishek Srivastava is an accomplished legal academic with over seven years of teaching and research experience. Currently serving as Assistant Professor at Amity University Jaipur, he has contributed extensively to the fields of Law of Evidence, Constitutional Law, and Cyber Law, which form his core areas of expertise. He has authored and co-authored multiple publications that reflect his commitment to advancing legal scholarship and bridging the gap between theory and practice. His teaching philosophy emphasizes clarity, accessibility, and comparative analysis, enabling students to grasp complex legal concepts with confidence. Beyond classroom teaching, Dr. Srivastava has played a pivotal role in curriculum design, exam paper development, and evaluation frameworks, ensuring academic rigor and fairness. His dedication to student-centered pedagogy, bilingual resources, and visual learning tools has empowered diverse learners and enriched legal education at Amity University. With a strong academic foundation and a vision for innovation in legal studies, Dr. Srivastava continues to inspire students and contribute meaningfully to the evolving landscape of law and justice.

Index

A

AI Ethics 125
Artificial Intelligence in Prisons 1, 3

B

Brain-Computer Interface 3, 5, 11, 17, 28, 56, 65, 68, 155, 168, 174, 176, 181, 184, 185, 187, 190, 199, 200, 234
Brain-Computer Interfaces 1, 2, 4, 8, 9, 18, 19, 20, 23, 24, 26, 27, 30, 32, 38, 40, 41, 57, 58, 66, 69, 70, 72, 79, 80, 84, 109, 121, 123, 127, 140, 155, 156, 159, 161, 163, 165, 171, 172, 177, 180, 184, 185, 188, 191, 192, 194, 195, 199, 200, 205, 210, 216, 220, 222, 233
Brain Data 22, 29, 41, 44, 47, 64, 65, 66, 69, 71, 73, 74, 75, 77, 78, 79, 80, 81, 82, 121, 122, 123, 124, 125, 127, 128, 129, 130, 133, 137, 138, 141, 142, 143, 144, 146, 148, 149, 151, 185, 188, 189, 203, 205, 206, 207, 208, 210, 220, 223, 224, 225, 226, 227, 228, 229, 231, 242
Brain Data Privacy 203
Brain Hacking 21, 55, 56, 58, 60, 66, 179, 182
Brand Loyalty 37, 38, 39, 40, 43, 47, 49, 50, 51, 52, 53

C

Cognitive Liberty 4, 8, 12, 16, 31, 58, 65, 70, 72, 74, 75, 76, 121, 125, 127, 128, 131, 137, 138, 139, 141, 142, 143, 145, 146, 147, 149, 151, 152, 153, 154, 157, 162, 165, 168, 173, 178, 179, 182, 204, 205, 208, 212, 213, 219, 222, 224, 227
Communication Skills Training 187, 188, 191, 192, 195
Consumer attitudes 201, 202, 210, 213, 214
Corporate Transparency 37, 40, 42, 48, 50, 210

D

Data protection 1, 2, 9, 11, 15, 21, 24, 29, 31, 45, 58, 60, 61, 62, 71, 74, 75, 78, 80, 81, 85, 117, 123, 126, 145, 150, 162, 166, 178, 179, 205, 220, 230
Digital Forensics 57, 67, 68, 87, 97, 102
Digital Inclusion 19, 20, 23, 24, 25, 26, 28, 30, 31, 32

E

Emotional Well-being 235
Evidentiary Admissibility 5, 14
Evidentiary Challenges 55, 63, 87, 95, 102

F

fMRI Lie Detection 110
Forensic Neuroscience 118, 119

G

Gender-Neutral Justice 155, 156, 160, 161, 163, 165
Generative AI Evidence 90

H

Human Resource Development 187, 188, 194, 195

I

Indian Policing 235, 239, 240, 241, 244, 245, 247, 248

L

Law Enforcement 3, 57, 62, 69, 71, 74, 76, 78, 81, 98, 99, 128, 162, 236, 237, 240, 244, 245
Legal Frameworks 28, 29, 41, 61, 110, 117, 137, 149, 160, 224

Legal Implications 67, 118, 171

M

Male Victims of Cruelty 162
Mental Health 1, 2, 4, 5, 6, 7, 10, 12, 14, 15, 27, 38, 42, 56, 57, 82, 114, 117, 139, 141, 148, 153, 155, 156, 157, 158, 159, 160, 161, 164, 165, 166, 167, 169, 180, 182, 184, 203, 205, 208, 210, 212, 214, 223, 225, 227, 237, 238, 240, 241, 244, 245, 246, 247, 248
Mental Privacy 2, 3, 8, 13, 15, 28, 31, 38, 41, 50, 51, 56, 57, 62, 64, 65, 66, 69, 70, 71, 72, 73, 75, 77, 79, 84, 85, 115, 117, 121, 125, 127, 131, 132, 137, 138, 139, 140, 142, 143, 144, 145, 146, 147, 149, 151, 153, 157, 162, 163, 165, 168, 173, 178, 182, 190, 193, 197, 202, 203, 205, 206, 208, 209, 210, 212, 213, 220, 221, 222, 223, 224, 225, 227, 228, 229, 233, 234

N

Neural Data Collection 37, 43
Neural Data Privacy 15, 202
Neural Data Rights 1, 3, 5, 7, 11, 201, 202, 203, 204, 205, 206, 208, 209, 213, 214
Neural-Derived Evidence 87, 88, 89, 92, 94, 99, 100, 105, 106, 108, 111, 114, 116
Neural Evidence 55, 57, 58, 64, 65, 66, 82, 88, 89, 90, 93, 94, 95, 96, 97, 98, 99, 100, 106, 108, 111, 112, 113
Neuro-Digital Workplaces 187, 188, 190, 196
Neuroethics 80, 118, 123, 125, 131, 133, 153, 165, 168, 178, 182, 233, 236, 238, 241, 242, 243, 247
Neurolaw 30, 58, 111, 113, 116, 117, 118
Neurorights 4, 8, 11, 12, 13, 14, 18, 22, 28, 32, 38, 39, 41, 42, 44, 46, 47, 48, 49, 69, 70, 71, 72, 73, 74, 76, 77, 78, 84, 121, 122, 123, 124, 125, 126, 130, 131, 132, 133, 134, 137, 138, 139, 140, 141, 142, 143, 144, 145, 146, 147, 148, 149, 150, 151, 154, 157, 161, 163, 167, 173, 176, 177, 179, 182, 197, 202, 203, 205, 206, 207, 208, 209, 211, 212, 213, 214, 219, 220, 221, 222, 224, 226, 229, 230, 231, 233, 234, 249, 250
Neuro Rights 57, 58, 62
Neuroscience 23, 32, 40, 51, 53, 56, 66, 71, 84, 106, 107, 108, 111, 113, 116, 117, 118, 119, 134, 135, 151, 153, 171, 172, 173, 174, 177, 178, 179, 181, 184, 187, 199, 215, 216, 217, 220, 227, 228, 233, 235, 236, 238, 241, 247, 249
Neurotechnology 4, 8, 12, 13, 16, 17, 18, 37, 39, 40, 41, 44, 45, 50, 51, 60, 61, 62, 66, 70, 71, 72, 74, 76, 77, 78, 79, 80, 81, 82, 83, 84, 123, 124, 127, 130, 131, 132, 133, 134, 137, 138, 140, 141, 142, 143, 144, 145, 146, 151, 153, 155, 156, 159, 161, 162, 163, 166, 167, 174, 180, 187, 195, 196, 197, 199, 201, 202, 203, 205, 206, 207, 210, 211, 212, 213, 214, 215, 216, 220, 221, 222, 224, 228, 229, 230, 231, 233, 234, 249
Neurotechnology Ethics 79, 82
Neurotechnology Regulation 4

O

Occupational Stress 246, 249

P

Patents 30, 157, 171, 173, 174, 175, 176, 177
Public Health 30, 158, 161, 164, 166, 171, 172, 173, 174, 175, 178, 179, 180, 181, 224

R

Resilience Training 246
Responsible Innovation 62, 69, 70, 71, 78, 79, 81, 82, 121, 122, 123, 124, 130, 134, 135, 148, 151, 166, 195, 204, 213, 219, 220, 221, 228, 231

W

Women with Disabilities 19, 20, 21, 22, 23, 24, 25, 26, 27, 28, 29, 30, 31, 32, 34